PRAISE FOR *VERONICA'S GRAVE*

"*Veronica's Grave* shows both the warmth of a loving family and the mistakes when secrets are kept. A compelling tale that gives wonderful insight to the readers."

—**MARY HIGGINS CLARK**, author of more than 50 best-selling novels, including *All Around the Town*, *Loves Music, Loves to Dance*, and *While My Pretty One Sleeps*

"*Veronica's Grave: A Daughter's Memoir* is a compelling account of how a young woman, confronted with the unexplained loss of her mother, relies on her own inner resources and determination to not only discover the family secret of who her mother was but, in the process, discovers her own self and her own unacknowledged potential."

—**PETER H. KUDLER, M.D**, Department of Psychiatry, NYU Langone Medical Center

"Readers who melt reading about the good old days will be charmed by the protagonist, a girl named after Saint Barbara, who can't shed her father's insistence on calling her Bob. We learn that for her those days were neither charming, nor good. From the moment we meet some of the quaintly named characters like Betty, Dot, or Agnes, we know we have time traveled to the fifties and sixties. The Bronx streets of her working class family—Decatur and Webster Avenues, the Third Avenue El—are forever beloved by Barbara even when she manages the extraordinary feat of escaping her mundane existence. If you remember Buster Browns, Betsy Wetsy, five cent cigars, Necco wafers, and Elsie the Borden cow, or Bendix washers, you will find yourself on a wonderful nostalgic ride. But Barbara's intelligence and persistence takes her on a journey far from her humble origins. You will cheer for her as she strolls confidently down Champs Elysees in her two piece jade green gabardine TWA uniform and later, as she dines on escargot at the romantic Le Coupe-Choux or sips a martini at the posh Algonquin Hotel in Manhattan."

—**ANNETTE LIBESKIND BERKOVITS,** author of *In the Unlikeliest of Places: How Nachman Libeskind Survived the Nazis, Gulags, and Soviet Communism*

"Donsky's coming-of-age memoir is a vivid portrait of a remarkable life. It is a deft rendering that begins by inhabiting the shadows of a childhood lost, later illustrating a person becoming slowly visible to herself. The images and sounds of her New York neighborhoods—as well as the perfume-scented rues in the Paris she discovers as a young woman—are defining brushstrokes to complement and frame this remarkable story."

—**RITA GARDNER,** author of award-winning memoir *Coconut Latitudes: Secrets, Storms, and Survival in the Caribbean*

VERONICA'S
GRAVE

VERONICA'S GRAVE

A DAUGHTER'S MEMOIR

BARBARA BRACHT DONSKY

SHE WRITES PRESS

Published 2016
Printed in the United States of America
ISBN: 978-1-63152-074-7 pbk
ISBN: 978-1-63152-075-4 ebk
Library of Congress Control Number: 2015956244

Cover design by Julie Metz Ltd./metzdesign.com
Interior design by Tabitha Lahr

For information, address:
She Writes Press
1563 Solano Ave #546
Berkeley, CA 94707

She Writes Press is a division of SparkPoint Studio, LLC.

Names and identifying characteristics have been changed to protect the privacy of certain individuals.

For my mother, Veronica Shanahan Bracht
My grandmother, Agnes Riester Bracht
And my husband, Richard Donsky

"One's philosophy is not best expressed in words; it is expressed in the choices one makes . . . and the choices we make are ultimately our responsibility."

—Eleanor Roosevelt
(Φ BK Harvard-Radcliffe, 1941)

Why isn't today like all my yesterdays? Riding my trike, I'm ringing the bell and having a good time—while waiting for Mommy to get up, waiting to go to the park. She says she has a tummy ache, doesn't want to get out of bed. When I pedal out of the room and she can't see me anymore, she calls: Barbara Jane, where are you?

Come find me, Mommy. When she doesn't, I pedal back to where she's lying in bed, listening to music and reading the paper. Usually, when the music's playing, we dance around the house, me riding on top of her shoes. Not today, she says, not today. When rounding the foot of the bed, the wheel of my tricycle catches on the tip of the bedspread lying on the floor. Before I know it, I'm flat on my back, sobbing as if my heart will break.

Tossing aside *The Irish Echo*, she leans over, grabs the straps on my overalls and pulls me up onto the bed with her.

Come, come, don't cry. You're all right, she says, kissing me on the forehead, running her hand through my hair. I know what to do, let's brush your hair. Saying that she hands me her silver mirror—what a pretty girl!—the one with a bird that has the longest tail I've ever seen. Pointing to it, I ask *what's this?*

It's a peacock, she says, can you say peacock? Say, pea-cock.

Before I can say a word, the silver mirror with the peacock slips out of my hand and onto the floor. I climb down to pick it up, and when I climb back up again she's gone. Is she playing hide-and-seek? I look under the spread, she's not there. I look under the bed, she's not there. Then the radio forgets how to play the songs it once knew, and the sun forgets to take naps on Mommy's bed. Everything's topsy-turvy. Mommy's gone, and she's taken away all the music. Nothing's the way it was yesterday.

THE DOORBELL rings and rings. The apartment fills with tears and sighs, with people coming and going for days on end. My aunts sit around in the living room, crossing and uncrossing their legs, not sure what to do with their hands, while my uncles are out in the kitchen smoking cigarettes and pipes and drinking the 'suds.' No one's laughing, no one's telling stories, no one's dancing—not the way they do when Mommy's here.

When the doorbell rings, I run to answer, but it's not my mother, it's only my grandmother. Someone moves over to make room for her to sit on the couch. The door to Mommy's bedroom is half-open, so I walk to the window to see if she's on the fire escape, but she's not. Opening the closet, I pick up her dancing shoes, the ones she calls her *Rita's* with the skinny straps that wrap around her ankles. Wherever she is, she's not dancing tonight—not without her dancing shoes.

In the kitchen, the air is thick and grey with smoke, but when I squint I see her standing in front of the refrigerator, her arms open wide. I run to her, but she disappears, and all I have left is an armful of smoke. Something's wrong—the wooden clock on the wall no longer says *tick-tock-tick-tock*. And the little boy and girl who came out to play have gone away.

Not knowing what to do with myself, I'm sitting on the floor sucking my thumb when Mommy's dancing broom falls over, hitting me on the head. I pick it up, put it next to me on the floor—hoping she will come looking for it, hoping she will come looking for me.

When I go to bed, a dark grey shadow is moving up and down, round and round, on the bedroom window—it's looking for the lock, looking for a way to get in. I scream and crawl out of bed, dragging my comforter into the closet where I sit hugging Mommy's dancing shoes. My father comes in and puts me back to bed. No one's there, he says, it's only a dream. Pulling the covers over my head, I tell myself it's only a dream, only a dream. But it feels so real. The following night the shadow returns, and once again I scream. Lickety-split, my father throws open the window and leans out, looking first one way and then the other, leaving his snowy fingerprints on the windowsill.

Go back to sleep, go back to sleep.

Before he can lock the window, the month of November comes rushing in—dropping chunks of cold moonlight on the bed, on the floor, and on me. When Daddy pulls up my covers, I can smell the tobacco on his hands and hear the cellophane on his Chesterfields making crinkly noises. Sucking my thumb for the longest time, I can't fall asleep. When will Mommy come home? is she lost? are the little boy and girl who lived in the clock lost? will I ever see them again?

I don't understand this. She's never left me alone before, not even when she goes to the mailbox. We're friends, the two of us going everywhere together. All day long, I'm listening for her footsteps in the hallway, listening for the key in the lock. No one calls my name, no one comes to play. The place is a mess—the walls are scared to death, the tiles on the bathroom floor are wet and dirty, and even the kitchen linoleum has lost its shine. Everybody's talking at me, but I don't hear a word. When will the rain stop? when will the sun come out? what's happening? No one tells me a thing.

Mommy and Me

When Daddy's working, Mrs Ryan, the lady who lives upstairs, sits around in our living room keeping an eye on me. When the doorbell rings one morning, it's my grandmother. She tries to kiss me, but I won't let her. I'm angry with Nana, angry with Mrs Ryan, and angry with Mommy.

What's the matter with you? Where's that smile of yours? C'mon, put on a happy face, she says, pushing up the corners of her mouth.

Go away, Nana. I want Mommy.

Tsch, tsch, tsch. You're as jumpy as a little Mexican jumping bean, you know that?

Don't touch me. And I don't want Mrs Ryan to touch me. She doesn't know how to play games, and when we go to the park, she doesn't talk to Mr Echo, not the way Mommy does. And you know what, Nana? Mr Echo doesn't talk to me anymore.

At that Nana jumps to her feet, saying: That does it. You and your father are coming to live with me. I've made up my mind, go get your coat.

Well, why not? My mother's been gone a long time, and there's no one to play games with me. And not only has the radio forgotten the songs it used to sing, but the dancing broom has forgotten the steps that Mommy taught it to do.

Nana, pinning her black hat, the one that looks like a stovepipe, to her snowy white hair says: I've made up my mind. It will be best for all of us—for you too, Mrs Ryan. I'm going to take my son and granddaughter to live at my house.

Mrs Ryan doesn't say a word, only shakes her head side-to-side, as if there's no use talking to Nana. Everyone knows that once Nana's made up her mind, that's it. Nana tells Mrs Ryan she's going home to switch the rooms around and give Daddy and me her bedroom.

If you do that, Nana, where will you sleep?

I'm going to turn the dining room into a bedroom. It's right next to the parlor, so that way I'll have me a suite of rooms. Imagine that, me with a suite!

A sweet? I don't know what she's talking about.

That night, Daddy says, we're moving to Nana's. Go get your dolls.

Well, why not? I don't like it here without Mommy. All

day long the windows are crying their eyes out and the living room walls are grey with shadows.

We have to straighten up this place, Daddy says, before we leave.

So that night, we wash the walls with our tears and punch the dust out of the rugs with our fists and pull down all the shades to make the shadows go away.

Did you pack your storybooks?

THE NEXT DAY my father takes me with him to Mr Kirkbauer's butcher shop on West Farms Road. It's a busy street, but I can see the green-and-white striped awning a block away. On one side of the building is a pink pig with a curly tail, dancing on top of the letters H-A-M. I know that word—it says ham. I like ham, and I like Mr Kirkbauer's butcher shop. When you open the door, a cowbell over the door jingle-jangles. But where are the cows?

Oh, liebkin, Mr Kirkbauer says, the cows don't come home until after dark.

Everything in the butcher shop is white—white tiles on the floor, white tiles on the walls, white tiles on the ceiling. There's even a white refrigerator big enough for the butchers to walk in and out of all day long and two white scales for weighing the bologna and liverwurst. The butchers—Otto, Hugo, and Mr Kirkbauer—wear white shirts with black bow-ties and long white aprons splattered with blood. The only thing not white is the sawdust clinging to my socks.

My father jokes with Otto, telling him to keep his finger off the scale. When I ask why Otto's weighing his finger, they laugh.

Liebkin, vat vould you like today? Livervurst or bologna? Mr Kirkbauer is very nice, but he has this funny way of talking.

A couple of days after my grandfather died, Mr Kirkbauer gave my father a job as a delivery boy. At first, they didn't pay him, not with real money. Instead, they gave him all the meat, chickens, and cold cuts Nana needed to feed her six children. After my father had been a delivery boy for a year, they made him a butcher. Today, we're here to pick up his knives and say good-bye. Daddy has a new job with the Great Atlantic and Pacific Tea Company, taking care of all the oil burners and refrigerators in the Bronx. Everyone's sorry to see him leave.

Don't be a stranger, Eddie.

Come back and see us, liebkin, Mr Kirkbauer says, patting me on the top of the head, flattening my pink bow.

When the cowbell rings, I look around to see if the cows are coming down the street. I wish I could see them—just once.

There are no empty rooms at Nana's, no creepy shadows on the walls. The kitchen is bright and sunny, and the radio plays music all day long. Sometimes when the music's playing, Aunt Betty dances me around the kitchen and down the hall on the tops of her shoes—just like Mommy used to do. Aunt Betty lives with us because her husband is in the Army.

After everyone leaves for work in the morning, Nana makes herself a cup of tea and pulls up a chair. Keeping one eye on the stove and the other on her prayer book, she says her prayers.

What are you praying for, Nana?

I'm praying for more money. It's hard to keep up with the bills.

Which saint has all the money?

The Infant of Prague, he's my little man.

Nana, look, I say, pointing to a picture of the Infant on her novena booklet. Does he keep the money in the ball he has in his hand?

No, that's no ball, she says. That's the whole wide world he's holding in his hand, shows you that he's thinking of us every minute. When I'm a smidge short, he comes through with a little extra for me. A dollar's not like a rubber band, you know, you can only stretch it so far.

Why, what happens then?

What do you mean *what happens then?*

What happens if you stretch it too far?

Off you go now. Be a good girl, go get me my glasses. I left them in the parlor on top of the sewing basket.

The statue of the Infant of Prague, the one she keeps on her dresser, is taller than a milk bottle but nowhere near as tall as I am. Every day, the Infant wears a gold crown and a red cape that Nana made for him, but at Christmas, she puts on his white cape with gold rickrack. I wouldn't mind having a cape like that myself. Under his feet is a card about the size of a picture postcard: *Ask and you shall receive. Knock and the door shall open.*

Which door do you knock on, Nana?

It doesn't matter, any door will do.

When you knock, who answers?

It doesn't work quite that way.

If I knocked on the back door, maybe my mother might be on the other side. Nana, how much money did you ask for today?

Not much, it changes from week to week and month to month. I let him decide. I simply say, here I am your poor child, Agnes, who needs your help. And then he helps me, as much as he can. There are a lot of people looking for help.

If Nana loses something—yesterday she lost her glasses—she goes to the ruby-red vase and takes out the Saint Anthony booklet. Then talking out loud, she says: Saint Anthony, Saint Anthony, look all around. Something's been lost and cannot be found. That's when Saint Anthony whispered in her ear to go check her housedress, the one rolled up in the hamper. Sure enough, she found her glasses.

Nana, can Saint Anthony find people who are lost?

I don't know about people, but he's found my glasses, my rosary beads, and my sewing scissors. He's got good eyes, all right, much better than mine.

My eyes are good, Nana.

Yes, but our eyes here on Earth are nowhere near as good as those up in heaven looking down on us.

Making a novena is hard work. Nana has to pray every hour for nine hours straight and do the same thing over and over for nine days. Nine is the magic number. No time-outs allowed. If you miss, you have to start all over again.

She keeps all the novena booklets in the ruby-red vase, the one Daddy gave her the day we moved in. My favorite is the one that has a picture of a young girl on the cover. They call her the Little Flower, Nana said, and she's a great favorite with all the angels and saints. If I pray to her, she might send me a rose.

All the way from heaven?

All the way from heaven.

Okay, I'll do it, I say, thinking a rose would be nice. Especially now when there's snow on the ground, not a dandelion in sight. Slipping the Little Flower's picture under my pillow, I take it out at night to talk to her. Sometimes I tell her what I did during the day, sometimes I ask what she's been doing and if she's seen my mother. So far, I haven't found a rose, and the Little Flower hasn't found my mother. Even so, I like talking to her. Talking to her is like talking to a big sister. If I had a big sister, then I wouldn't be all alone. It's not the same having a baby brother who's in the hospital.

Veronica and Ed

A few days ago, Nana got a phone call from Mother Theophilia, the superintendent at St. Elizabeth's Hospital. Mother Theophilia has been taking care of my baby brother ever since they found him at the hospital. It's a big job, because he's so tiny, not much more than three pounds. Mother Theophilia calls the house all the time to let Nana know how he's doing. That day he wasn't doing so good, and Mother Theophilia was worried.

Agnes, she said, I'd like you to come down and take a look at the baby. I'm wondering how you would feel about taking him home.

Taking him home? What do you mean, Sister, taking him home? How can I take him home? He's still in the oxygen tent, isn't he?

That he is, Agnes, that he is. But the poor little thing's not gaining any weight, not even an ounce. He's no bigger than a baby bird. I'm afraid he's not going to make it, but we don't know what to do for him. Do me a favor, Agnes, come take a look at him.

But Sister, can he breathe on his own, without the oxygen?

He can. We take him out for a feeding or to change the diaper, but the trouble is he's not gaining weight. You have to see the little arms, no bigger than matchsticks.

Are you sure he's warm enough, Sister? Do you have a blanket on him?

The doctors say he doesn't need a blanket, Agnes—the incubator's warm enough.

Don't listen to them, Sister, do what I tell you and put a light blanket over him. If nothing else, it will make him feel good. Otherwise, the poor little thing is flailing about, half-frightening himself to death. And Sister? Put a cap on his head, it will help keep in the warmth.

But, Agnes, you will come, won't you?

Of course, I will, Sister.

FLINGING HER BIBBED apron over the back of a chair, Nana tucked a few strands of silky white hair into the top of her stovepipe hat and pinned it together with a six-inch hatpin that, at one end, has the biggest pearl in the world. After that, she took a large shoebox and buttoning her long black coat—everything's long on her because she's so short—took the subway downtown and caught the cross-town bus.

When she got to the hospital, Mother Theophilia was waiting in the lobby, her face like a white star in a black universe. That's what Nana said: Her face was like a white star in a black universe. Mother Theophilia was upset because she has not forgotten that day, months ago, when the baby arrived at the hospital and Mommy disappeared.

When Daddy brought Mommy to the hospital, the nuns told him that they had called the doctor and he was on his way. That he should go home, get himself some rest, and they'd call him as soon as they knew anything. He had a lot of errands to do and never got back to the hospital until six o'clock. By that time, Mommy was missing. The nuns ran all over the place looking for her, and they even called the priest asking for his help, but it was too late. She was gone.

When Daddy heard this, he went crazy—yelling at the doctor, yelling at the nuns, yelling at the nurses, and yelling at Mother Theophilia. No one yells at Mother Theophilia, but he did. She told Nana that what happened next she would never forget—the way he tore the sheets off the bed, knocking over a lamp and leaving it in smithereens. He was like a raging bull, he was. That's what she called him—a raging bull. And the language! She had never heard such language in all of her born days. As if it was her fault

Mommy was missing. Mother Theophilia never wanted to go through that again, not on your life. That's why she called my grandmother.

With a shoebox tucked under one arm, Nana went into the nursery and saw my baby brother kicking his blanket.

See that, Sister? He's getting stronger every day, she said. I think he's ready to go home, yes I do.

When she heard that, Mother Theophilia breathed a sigh: Praise God!

Sister, get me a roll of the cotton batting.

When she got her hands on it, she pulled it apart like cotton candy and lined the shoebox. After that, there wasn't much for her to do, other than sign a paper saying she was taking the baby home, and that the hospital was not responsible for him. All the nuns at the hospital were so happy to see him go home, and when they said their evening prayers, they said a special prayer for baby Eddie. Praise be!

When Nana brought him home to 3272 Decatur Avenue, we emptied a dresser drawer and lined it with hot bricks, and after that we covered the bricks with bath towels. She put the drawer in the kitchen near the oven, but not in the draft that comes whistling through the back door.

Well, missy, Nana said, it's time for us to put your baby brother in his bassinet. So we did. And that's how you turn an empty drawer into a baby's bassinet.

Now, don't touch the baby, she says, as I stand tippy-toed, trying to get a good look at him.

He's small, Nana. Hello, Eddie! Look, he smiled at me, Nana.

He's no bigger than a baby bird, but you give him time, and he'll be a big boy one of these days.

Nana walks around the house carrying him on her shoulder all day long. She says you have to hold tiny babies a lot, so they can hear your heart beating. She says that when he gets bigger, I'll be able to hold him, and then he'll be able to hear my heart beating too.

Now, Daddy, Eddie, and me are living on Decatur Avenue with Nana, Uncle Fred, and Aunt Betty. Everyone's here except my mother who's still missing. How will she find us? what if she goes back to our apartment on Ryer Avenue? will the super tell her we moved to Decatur Avenue?

WEIGHING IN at three pounds, two ounces, my baby brother takes the neighborhood by storm. News of his arrival spreads like wildfire up and down the block. It's a miracle, everyone says. Such a tiny tot and still alive. Mercy, mercy! Like a Tom Turkey before Thanksgiving, Nana wants to fatten him up, so she feeds him all day long using an eyedropper . . . *drip, drip, drip.*

Every one of my grandchildren is the picture of health, she says, and this little one will be, too. Mark my words. Not today or tomorrow, but one of these days.

For his sake, I hope he doesn't get sick. When I'm croupy or coming down with a cold, she mixes a teaspoonful of yellow mustard seed powder with a few tablespoons of white flour and adds enough water to make a gloppy paste. Then she smears the stuff on a piece of flannel and puts the flannel on my chest. I don't like it one bit, but by morning the germs are gone. They don't like it either.

One night, when I was coughing like crazy—half-asleep, half-awake for hours—I heard her slippers *slap-slapping* the linoleum in the hallway. When she bent over my bed in the dark, I said: Hi, Nana! She jumped a mile, and I laughed out loud.

Oh, hush! You scared the daylights out of me! Open the top of your pajamas so I can see if you're getting blisters. She says people with freckles and light skin get blisters.

Another thing she does when I don't feel so good is mix apple cider vinegar with honey and warm water. When I have a tummy ache, she says drink some. For a sore throat, let me hear you gargle. Eddie's lucky he doesn't have to do any of these things.

Most people never bother to ring the bell, they just walk on in and come on down the hall to see what's cooking. One of my aunts usually stops by in the morning to see if Nana needs anything from 204th, and one of my uncles comes by at night to see how we're all doing. Everyone calls Nana by a different name. My Uncle Jack—a New York City fireman who keeps barbells in the hall closet—calls her Aggie. My Uncle Walter—he works at Con Edison during the day and at Prentice-Hall at night—calls her Mother, but she's really his mother-in-law. The Franciscan nuns call her Agnes. The neighbors call her Mrs Bracht. My father calls her Mom. I call her Nana.

Uncle Fred, who calls her Ag, wants to plant the spring bulbs in the backyard. Last week, they finished the fall planting over at Woodlawn Cemetery, and the foreman gave him a bagful of bulbs to take home.

Why can't we plant roses, Uncle Fred? If we had roses, then the Little Flower could put a rose on my pillow.

If we had roses in the yard, he says, I could put a rose on your pillow.

No, that doesn't count, because it wouldn't be a miracle. I want a miracle, a real miracle. If the Little Flower left me a rose, I'd know for sure she can hear me when I'm talking to her. Otherwise, how do I know for sure?

Uncle Fred doesn't know a thing about the saints or the Little Flower, not the way Nana does because he's a Protestant.

You know, Fred, Nana says, if you plant the bulbs in the backyard, the children will be walking all over them. It's going to be a muddy mess. Why not put them out front, where people can see them when they're going by?

Nope, he doesn't want to do that. He wants to plant morning glories out front and daffodils and irises out back.

Nana's right about us kids walking all over the yard. Rain or shine, every day of the year, a half-dozen pair of Buster Browns crisscross the backyard—going from the swings to the gliders, from the gliders to the sandbox, and from the sandbox up the rickety old back steps to the kitchen. Looking for a Band-Aid, looking for sympathy. That's why our backyard has hundreds of dandelions, not much grass.

There's nothing tougher than a dandelion, Uncle Fred says. He ought to know because they've got a million of them at the cemetery.

Don't worry, Ag, the bulbs will be fine out back. That way you'll be able to see them from the window.

See them from the kitchen window? You don't say! You must think I have nothing better to do with my time than sit around watching the flowers grow, she says, shaking her head side-to-side, as if it's the dumbest thing she's ever heard him say.

When we're all around the table after dinner—except Eddie who's in his crib—Uncle Fred's looking at a garden catalog from the W. Atlee Burpee Company, at the seeds for spring planting. On the cover is a yellow tomato, something no one in my family has ever seen. I want him to buy those seeds, but Uncle Fred says he's not going to waste his money on yellow tomato seeds, because they couldn't possibly be as juicy as the reds.

He buys his seeds from W. Atlee Burpee. Last year, he bought zinnias and morning glories that cost fifteen cents a pack. The white cabbage seeds were only ten cents, but we like flowers better than cabbages. Best of all are the morning glories that race up the strings to the top of the front porch—like trapeze artists at the Barnum & Bailey Circus. The time Aunt Dot took Aileen, Sis, and me to the circus, she bought each of us a cupie-doll on a stick. The dolls were so pretty—with pink feathers and spangles—we almost forgot to watch the clowns tripping over their own shoes and the dogs jumping through the high hoops.

THIS MORNING, Nana woke up with a toothache and had to go see the dentist. I'm staying at Aileen's until she comes back. After we finish our peanut butter and jelly sandwiches,

Aunt Dot says we have to take naps. Sharing a bed with my cousin is fun, but it's hard for us to fall asleep. We keep peeking at one another and giggling. Each time I open my eyes, Aileen's watching me, and when she closes her eyes, I stare at her until she opens them again. Then we laugh and laugh. Until she snatches my doll.

She's mine! Give her back!

No, it's my house, she says.

What a snip! I pull her hair, but she won't let go of Betsy-Wetsy. She's jealous because her dolls don't drink water and wet their diapers—not like Betsy-Wetsy does.

You're too heavy, I tell her. You're smothering her. Get off, get off.

All this time, my aunt's ironing the sheets and pillowcases on her ironing mangle in the kitchen and can't hear a thing. Other than the thumping and bumping of the roller as it hits the ironing board.

Not sure how to get back Betsy-Wetsy, I bite Aileen on the arm. When she sees the tiny tooth marks, she lets out a scream that has my aunt running like a dog with its tail on fire.

She bit me, Aileen said, between sobs and sniffles.

She took my doll and won't give her back, I say, scooting to the far end of the bed, but not fast enough. Before I can say another word, my aunt grabs my arm and bites as hard as she can. Tit-for-tat! We don't bite people.

Living on Decatur Avenue with all the cousins, there's always someone to play with, something to do. In the morning, the Dugan's truck comes down the street, and if Nana needs anything, we stick a sign with the letter 'D' in the front window so he knows enough to stop. On Wednesdays, when the Prudential Life Insurance Company agent drops by to pick up Nana's payment for her life insurance policy, he stays for coffee. Everyone likes to talk to Nana, and Nana likes to talk to everyone. As soon as I hear him coming down the hall, I run to get her payment booklet from the top drawer of her bureau. She pays him ten cents a week for a policy to cover the cost of her funeral.

Nana, don't pay him! I don't want you to die. When people die, they go to heaven, and you don't see them anymore.

Nana says she's not going to die, not yet, but that when she does, she doesn't want anyone paying one red cent for her funeral. Not one red cent.

Lighting up a White Owl cigar, the Prudential agent hands me the gold paper band. I slip it on my pinky hoping it doesn't break, but they all break. For Christmas, I'm going to ask Santa for a real ring. The only jewelry I have is a medal and, for all I know, I may have been born with it.

You can't beat a five-cent Havana, the agent says, they're the best money can buy.

If they're as good as he says, how come they stink up the house to high heaven? Cigar smoke gives me headaches, pipes not so much. As soon as he's gone, I run around like a chicken without a head, flapping a dishtowel, chasing the smoke out the backdoor. Nana doesn't mind the smoke, but she doesn't like him using a saucer as an ashtray.

Good riddance to that cigar, she says, as she pinches her nose with one hand and tips the saucer with a stogie, all wet with spittle, into the garbage pail.

Nana, your face looks funny scrunched up like that!

On Fridays, the agent from the Metropolitan Life Insurance Company comes by, but instead of a pocketful of five-cent Havanas, he has a pocketful of Necco wafers. The Metropolitan Life Insurance Company—they're very strict—gave her a booklet with all the rules.

- Premiums are due each Monday, in advance.
- If the Agent does not collect the premiums when due, send them to the District Home Office in New York or to the Head Office in San Francisco, California.

- Checks or money orders should be made payable only to the Metropolitan Life Insurance Company.
- An Authorized Agent must enter premiums in this Premium Receipt Book.
- A policy on which premiums are unpaid for more than four weeks is lapsed. Be safe, pay the premiums in advance.

Nana might skip a week once in a while, but never more than one. If she's short money, the agent still stops for coffee and Dugan's.

What she never does is send payments all the way to San Francisco because she says that's demented.

What's demented?

Sending a dime to San Francisco, that's demented.

When you die and go to heaven, Nana, will you see Grandpa?

Heavens to Betsy, no! Not after what that man did to me.

Swallowing hard, I ask what he did.

What did he *do*? I'll tell you what he did. He dropped dead at a traffic light on me, that's what he did. Can you imagine? Forty-one years old, he was, and perfectly fine when he left home that morning. I made him breakfast, packed him a lunch, he walks out the door and that's the last I see of him. Three hours later the neighbors come running to tell me he's dead. I collapsed right there in the doorway, fainted dead away. They even put that about him dying and me fainting in the newspaper. Can you believe that?

He died so fast?

Like that, she says, snapping her fingers. And me living out there in the sticks in East Williston with six kids. No job, no money, no way to pay the rent. Nothing.

When she says that, tiny beads of perspiration break out on her forehead. I kiss her on the cheek. Her Grandma-skin is cool and clammy.

Don't be sad, Nana, but tell me what happened.

Well, the first thing I did was move us out of East Williston and back to the city. We were city folks. When I met your grandfather, he was living on West 164th Street. But there was no talking to that man.

He liked living out there in East Williston, liked that big old house we had on Sagamore Avenue. Right next door to the firehouse, it was. He volunteered so often, they made him captain. And what did he do? He got rid of the bell, and put in a siren to call in all the volunteer firemen. You could hear that thing a mile away. Every time it went off, I'd jump out of my skin. That story made the papers too. He liked things up-to-date, your grandpa did. The man didn't have a lazy bone in his body. When he wasn't working on other peoples' cars, he was tinkering with his own. I'd go out looking for him, and all I could see was a pair of legs sticking out from under the car.

I laughed when she said that.

Your grandpa was the shop foreman for Mack Markowitz, in Mineola. Mr Markowitz was the biggest Oldsmobile dealer on all of Long Island, and he wouldn't let anyone but your grandpa work on his cars. That's what he was doing, testing a car for Mr Markowitz when he stopped at Main and Second and had a heart attack. When it came to cars, your grandpa was a genius.

I bet he'd like Daddy's truck. Did Grandpa have a truck?

No, he had something better. He had a 1923 Model T Ford. It was a coupe—a big open-air car with a spare wheel up front on one side and leather seats. A grand car, it was—the headlights bigger than dinner plates. And he had something else! A chauffer's license. Not many people in those days had a chauffer's license, but your grandpa did. When we lived in the city, he drove for Mr Seaman, a big shot at Birmingham & Seaman Company. They were paper manufacturers with an office at 200 Fifth Avenue—the lobby of that building was something to see. When we rode down Fifth Avenue in that car, I felt like her Royal Highness, Miss High-and-Mighty. Mr Seaman was a gentleman, he was. They don't make men like him anymore. When the company had a good year, he'd send his employees a letter thanking them for their loyalty and hard work and giving them ten percent of their wages as a Christmas gift. I kept the letter, still have it.

Where's Grandpa now?

He's in Brooklyn at the Green-Wood Cemetery.

Listening to her, I feel sorry Grandpa's all alone in Brooklyn—waiting for Nana to come visit, waiting to hear what happened to his 1923 Model T Ford. Nana doesn't know how to drive, doesn't own a car. Maybe that's why she doesn't want to go to Brooklyn when she dies.

ONE DARK nippy winter night, an insurance agent I never saw before comes to the house after dinner. When I run to answer the bell, he asks if my father's at home. The agent is dressed head-to-toe in brown—a brown suit, brown hat, brown shoes, and a brown leather briefcase stuffed with papers. He looks important, his briefcase looks important.

Yes, he's home, I'll show you. Skipping ahead, leading the way down the hall, I have no idea he's here about an insurance claim. What happened is that Daddy was driving down Parkside Place, two blocks from the house, when his car burst into flames. The flames came pouring through the front of the car, and his pants caught on fire. Thinking fast, he jammed on the brakes and slapped at his legs, trying to put out the flames. Then he crashed into a pillar of the Third Avenue El, right where Parkside Place runs into Webster Avenue. Aunt Betty and I walked down the hill to see the dent in the pillar. Nana says he was lucky to get out alive, that he could have died. His legs and feet are a mess—red and raw with big watery blisters—and he needs crutches to get around. Yesterday, Nana was busy and wanted me to put the salve on my father's feet, but I couldn't do it. Looking at his feet made me sick to my stomach. I ran back and told her I was going to puke.

You're going to puke, Nana says, is that so? I'll tell you one thing, missy, don't be a nurse when you grow up. That's not for you. Let me have the ointment.

When the agent enters the bedroom, my father's propped up in bed on pillows, his bandaged legs straight out in front of him, stiff as ironing boards. I run back to the parlor where the announcer's saying: *Wheaties, the Breakfast of Champions is bringing you the adventures of Jack Armstrong, the All-American Boy.*

Before we can find out what Jack's up to tonight, we hear angry voices coming from the bedroom.

Go see what's happening, Nana says. See if your father's all right.

Standing in the doorway of the bedroom, wanting to hear what they're saying, but not wanting to miss what Jack's saying, I think it's all about the money. The insurance agent doesn't want to pay my father the money he owes him.

It was an accident, my father says, and my policy covers that. You know it does, it was an accident.

It doesn't matter. I need you to sign these papers.

No, I've paid my premiums. You owe me that money.

The company doesn't see it that way. You need to sign the release papers.

No, it wasn't *my* fault that the engine exploded. It was an accident, the policy covers accidents. You can see for yourself, go look at the car if you want to. It's over at the garage.

Uh-oh. With their voices rising, my heart gets panicky. When my father puts the rubber tips of the crutches on the floor, the agent yanks one of the crutches out of his hand. Is he going to hit Daddy with it? I run across the room, shouting: You leave my daddy alone! And for good measure, I kick him in the shins.

Surprised by the sneak attack, he tries to hold me at arm's length. My father tells me to calm down, says it's okay. But it doesn't feel okay to me. I feel as if I've had a narrow escape. I've already lost my mother, what if something terrible happens to my father?

You'll hear from my company, the agent says, buttoning his overcoat and heading into a night that's as black as shoe polish, leaving the insurance papers scattered all over the floor.

Falling asleep that night, I dream I'm riding in the backseat of our Buick. There's an explosion, and the car bursts into flames. A big brown bear jumps onto the running board, growling: Sign the papers, and I'll let you out.

I wake in a sweat, my heart hammering. Calm down, take it easy, I tell myself, it's only a dream. Dreams aren't real, they just feel that way.

After everyone leaves for work in the morning, the house gets as quiet as paint drying on the backyard fence. We've been living at Nana's for about a year, and one of the things I like doing is walking room to room, listening to all the quiet that rushes in when everyone goes off to work. It's as if I'm looking for something, but don't know what. Something's missing, I've got to find it.

In Uncle Fred's room—Uncle Fred is my father's uncle, Nana's brother-in-law, and my great-uncle, although I don't think he's all that great—there are no holy pictures on the walls, only a picture of a cat with one eye open, one eye shut. The whole time I'm in the room, that cat's watching me. It's really spooky.

The room smells sweet and tangy, like the Prince Albert tobacco on the dresser. Prince Albert wears a red coat with shiny brass buttons and a flower pinned to his lapel. No one I know dresses as nice as he does, but I don't like that kinky black beard. No one in our family has a beard. In fact, if Nana gets even one tiny hair on her chin, she plucks it out, saying it's not very attractive. I think she's right.

Why doesn't Uncle Fred have a crucifix in his bedroom?

Nana says it's because he's Protestant, that only Catholics have crucifixes on the walls.

Is that why he doesn't go to church with us on Sunday?

All the questions! Skedaddle. Go out and play.

When Uncle Fred left for work this morning, he told me not to touch his things, to stay out of his room. That's because last week, I accidentally knocked over the tobacco jar. Even though I scooped up all the bits and pieces and put them back in the tin, he could tell I'd been in his room and didn't like it. Yet—this is true, cross my heart—if Eddie had knocked over the tobacco jar, it would be a different story. My uncle wouldn't have said one word.

How come you never scold Eddie?

Eddie's younger than you are, he says, he doesn't know any better, but you do.

I think he likes Eddie better, because Eddie's a boy. He lets Eddie play with the peewees from Germany. I asked if I could play with them, but he said girls don't shoot marbles. I told him I'd shoot them, if he'd let me, but he won't. When I asked if I could have one of the tobacco cans for my crayons, he said I could when it was empty. I'm waiting.

UNCLE FRED was too old to go to war, so he signed up for classes and learned how to fix broken water lines and repair the electric wires—in case the Germans bomb us on Decatur Avenue. When he went to the police station to register, they took his fingerprints and his picture. Daddy said he'd better be careful or he might end up in the hoosegow.

What's a hoosegow? A jail, he said. But they didn't send him to jail. Instead, they gave him a badge for *The Civilian Defense of the Homeland.* When the air-raid sirens go off, he puts on his white helmet and walks around the neighborhood, checking to see if the shades are down. If he sees a scrap of light coming from a window, he raps with his nightstick: Put out that light, the Krauts are coming!

Most nights after dinner, he goes to his room to listen to Gabriel Heater on the radio saying: There's good news tonight! Everyone wants the war to end, wants the lights to come on again all over the world. My father doesn't have to go to war, because President Roosevelt wants him to keep the oil burners and refrigerators in the Bronx working. Nana's worried he's going to be called up any day, and then what? That's what she says: And then what? I don't know. Everyone hopes that it will be like the song Aunt Betty sings, the one about when the war is over there'll be no more good-bye kisses, only hello kisses.

Maybe then, Fred, you, too, can find yourself a lady friend, says Nana, and say hello to love.

Everyone laughs, except my uncle, who says he doesn't know about *that.* He hasn't found any live wires at the cemetery.

With everyone back from church, it's time for Sunday dinner, which, for me, is the best time of the week. Nana takes the roasting pan with the chickens from the oven, which is the prettiest thing in the kitchen. If most ovens are white, Nana's oven is pale green, with four pale green legs, each as thick and round as a bunch of celery. Nana likes having a high oven because that way she doesn't have to bend over.

As she places the chickens on the carving board, my father takes out the steel to sharpen the knife. No one carves chickens or turkeys better than he does. There's only one way to sharpen a knife, he says. You start by running the blade of the knife down one side of the steel, turn it over at the bottom, and then bring it back up on the other side. The steel is like a magic wand, sparks flying every which way. Eddie and I laugh and jump out of the way.

Aunt Betty and I take out Nana's good china—white plates with pink flowers in the center and gold along the edges—to set the table. Then we bring over a bowl of mashed potatoes with a lump of butter in the center, a bowl of green beans wet and shiny with melted butter, and a basket of Bisquick biscuits with the butter on the side. Everyone loves butter. Nana says the more butter you use, the better everything tastes. Aunt Betty slices the Ocean Spray cranberry sauce, trying to keep all the slices the same size, so no one is cheated.

Before anyone has a chance to shake out a napkin, I lean over and snitch a pinch of stuffing. I love stuffing even more than mashed potatoes. Ouch! It's hot. Popping it into my mouth to stop my finger from burning, I swallow fast and let out a big burp.

Are you all right? Aunt Betty says, her eyes narrowing the way Bambino's do when I tickle him behind the ears. Bambino is a golden-haired tabby with brown stripes and green eyes who lives next door with Mrs Bernacci. Every morning, he squeezes between the wooden slats in the fence and prowls around in our backyard, with his stomach pressed to the ground. Like a lion on a hunt.

Say you're sorry or leave the table, my father says, pulling out his chair, about to sit down.

I look at Nana, who's giving my father a bug-eyed look, her lips pressed together, as she pours gravy from the saucepan into the gravy bowl.

I said, say you're sorry or leave the table.

With all eyes on me, the word *sorry* gets stuck in my throat, along with the stuffing. Holding onto the sides of the chair, I swing my legs back and forth, without saying a word.

Say you're sorry.

A minute ago, the kitchen was full of happy faces—chairs scraping, napkins flapping, everyone waiting for someone to say grace—but now all the happiness has flown out the back door.

It was only a burp.

I don't care what it was, say you're sorry or leave the table, my father says, his eyes drilling holes into my head. I study my dress, saying:

I didn't do it on *purpose.*

It doesn't matter if you did it on purpose or not, say you're sorry.

Actually, I couldn't help it. (At five going on six, *actually* is a new word.)

Don't answer me back. Say you're sorry or go to your room, my father says, his face getting redder, still holding the back of the chair.

Do what your father tells you, Uncle Fred says, his sunburnt hands passing the basket of biscuits in front of me, not even slowing down for me to take one. Don't be a little fresh mouth.

That does it: *little fresh mouth* breaks the spell, lifting a curtain of fear that's been hanging over the plates and glasses.

Pass the cranberry sauce, Uncle Fred says, folding his cuffs back before cutting up a piece of chicken for Eddie who's seated in the high chair next to him.

My head hurts, Nana, I say, turning away from my father. Before she can say or do anything, my father interrupts:

I don't want to hear anything about headaches. Children don't get headaches. For the last time, say you're sorry or go to your room.

You can't make me, you're not my mother.

When those words spill out of my mouth, the warm air in the kitchen follows the happiness down the back steps. Shoes shuffle under the table. Uncle Fred clears his throat, something he does a lot anyway. It's as if no one knows what to say, their eyes darting back and forth like windshield wipers on a rainy night. My father moves around the table, grabs me by the arm and pulls me after him. I do a Raggedy Ann, go limp all over, dragging my patent leather Mary Janes across the linoleum.

Aunt Betty puts down her napkin, jumps up saying: Oh, Ed, please. Let her have her dinner. My aunt takes my hand from his, saying: She can lie on my bed.

I like that, because my room is halfway down the hall, but hers is off the kitchen. That way I could hear everything they're saying, if only my head didn't hurt so much. My aunt unbuckles my Mary Jane's and pushing a few strands of hair off my face, says: I hope you're not coming down with something. You feel hot.

My head hurts right here, I say, rubbing my forehead. However, rubbing it doesn't take away the pain. She goes to the window, pulls down the blackout shades, and in a split-second the bedroom goes from daytime to nighttime.

I'll be right back, don't move.

Move? How can I move? My head weighs a ton. I think I'm going to throw up.

She returns with an ice pack. Here, she says, take a nap, and you'll feel better when you wake up. I'll bring you something to eat in a little while.

I don't want to eat. My tummy's sick. Nana says I can have tea with milk when I have a headache.

Okay, I'll bring you tea with milk, but take a nap.

Nana doesn't know why I get headaches, because no one in our family gets headaches. Dr. Deganhardt says I'm not to eat pork or chocolate. I don't mind not eating pork, but I miss not having Hershey's in my milk. He said that when I have a headache, she should let me lie down in a dark room. And that's what I'm doing—the ice cubes melting and the water trickling over my forehead and down behind my ears and onto my aunt's pillow that smells like Yardley's English Lavender. Like a hug in a bottle. And even though my forehead hurts, my heart is breathing a little bit easier.

Nana keeps her *4711* from Germany in the icebox. Every time I open the door, there it is—a bottle of blue sky on a shelf. Aunt Betty says *4711* is a grandma's perfume, but that Yardley's is a modern perfume—one you can wear to work, to church on Sunday, and to the roller rink.

When I get sleepy, I meet Br'er Rabbit. We walk and walk and talk and talk as we cross a briar patch filled with stickers and thorns. The longer we walk, the better I feel. By the time I wake up, my headache's gone. From the kitchen, I hear my aunt saying: You're too hard on her, Ed. She's just a child.

She's right, I'm just a child.

A cool breeze comes through the back door. Nana, her silky white hair pinned up with black bobby pins, is helping me into a dress she made for my first day at kindergarten.

Hold still, she says, trying to puff up the bow in the back. As antsy as they come, I'm jiggling foot-to-foot, watching the sun climbing over the rooftops of the houses on Parkside Place.

Here comes Aunt Dot!

I can tell it's my aunt. She walks heavy on her feet, but when she's dancing the Charleston—arms and legs swinging, knees crisscrossing—she's as light as a feather.

Ooohhh la-la, how pret-tee you look, she says.

How come you're wearing lipstick today?

Because it's your first day at school, and I want to look nice when I meet your teacher. Do you like it? It's *Victory Red*, she says, puckering up as if she's going to kiss me. I'm too quick for her, jumping out of reach.

Okay, no kisses, but turn around so I can see the back of the dress. Mom, did you embroider all those cross-stitches by hand?

My grandmother and aunt know everything about sewing dresses, knitting sweaters, embroidering tablecloths, crocheting doilies, and baking cakes.

Will you look at the clock! You better skedaddle, Nana says. We don't want you late for school, not the first day.

Until this minute, I haven't given any thought to who's taking me to school.

Nana, I want you to come.

Sweetheart, I can't do that, she says, tugging the hem of my dress, wanting to make sure it's even all around. Aunt Dot's going to take you today.

Then I don't want to go.

If you don't go to school, how will you ever be as smart as Aileen? Pulling away, I'm heading for the back door.

You stop right there, missy. Don't make me angry.

But I don't know anyone at school. Why can't I stay home with you? I say, pulling a long face—my chin quivering, the tears welling in the corners of my eyes.

Temper, temper, my aunt says. Someone's getting too big for her britches.

Just look at me, Nana says. Do I look ready for school? Drawing her housecoat around her, she sits down to a cold cup of coffee.

My eyes jump from my grandmother to my aunt, from the faded housedress to the Buttermilk pattern. Nana, please come.

My poor knees are hurting. Climbing the steps at school

is too hard on them. Be a good girl, go with Aunt Dot. She knows all the teachers, I don't know a one. Who knows? You might have the same teacher Aileen had last year. Wouldn't that be nice?

It's true that her knees are swollen, big as elephant knees. Whenever we're playing in the yard—fighting over dolls and carriages, deciding who should sit where on which glider— she yells down from the back porch: Don't you make me come down or there'll be trouble. We laugh, because she doesn't mean it. She never comes down those rickety steps. If she did, she'd have to go up again.

My aunt hands me a pencil box and a handkerchief embroidered with a pink and purple flower saying: Time to go, Babs. Let's get this show on the road.

When we reach PS #56, at the corner of Decatur and 207th, I see right away that Nana was wrong, that there are no steps to climb. All we do is open the door and walk right in. And when we do, there's a problem. I've been assigned to a teacher who is new to the school, new to my aunt. When we finally find the right classroom and my aunt leans over to give the teacher my name, the teacher smiles, saying:

Barbara, why don't you let go of Mommy's hand. Would you like to go play with the girls in the dolls' corner?

Let go of Mommy's hand? My mind goes blank, my heart stands still. What's she talking about? doesn't she know this is my aunt, not my mother? should I tell her? There's so much going on in my head it's hard to hear what the teacher and my aunt are saying to one another. Is there some sort of rule that your mother has to bring you to school the first day? Seeing all the kids with their moms, my heart loses its confidence. If my teacher finds out, will she let me stay?

With all the questions spinning round and round in my head, I hold onto the edge of the teacher's desk and bite down hard on my bottom lip. I don't want to cry. If I cry, the kids will call me a crybaby.

Seeing my aunt getting ready to leave—wiggling her fingers free of mine, scooching a handbag under her arm—I beg her not to go: Stay! Stay!

The teacher tries to pry open my fingers, to pull them off my aunt's skirt. All my worries and fears are making it hard for me to breathe, hard for me to think. My cheeks are burning, my ears on fire. Filled with anger and shame, I don't know what I'm doing. The next thing I know, I bite my teacher on her wrist. I wasn't planning to bite her, I didn't want to bite her—it just happened. She lets out a cry of surprise.

Babs! Shame on you! Say you're sorry, says my aunt. You know better than that. We don't bite people.

Keeping my eyes fixed on my shoes, afraid to look up for fear I might fall over, I mumble *sorry*, hoping my aunt won't bite me, not like she did the last time—not in front of the teacher, not in front of the kids with mothers who never bite them. If I had a mother, I know she would not bite me.

A woozy feeling is moving up, up, up—from the tips of my toes to top of my stomach. When it reaches my head, I will become invisible.

∽

Aunt Betty invites a friend, Miss Marge, for Sunday dinner. What I notice right away is that they both wear their hair the same way—with the sides rolled up and pinned on top like bratwurst— and they both work at the Horn & Hardhart retail store on Fordham Road. On their days off, they like to skate at the roller rink on Jerome Avenue. It's packed all the time, they say, but there are guards who skate around to make sure there are no pile-ups. I'm hoping my aunt will take me one day, rent me a pair of those white leather skates with purple pompoms. When not skating or working, they like watching women's roller derby—say that the best skaters are Toughie Brasuhn, Gerry Murray and Kitty-from-Hell. Both Miss Marge and my Aunt Betty laugh—Oh, Ed!—at anything my father says. Clueless when it comes to matters of the heart, I'm surprised when Aileen tells me they're dating.

Who's dating?

Your father and Miss Marge.

Like how?

She's not sure, and I don't know either. So far, Eddie and I haven't been invited on any dates. My heart begins to climb a wall of worry. Dating, what does it mean?

COME SUMMER, all the men in our family stay in the city while the aunts and kids go to the country. This summer we're staying at Aunt Nellie's farm in the Catskills—a real farm with cows and chickens near Kingston. Aunt Nellie has ladies from town who help in the kitchen, and Claude who takes care of the farm all year round. When the cows are in the pasture, Claude lets us go into the barn and jump in the hay, but when they're in their stalls, he likes to keep things quiet, doesn't want to spook 'em, not when he's milking.

You have to go gentle with cows. If you rush 'em or talk too loud, they won't give milk. And you want to move real slow, he says, stretching his words out like rubber bands, so you don't make 'em nervous. When it's time to milk them, he pulls up a low stool and rests his head against the cow's side.

All the cows have names: Jessie and Bessie, Jumbo and Dumbo, and there's even one called Elsie, like Elsie the Borden cow.

Is there an Elmer?

Nope, no Elmer.

Elsie the Borden cow has a husband named Elmer.

Yup, I know, but this Elsie doesn't have a husband.

Even on the farm, there are rules. Rule One: Don't enter

the dining room until after the farm bell rings. Rule Two: When the bell rings, don't dilly-dally or your food will get cold. We kids never dilly-dally. Nana and the aunts hurry over from the cottages where they've been hanging up wet bathing suits and towels, and Claude, in his bib overalls with the metal snaps, washes up at the outdoor sink. In our seersucker sun-suits and leather sandals, we race around the table—Sit here! Sit with me! Babs, you promised!—everyone wanting to sit next to everyone else.

We like living in the cottages more than in the main house, because we can go in and out all day long—the screen doors banging, the floorboards creaking—without bothering anyone. And there are no steps for Nana to climb.

The cottages are like dollhouses for families, with everything in its place. What's good is that there are no kitchens, so we take all our meals together over at the main house. What's not so good is that there are no bathrooms, only a stinky outhouse with nasty horseflies buzzing around, trying to sting your butt. And there's no toilet paper, so we tear pages from the Montgomery Ward and Sears Roebuck catalogs.

At Aunt Nellie's farm, we catch butterflies with long floppy nets and grab frogs and salamanders with our bare hands. After dark, we capture fireflies and put them into empty Hellman's mayonnaise jars, but not before punching holes in the lids so they can breathe. Nobody wants to wake up next to a jar of dead bugs, so we let them go when we turn in for the night.

Climbing into bed—*now I lay me down to sleep*—I'm fast asleep before my head hits the pillow. A good thing, because there's not much time for me to worry about my father dating Miss Marge or about the Little Flower still not finding my mother. I wish I could stay at the farm forever.

One weekend, Daddy and Miss Marge drive up to Aunt Nellie's to see how we're doing. Everyone's happy to see them because we didn't know they were coming. I know one thing—Daddy and Miss Marge are still dating.

Holding onto my father's arm for dear life, I ask if I can stay all summer. Pul-lease? Are you and Miss Marge going to stay?

No, we're staying for lunch, but then driving back to the city.

That's probably a good thing, because there's no room in the cottages for them. Miss Marge is nice and smiles a lot. She picks up Eddie—anyone can lift Eddie, even soaking wet—and gives him a hug. I wonder if Daddy likes her as much as he likes my mother. Aileen says they're getting engaged, that she heard her mom and Aunt Betty talking.

Engaged, like what?

Before you get married, you get engaged. The man gives the woman a diamond ring, and it's for keeps.

Lying awake that night, I'm worrying about everything—worrying about my mother who's been gone so long and my father who's dating. No one tells me a thing. Saying my prayers, I pray that my mother will hurry up and find us before it's too late.

At St. Brendan's, Sister Mary Louise is teaching us how to write in script, the Palmer Method. Once we learn how to string our letters together, it will be easier than printing—like we did in kindergarten. Sister says you have to keep the pen moving across the paper, connecting all the letters in each word. To make it easier for us to learn the correct way to make each letter—capital and lowercase—Sister gave out penmanship cards, with arrows showing where to start each letter. Wanting to practice my letters after school, I took the card home yesterday and can't find it. Before going to bed last night, I put it inside my book, *Sally and Puff,* I know I did, but it must have fallen out on the way to school.

When Sister Mary Louise tells us to take out our penmanship cards, I don't know what to do. Watching her coming toward me down the aisle, I'm scared to death, my heart stuck in my throat. Psst! Jesus, can you hear me? Please, please, please . . .don't let her stop at my desk, make her stop at someone else's desk, tell them that they're holding the pen the wrong way.

Don't lift that pen off the paper, she says to the boy ahead of me. Keep it going, keep it going. Start the capital 'T' with a down stroke, not a loop.

Two shiny black shoes stop right next to my desk.

Where's your writing card? she asks in a squeaky little girl voice.

I can't find it.

I can't find it, *Sister*, she says, her face as squished as a wet Lipton's teabag.

I can't find it, Sister.

And why can't you? Take out your books right now and look for it.

I take out *Sally and Puff, Spot Helps Mother, Big and Little.*

What are all those books doing in your desk? You can only read one book at a time, isn't that so?

Yes, I answer sheepishly, not meeting her eyes.

Yes, *Sister!* I want you to put those books on the bookshelf where they belong. Yes, Sister.

It's that I love the stories about Dick and Jane and Sally and Spot and Puff. When you read the words, you see pictures in your head. Reading a book is like opening a box of Crackerjacks—when you get to the end, there's a surprise. After school, sometimes I read the books to Nana or, if she's too busy to my dolls.

Oh, oh. (Turn the page.) Look, look! (Turn the page.) See, see! (Turn the page.) Look what Mother found in the kitchen.

Who knows, one of these days I might find my mother in the kitchen.

With Sister Mary Louise glaring at me, making me panicky, I drop one of the books.

Is this how you treat school property? Pick it up, right now.

But I didn't…

But, *Sister*, I didn't…

But, Sister, I didn't…

Don't answer me back!

I want to tell her that I didn't do it on purpose, that it was an accident. I would never throw Dick and Jane on the floor.

First, you disobey and take home your writing card, and then you lose it. See? God's punishing you for not listening. What if we all behaved this way?

Biting my lower lip, I don't say a word, only stare.

And take that look off your face right now, she says, before giving me a whack on the back of my head. Seeing stars, I wave a hand in front of my face, thinking I could brush them away, but it doesn't work. I'd like to hit her back, but you're not allowed to hit nuns. What would Nana say?

After all, Nana's sister was a nun, Sister Bernadette of Lourdes, who died very young. At Christmas, Sister's friends—Sister Innocencia and Sister Evarista—visit, and we make Manhattans with Maraschino cherries. Before you can say cheers! everyone's laughing and having a good time. Last year, Sister Evarista, a principal of a grammar school, picked up the hem of her skirt and danced an Irish jig. I never knew nuns had legs like real people.

When Sister Mary Louise grabs me by the ear, I stumble after her to the front of the room where I have to stand with my back to the class. What if my mother walked in and saw me standing here like the class dummy? would her feelings be hurt? would she be angry with me or angry with Sister Mary Louise?

My stomach's sloshing like a washing machine. Afraid to look left, afraid to look right, my eyes travel upward to the crucifix above the board.

Psst! Jesus, can you hear me? Sister Mary Louise is so mean, as mean as one of the Roman soldiers. That's the truth.

Feeling woozy, I hold onto the ledge of the chalkboard. I feel ashamed—my cheeks, ears and neck red-hot. All I wanted to do was to practice my letters, and now look.

Stop playing with the chalk, Sister says. Put your hands by your side. Of all the children in this class, you are absolutely the worst one! I should send you to the principal's office. Maybe then, you'll remember what happened to your writing card. Take that look off your face.

Staring at my shoelaces, I'm wondering if nuns ever tell lies. Am I really the worst one in the whole class?

Sniff, sniff...

Crying's not going to find your writing card, Sister Mary Louise says.

When the lunch bell rings, I make a beeline for home.

Nana, you have to find my card. I can't go back to school unless I find it.

Don't be a silly goose. If you tell Sister you lost it, she'll give you another. Ask her, you'll see. Come, have your chicken noodle soup.

My grandmother doesn't know Sister Mary Louise, not the way I do. If only I had someone to help me. If my mother was here, she could go over to the school and talk to Sister, and then all kids would see I have a mother too.

On New Year's Day, the family—all the aunts, uncles, and cousins—gets together at Nana's. It's that time of year when she makes the eggnog with rum and the pound cake with raisins. That's when Daddy and Miss Marge tell everyone they're getting married in a few weeks, that they've found an apartment in Yonkers. Yonkers, where's that?

Everyone's laughing and happy for them, but at seven-going-on-eight, I'm wondering what it means for me. When you stop to think about it, why would I want to move to Yonkers? The best people live in the Bronx, the beautiful Bronx. Besides, Nana's good at finding places for people to sleep, so maybe she can find a place for Miss Marge.

No one asks my opinion about anything: How do you feel about leaving the Bronx, moving to Yonkers? So, you're going to another new school—your third, right? aren't you the lucky girl, your dad has found you a new stepmother? I'll tell you how I feel—I'm worried.

When I tell Daddy I want to stay at Nana's and don't want to move to Yonkers, Nana doesn't say a word, just sits watching. He says Sherwood Park is much nicer than the Bronx. How can it be nicer than the beautiful Bronx? When I tell him I don't know Miss Marge all that much, he says I'll get to know her once we move. The only time we see her is when she comes to the house for Sunday dinner. Though last month, she and Daddy took me to the Bronx Zoo where I rode a pony. Eddie's too small to ride a pony so he stayed home with Nana and Uncle Fred.

My father says when we move, I'll have a room of my own. My cousins will be surprised because they all share.

Can Nana come?

Nana has to take care of the house and look after Uncle Fred, but you can come down to see her whenever you want.

How far is it to Sherwood Park?

Three miles, that's all.

It's easy for him to say, because he has a car and a truck. Can you walk three miles? I might as well be living at the North Pole.

When it's not quite February, I'm helping Nana in the kitchen, saying something or other about Miss Marge this, Miss Marge that.

I don't want you calling her Miss Marge, my father says. I want you to call her Mother.

Mother? I don't want to call her mother. She's not my mother, and besides I hardly know her.

She's going to be your mother, he says, and if Eddie hears you calling her mother, he'll do the same thing.

Why can't I call her Miss Marge?

Because children don't call adults by their first names.

But I do, I call her Miss Marge now. You never said not to call her that before.

It's different. She's going to be your mother, so I want you to call her Mother. And stop arguing, not another word.

What choice do I have? The idea of calling Miss Marge Mother doesn't feel right. I'd rather call Aunt Betty *mother* because at least I know her. Miss Marge doesn't have any kids, so won't it sound weird to suddenly have Eddie and me calling her Mother? does he think that if I call her Mother, she'll get confused and think I'm her daughter? what if my real mother finds out about all this? will her feelings be hurt? will she think I've forgotten her? My head hurts.

C'mon, I tell myself, pretend it's a game. What game? *Can You Keep a Secret?* The problem with pretending is that once you start, it's hard to stop. And adding another player to the game only complicates things. My father says that if anyone asks any questions about our family, I'm to say that Miss Marge is my mother, that she's always been my mother. Not to say she's my stepmother.

The truth is that whenever I hear the word *stepmother,* I think of poor Cinderella whose father married the stuck-up Lady Tremaine all because he thought Cinderella needed a mother to guide her. What a mistake! Her stepmother was so mean and her stepsisters so dreadful, that just thinking about them gives me the shivers. At least, I don't have to worry about any stepsisters, because Miss Marge has never been married.

Maybe my father's hoping that our new neighbors will think we're the All-American family, and that he and Miss Marge are like Ozzie and Harriet. Fooling the neighbors is one thing, but pulling the wool over Eddie's eyes doesn't feel right. What if Eddie never learns the truth? when will I be able to stop telling lies? is telling lies a mortal sin or a venial sin?

Having a room of my own would be nice, but not nice enough to move to Yonkers. Besides, if Daddy, Eddie, and Miss Marge moved without me, I'd have a room of my own at Nana's. Though for all I know, Nana might have a waiting list for the rooms. Gosh! I'm going to miss Decatur Avenue. Miss the insurance agents who stop for coffee. Miss buying the boxes of Dugan's cupcakes—the icing so thick you can peel it off in one long strip. Miss the young man who delivers the crystalline bleach in old wine jugs, and the old man who sharpens the knives and scissors and has a pet monkey on a chain.

What a dingbat! Nana says. No one in his right mind keeps a monkey in a house. Mostly, I'll miss Nana's kitchen, with everyone coming and going. Usually Nana is so busy cooking, she doesn't have time to play games or read stories, not the way Mommy did, but she's smart. When she bakes, for instance, she never measures a thing—she uses a handful of this, a scoop of that and a few drops of vanilla. Everything she bakes is delicious, especially the warm rice pudding. Nana likes having people around. When I told her one day she was lucky Eddie and I moved in to keep her company, she laughed and said, Is that so?

M y father and Miss Marge got married last week, everyone throwing rice and confetti. Someone hung a sign—Just Married!—on the back of our Buick. Eddie and I did not go to the wedding, because we were not invited. Aileen says it's not fair. She says that we should have been the flower girls and that Eddie should have carried the ring on a pillow down the aisle. After all, that's what they do at real weddings. Aileen knows a lot about a lot of things. She knows, for instance, how to do subtraction and showed me how to do *take away* on my fingers. Aileen's my best friend, but if I told her anything about my mother, how she's been missing a long time, she'd tell her mother who would then tell my father, and I'd be in big trouble. My father has never said a word about my mother. I've never heard him say her name, never found a picture of her in the house. When Nana doesn't want to talk about something, she says: No sense in opening a can of worms. I think she's right. Who wants to open a can of worms in a house?

Today's moving day, with the house full of people, everyone wanting to say good-bye, good-bye, good-bye. Walking from room to room, I'm looking at this and that, looking at all the things I'm going to miss seeing. At Uncle Fred's pipes lined up in his pipe rack, the one he bought at the tobacco shop down on Gun Hill Road. At all the lipsticks, reds and pinks, on Aunt Betty's dressing table. At Nana's sewing basket filled with spools of thread, all of them with J&P Coats Company stickers on the bottom. Nana says J&P Coats thread is the best because it doesn't get knots.

What I remember is that when we moved in five years ago, I was so cold—as if someone had left me standing on a corner in a blizzard. Now, we're moving again, moving closer and closer to the North Pole. If this keeps up, how will I ever get warm?

By ten in the morning, the kitchen is up to its elbows in chopped tomatoes, onions, and parsley.

These onions are strong enough to make a grown man cry, Nana says, wiping away a tear. Here, I want you to take this with you, she tells Miss Marge, handing her a large jar filled with tomato sauce and meatballs. This way, you'll have yourself an easy supper. Cook up a pound of spaghetti, and you, Ed, and the children will be all set.

I can never make up my mind if Nana's more like Mary or Martha. Sister Mary Louise told us about the day Jesus stopped to visit the two sisters. Right away, Martha ran to get a bucket of water and an armful of firewood to start fixing dinner. On the other hand, Mary never helped her sister, not one bit. All she did was sit around all afternoon talking with Jesus. When Martha complained, Jesus said that Mary had done the right thing. I don't know about that. What if Nana sat around talking all day, who'd fix us dinner?

Cleaning out a closet, my father hands me a pair of scuffed shoes, saying: Throw these out, will you?

How come you're throwing out your dancing shoes, don't you want to go dancing anymore?

No, they're shot. Let's get rid of them.

When it's time to leave—everyone hugging and kissing, as if we're going to the end of the world—Uncle Fred promises to put up a birdhouse the next time Eddie and I come down. He's seen one at the hardware store with little cubbies, like an apartment house for purple martins.

Why can't we have a birdhouse for the bluebird of happiness?

Bluebirds are country birds, he says. They like wide-open spaces, fields and farms. I've seen a couple over at the cemetery, but not in backyards. But purple martins are city birds, and they eat a ton of insects.

I don't know which is better, a city bird or a country bird. All I know is that I feel like a baby bird being pushed from its nest. When I lost my mother, I lost the house that danced down on Ryer Avenue—lost all the songs, the games, and the dance steps. Now, again, I'm losing my mother—I mean, my grandmother—and the house that laughs on Decatur Avenue. My father says we're moving to a nicer place, but what could be nicer than living here in the beautiful Bronx? He's says he's found me a new mother, but who could be nicer than my old mother? I'm not even eight years old yet—two weeks to go!—and this will be my third mother, my third school, and my third house.

You're as jumpy as a Mexican jumping bean, Nana always tells me. You've got to settle down, missy. Settle down.

But if I keep jumping around like this, how will I settle down?

With Miss Marge helping my father pack up in the bedroom, and Nana and my aunts yakking around the kitchen table, I'm hanging out like a ghost in the hallway when I hear Aunt Dot say: Mom, has Babs ever asked you about Veronica?

Veronica? Who is she talking about?

Placing a finger over her lips, my grandmother shushes her, looks around to see if I'm listening. Aunt Betty interrupts, saying: She was way too *young* to remember . . .

Hiding in plain sight, I don't say a word. Grabbing Betsy-Wetsy under one arm, I pack up my crayons and paper dolls and get ready to move.

W here's the door?
        Where's the door? What do you mean *where's* the door? It's downstairs, my father says, we just walked through it.

But that's the outside door. Where's the inside door, the door to the apartment? Anyone could open the downstairs door and climb the stairs, the way we did.

What are you talking about? Walk upstairs into this apartment? That's nonsense.

I look from him to Miss Marge, but she's not saying a word, just looking around—checking out the cupboards, checking inside the refrigerator, checking the view from the kitchen window.

Are you *sure* this is a real apartment? It's not like Aunt Dot's apartment. It's not like Nana's house. Nana has a front door, a vestibule door, a door going into her apartment and a back door.

What kind of a question is that? Of course, it's a real apartment.

Then where are the doors?

Bang-bang, he shot me down, all my worries hit the ground. How can it be an apartment if it doesn't have a door with a lock?

You want a door? Look at these, he says pointing to a pair of pocket doors separating two rooms, one of which is going to be my bedroom, the other the living room.

What do you think of that view, huh? he says, his powerful freckled hands spread wide on the windowsill, shoulders hunched. Following his gaze, all I see is an empty lot with black weeds poking through dirty patches of snow.

It's nice, I say wanting to be agreeable. Miss Marge says he might want to put a hook in the closet for my bathrobe.

Where's Eddie's room?

He's going to have the room off the hall.

That room is about half the size of mine, but Eddie won't mind, because Eddie's a happy-go-lucky kid. He doesn't know a thing about our mother being lost, so he doesn't have to worry about her the way I do. He doesn't miss her, because he never knew her. And he doesn't have to worry about forgetting her, because he doesn't remember. It's easier being Eddie.

I'M AS jumpy as can be when Miss Marge and I register at PS #14. Arriving promptly at 8:30 a.m., she's not sure which is the main entrance, so we walk up the hill to the Villa Avenue side. Opening the door, sunlight comes rushing in, slipping and sliding past us on wooden floors as shiny as those down at the roller rink. Chalk dust hangs heavy in the air. An up-arrow in a stairwell points to the principal's office. Coming from a classroom, we hear the singsong voices of children pledging allegiance to the flag of the United States of America and to the republic for which it stands.

On the phone as we enter, Mrs Julia B. Gregory motions for us to take a seat on a bench by the wall. Miss Marge keeps opening and closing her handbag—what's she looking for?—while I kick my legs back and forth in time to a tune stuck in my head. The longer we sit, the more nervous I feel. It's that Miss Marge and I have never done this sort of thing before—she pretending to be my mother, me pretending to be her daughter. If Mrs Gregory is half as smart as she sounds, we're not going to get away with it. She'll see through us in a minute, see we're imposters. Making believe all the time is hard work.

There's a problem, but not any I expected. It's that there's a Catholic school way of doing things and a public school way. At St. Brendan's, for instance, I've completed grades 1A and 1B and should be going into 2A, whereas here at PS #14, everyone is in 2B, the second half of Second Grade. Swallowing hard, I'm hoping Mrs Gregory won't send me back to Sister Mary Louise. After looking over my school records, she calls in the school psychologist and tells Miss Marge that it's all right to leave me here. I'm not sure how I feel, but I think Miss Marge is happy to leave before the principal discovers she's telling a fib.

The school psychologist brings me into an empty class-room where we sit knee-to-knee, she asking questions, and I answering best I can. Easy questions like: What should you do if you lose a ball that belongs to someone else? Say you're sorry, get them another one. That sort of thing. After an hour or so, we go back to the principal's office, and Mrs Gregory has me follow her downstairs, where she introduces me to my new teacher. This must be my lucky day, because like magic I'm promoted to 2B. What's going to happen when my teacher finds out I haven't done any 2A work?

WITHIN MONTHS of our moving to Crescent Place, the whole family comes to visit, bringing with them our favorite foods—a strawberry Jell-O mold with Dole's fruit cocktail. A German-style potato salad slick with oil and topped with crunchy bacon bits. A bowl of elbow macaroni, each little elbow doing the backstroke in a pool of Hellman's mayonnaise. Aunt Dot bakes her famous German Bee Sting Cake—all custard-creamy on the inside, crunchy with almonds and honey on the outside—and Miss Marge bakes a finger-licking good Pineapple Upside-Down Cake. It's a battle of the vanillas.

Surrounded by my cousins—This is like living in the country! Look at the grass! Watch out, it's a bee!—the place begins to feel more like home. First thing we do is walk around the block to see what's on the other side. Then, we take turns jumping rope in front of the garage: *All in together girls how do you like the weather girls? January, February, March . . .*

Whoops! The rope snags my ankle, bringing me to the ground, leaving me with a bloodied knee. Stuffing my wounded pride into my pocket, I call back over my shoulder that I'm going to have my mom put Mercurochrome on it . . . Aileen—her pale eyes squinting, her mouth puckered with exasperation, the fists planted firmly on her hips—interrupts: She's *not* your mother. Stop saying that. Your mother's dead. My mother said so.

What did she say? My mother's *dead*? Stung to the point of tears, my throat closes down. I want to shout—Liar, liar, your pants are on fire!—but I can't get the words out. Aunt Dot said *that*? My make-believe world with a happy ending crumbles like a sandcastle at the beach. Aileen, head tilted to one side and a simper on her face, calls after me: If you don't believe me, go ask your father.

Ask my *father*? Whoa, not so fast, Cinderella. Looking back over my shoulder, I see my cousins shaking their heads in unison: Go ask your father.

Why should I? He's had plenty of chances to talk to me. If only I had been a steady-ender, none of this would be happening. ◗

Living in a house without a door is like living in a three-sided cabin. No one has to tell you something's wrong—you can feel it. With us living upstairs and Mrs Schwartz and Seymour down below, you'd think we were all one big happy family.

When Eddie's vacuuming the steps Saturday mornings, Mrs Schwartz is two steps away from him dusting the bookcase. It's as if they're a team—like Spic 'n' Span. Do my parents care? Not on your life. And Eddie? He's in a world of his own. If I complain we have no privacy in this apartment, my father says: what are you talking about? who are you to need privacy? where do you get these whacky ideas?

I don't know, they pop into my head when I'm not even thinking about them. But I don't tell him that. What I do say is that I don't like Mrs Schwartz knowing what I'm doing all the time, that it makes feel me uncomfortable.

Uncomfortable? I guarantee you, he says, Mrs Schwartz is not the least bit interested in what you're doing.

I'm not so sure about that. Last Saturday, when I was cleaning the bathroom, she came to the bottom of the stairs: Barbara? Yoo-hoo, Barbara. Well, I couldn't pretend I didn't hear her, not when she can hear me walking around.

You've had that water running in the tub for a good ten minutes, she said. Go turn it off before we have a flood.

I told her not to worry, that the stopper was out and that I still had to wash the floor.

It doesn't take that long to clean a tub, she said, now turn it off. Now. You're wasting water.

ANOTHER NIGHT, another story. If you think about it, Daddy, when we're not here, what's to keep Mrs Schwartz from coming upstairs and walking around. She could open the refrigerator, sit on the couch, go through my desk, and we'd never know if she did any of those things.

At this point in my tale of high drama and skullduggery, my father lets out a horselaugh, saying Mrs Schwartz has better things to do with her time than to go snooping in my desk.

Maybe so, but why we can't live in an apartment with a door? The Tudor houses in Scarsdale and Bronxville have heavy oak doors. Just like Nancy Drew's house in River Heights.

We're not moving to Bronxville, so get that out of your head.

Trying to bolster my case for moving, I throw in mention of Seymour.

Seymour? What about Seymour?

You have to admit Seymour's odd. All the kids say so. If he wanted to, he could creep up the stairs in the middle of the night and murder us in our beds. We'd have no protection. None.

You think Seymour's a killer and you have no protection? Your problem is that you're reading too many of those mystery books.

All I'm saying is that he *could* creep up the stairs, if he wanted to. I'm not saying he's a cold-blooded killer. But tell the truth, don't you think he's a bit strange?

My father shakes his head, returns to reading the paper. What's true is that Seymour, with his weak eyes and thick glasses, looks more like an accountant than a murderer. All he needs is a green eyeshade, like the one worn by the newspaper publisher in one of the Nancy Drew mysteries. Watching Seymour shuffle up the hill, his eyes glued to the pavement, his head flopping side to side, I feel bad for him. All the kids ask *what's the matter with Seymour?* I haven't a clue. *The Case of the Mysterious Downstairs Neighbor.* When I showed Nana the way he walks, she said he most likely has fallen arches.

Fallen arches? That's silly, Nana. It's not his arches, but his head that's the problem.

I'll bet he has flat feet. If you have flat feet, your head wobbles side-to-side, did you know that?

Rolling my eyes upward, indicating the idea too fanciful for words, I ask: Are you saying his feet are too tired to hold up his head?

Was Seymour in the Army?

I don't know. I don't know anything about him. He doesn't say hello, doesn't talk to any of the neighbors. If I acted like that, the neighbors would tell my mom—Mrs Bracht, do you know Barbara walks by without saying hello?—and I'd be in trouble. Seymour walks with his chin almost touching his chest. I think he's the shyest person I know.

Maybe so, but the Army will still take you if you're shy, but they won't take you with flat feet. You have to be able to walk a lot when you're in the infantry. Find out if Seymour was in the Army.

Maybe I will, maybe I won't. I have more to think about these days than Seymour. I have a new baby brother, and with my mom still in the hospital and my dad working, my aunts have been taking turns staying with me and Eddie—one baked us a cake, another made strawberry Jell-O. The baby's name is Kenneth James, but we're going to call him Kenny. My dad says he's cute as a button, with blond hair and big blue eyes. He's coming home tomorrow. What's really good is that tomorrow's Halloween—trick or treat! I'm going as a princess.

The Cousins

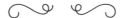

L evittown? There's nothing there but potato farms and hayseeds, my father says. I don't know what Gert and Joe are thinking, moving the kids from Astoria all the way out to the boondocks.

A few of my cousins, lucky stiffs, have moved into a house on Long Island, not an apartment but a house. We're driving out Sunday to see them, to see the house. I can't wait. I wonder what it would be like to have a house without Mrs Schwartz—Walk, don't jump on the stairs!—knowing when I'm coming and going all the time.

Let's hit the road early, my dad says, so we can beat the traffic.

On Sunday, with all the churchgoers still in the pews, it doesn't take much more than an hour for us to get there, where we drive up one lane and down the next, wanting to see *the miracle of Levittown*. What I notice is that all the streets have wonderful sounding names—names like Winding Lane, Windmill Path, and Snapdragon Road. But where are the hayseeds and where are the potato fields?

We stop at a Sales Office to see the two models—a ranch house like the one in *The Secret at Shadow Ranch* and a Cape Cod saltbox like that in *The Bungalow Mystery*. Choose one, I tell my heart, either one is fine with me. Watching a sizable crowd milling about in front of the house, I'm suddenly afraid that someone's going to beat us to it, going to plunk down their money before we have a chance. How many houses are for sale?

Digging deep in my pocket, I give a rabbit foot key chain a rub for luck.

Welcome to Levittown, booms a salesman coming over to the car. Welcome to suburbia! Which of our models would you like to see first? How about you, little lady, what's your choice?

Unable to say a word, choking on excitement, I'm thinking: I'll take the Cape Cod with the ocean breezes coming through the windows. Don't bother to wrap it, I'm in a hurry.

Scrutinizing my father's face for any sign of interest in a $7,990 house, I'm beginning to wonder if we have enough money. Anyone can see that a $7,990 Levitt house is a good deal, but do we have enough? When my father asks about the easy financing terms, my hopes soar on eagles' wings.

Are you a veteran? If you're a vet, the salesman says, you don't have to put anything down. Zero percent. Can't beat them terms for easy financing, can you? If you're not a vet, all you have to do is put five percent down.

I'm thinking *how much is five per cent down? is this how my dream ends?*

We have thirty-year mortgages available with low payments—$56 a month for vets, a shade higher for non-vets. And for that, you get a new house with GE appliances in the kitchen, a Bendix clothes washer, and tiled floors throughout the whole place. It's quite a deal. With three kids, you might want to look at the Cape Cod because it has an unfinished loft that could be made into another bedroom or two. All the backyards run together, so there's plenty of open space for the kids to play. Mr Levitt doesn't want any fences—no walls and no fences.

Listening to him, it sounds as if all we have to do is select a model, pick a property, and move in within months. Maybe right next door to my cousins on Crag Lane. Wouldn't they be surprised?

No need to pay it all up front, the salesman says, all you have to do is give us a small down payment.

Dizzy on hope, my brain's doing somersaults. My dream of living in a house has never been this close before.

Yep. Pick a site. We pour the concrete. We're using prefabricated panels and have shipments arriving from the factory every day. Why, little lady, he says, mussing my hair, your house could be rolling off the line in months.

He doesn't have to convince me, I'm sold. But why months, not weeks? Seeing a solution at hand: Daddy, can we buy one of the models?

No, they're not selling the models, not yet. They need them to show people what they're getting for their money.

In less time than it takes to say Rumpelstiltskin, a funny feeling creeps over me, making it hard for me to think straight. Until now, I've been filling my notebooks with sketches of old Tudors with slate roofs, pachysandra edging the walkways and wisps of smoke curling from chimneys. Psst! Heart-of-Mine, will you be terribly disappointed if we don't live in a Tudor? what if we lived in a Cape Cod with sea-blue breezes? or a ranch house with a hitching post out front? what do you say?

C'mon, says the salesman. Don't be bashful, look around.

I thought he'd never ask. Following him up the walk, I feel like Dorothy on the yellow brick road to Oz.

Get a load of the GE appliances in the kitchen, says the salesman, elbowing his way through the crowd. Sure to please the lady of the house.

The lady of the house? I look around to see if my mom's paying attention. When he says it wouldn't take much to turn the loft into an extra bedroom, I know exactly where to put the bed. Eddie and Kenny can have the room downstairs next to the bathroom. Where my father sees raw beams, sloping eaves and a lot of work, I see a room with a door—Please Knock. Just thinking about it, I sigh the longest of sighs. Wouldn't it be *wonderful?* A four-poster bed, a shaggy rug and a radio playing music all the time.

If my mom likes the fully equipped kitchen and my dad approves of the overall layout, I'm head-over-heels in love with a cream-and-burgundy wallpaper in the living room. No one we know has wallpaper, only paint on the walls. Checking to see if anyone's watching, I run a finger over a fuzzy Victorian design that's about the most stylish thing I've ever laid eyes on. How soon could we move in?

Mom, come look at this! I say, pointing to a Bendix washing machine with three cycles—wash, rinse, and spin—tucked under the steps that lead to the loft. Isn't this the greatest? Think about it, no more floods. A cardboard advertisement propped on top of the washer shows the woman-of-the-house beaming like a kid at Christmas, so happy to be doing the laundry: It's a snap with a Bendix.

Can we buy this house, Daddy? Pul-lease! Pul-lease! Pul-lease! Would Mr Levitt let us keep the wallpaper? My father ignores the question, tells the sales representative that he'll think about it and get back to him. What he doesn't do is give him any money as a down payment. I don't know who's more disappointed, the salesman or me. I look around at all the families going room to room, wondering which one will end up with the fuzzy wallpaper.

When we pull up to 10 Crag Lane, there sits a white Cape Cod saltbox with black shutters on a curve in the road. It's love at first sight, a love colored with craving and envy.

The cousins come running out, asking if I want to see their pool. A pool? We race three blocks to the South Village Green on Acorn Lane—Leapin' lizards!—to find a huge pool that's not yet filled, a playground with swings and slides, and a delicatessen newer and nicer than Alphonse's. With my head-in-the-clouds at the prospect of swimming in a pool only three blocks from their house—swan diving off a ten-foot platform, doing laps like Esther Williams—I ask who can swim there.

You have to be a member, they say pulling out their passes. See? It's private.

I'm crestfallen, but only for a second, only until they say I can come as a guest. Can Eddie come too?

Rosh Hashanah, the Jewish New Year, is coming up, and Mrs Schwartz has invited her family for dinner. Last year on Rosh Hashanah, I worked downstairs for nearly six hours, washing and drying the dishes, scrubbing pots and pans, and even cleaning the oven and sink. After which she gave me the sum total of one dollar, which was much more than she usually gives me, but not enough. Usually she gives me a penny—a penny to go to Alphonse's for bread and milk, a penny to go to the butcher shop on Yonkers Avenue, and a penny to sweep the walk.

Don't worry about the money, my mom says, do it as a good deed. After all, it's hard for her to do all the cooking and cleaning when her family's coming for the holidays. She'll give you something, she always does.

Why doesn't she ask Seymour to help? Seymour's like a prince, he never does any work around the house.

Seymour? Seymour's no good in the kitchen. Besides, you know where everything goes.

And he doesn't? He lives there. It's not as if Mrs Schwartz is my grandmother, and I want to help her.

I've told her that you would.

Why did you *do* that? You always do that without asking me.

What else are you doing? You have time to help.

That's not the point. You know, Hannah Gruen would *never* do such a thing.

Hannah? Who's Hannah?

Hannah? You don't know Hannah Gruen? She's the Drew's housekeeper.

Not knowing Hannah is like not knowing who's president of the United States. Before she can say anything, the telephone rings, with one of my aunts calling. Seeing an opportunity, I run downstairs to sort things out for myself.

When Mrs Schwartz comes to the door, I tell her that if I help in the kitchen on Rosh Hashanah, I'm wondering how much I'm going to get.

How much you're going to get? How much *money*? Taken back and annoyed, she has a way of making *money* sound like a dirty word.

Well, I gave you a dollar last year, didn't I?

Yes, but it took me almost six hours to do everything.

It won't take that long this year.

Did my mom tell you I've raised my babysitting rates? I get thirty-five cents an hour, and babysitting's a cinch compared to working in the kitchen. After the baby goes to sleep, all I do is read a book or listen in on the party line.

You do *what*?

Listen in on the party line. On Friday nights, when I babysit at the Wilkinson's, the same guy calls his girlfriend from the bowling alley. You can hear the pins scattering in the background—*ka-boom!*

From the look on her face, you'd think I was listening in on her party line.

Does your mother know you do that?

Do what?

Listen in on other people's conversations. That's rude.

As for working on Rosh Hashanah, I tell her two dollars would be nice. She says she'll think about it, but doesn't want to talk about it anymore. What she wants is that I come down early to set the table before the family arrives.

WHEN THE Jewish New Year comes around, the kitchen looks like a china shop, with all the plates and soup bowls stacked on the table, on the counter and even on the stove. Working in the kitchen isn't all that bad, not when I can snitch a taste of the holiday dishes Mrs Schwartz makes. In the not-so-good I'd put the matzo ball soup—the broth is nowhere near as tasty as Campbell's and the matzo ball is as heavy as a musket ball. Because it's the Jewish New Year, a lot of the dishes are made with apples and honey—like the sweet potato tzimmes, honey-glazed carrots, and a noodle kugle with yellow raisins and apricot jam. Eating kugle is as good as eating cake.

When the family sits down, they light candles. Mrs Schwartz once told me that if you light a candle in your home, you will never run out of goodness in your heart. The only candles we have are birthday candles, so I don't know if they count.

Later that evening, after the last pan is scrubbed and the last glass back on the shelf, her son, Jack—a lawyer married to the gorgeous Billie who wears her black hair in a chignon like a Spanish senorita and lives in a Tudor house in Scarsdale—comes into the kitchen to thank me for helping, giving me not one but two dollars. How do I feel about that? Pleased as punch, but had I been babysitting this long, I would have made $2.10.

Mrs. Schwartz has an eye for iris. She grows the bearded iris—the purple ones as dark as night, the yellows as bright as a summer day—in a sunny patch at the front of the house. Finding her down on her knees weeding one Saturday morning, not able to decide myself, I ask which ones she likes best, the purples or the yellows.

I like seeing them in a mixed border, she says, but what I don't like is the carroty smell.

Sniffing one, I'm not sure it smells like a carrot, but it sure doesn't smell like a rose. Rubbing a finger lightly over the bushy hairs on a petal, I ask why they call them bearded iris, is it because of the fuzzy strips. They look more like caterpillars to me, don't you think?

What I think is that if you keep doing what you're doing, you're going to knock that flower off its stem.

All year long, no one pays a bit of attention to the irises, not until early in June. Then they're showstoppers, all the neighbors pausing to admire them. When coming up the hill at lunchtime, I can spot them a block away, their fluffy heads dancing in a breeze—like the Rockettes at the Radio City Music Hall.

Do the roses have names?

No, they're just plain old-fashioned roses.

When I grow up, I'm going to get me some old-fashioned roses, but I'm going to give them names.

Names?

Pretty names like Summertime Beauty and Easy Does It.

ONE MUGGY summer evening, I'm sitting on the back steps near the garage, listening for the Good Humor truck. Mrs Schwartz is out in the yard reading, no more than fifteen feet from me. We're both escaping the heat that builds up in the house, week after week and month after month, all summer long. By August, the attic is like an oven, with all the rolled up winter rugs burnt to a crisp. My parents have warned me that when Mrs Schwartz is in the yard, I'm to say hello and go on about my business, not to pester her with questions. Above all, I'm not to go into the backyard or to swing in the hammock, as that is her private space.

When she puts down the book to go inside for a glass of water, I walk over to see what she's reading and to give the hammock a push. It's a dictionary with pictures of flowers arranged in alphabetical order. A Pictionary. The one called 'Goat's Beard' makes me laugh, because it really does look like a grey goat's beard. Flipping through, I'm hoping to find a picture of the periwinkle blue flowers growing alongside all the parkways, the ones that bow their heads low to the ground as we drive by and then pop right up again. Last year, we saw them growing all over Lake Placid up in the high Adirondack Mountains, not far from the Canadian border. Up there, the air is evergreen and all the lakes are a sapphire blue. Looking at a blue flower, any blue flower, makes me feel ten degrees cooler.

When the screen door bangs, I jump a mile. Pushing her eyeglasses to the top of her head, Mrs Schwartz asks if my hands are clean. You're holding a library book.

Tucking the book under one arm, I rub my hands on my shorts, take a quick look and hold them out for inspection, telling her I was looking for the blue flowers over by the Bronx River Parkway.

Most likely, they're cornflowers. Some people call them Bachelor's buttons.

Cornflowers? I wonder how she knows that. She doesn't own a car, doesn't know how to drive. However, she reads a lot of books. My mother used to read to me when I was little. I wonder if she was as smart as Mrs Schwartz.

∽

Miss Marge and Me

Returning home from my Wednesday Girl Scout meeting, I find my mom flipping mad. As soon as she hears me coming up the stairs, she says: I want to see you in here, right now! I can tell by the way she says it, I'm in trouble. Making sure to keep my distance from the flashing eyes, I ask what's wrong.

I'll tell you what's wrong, she says, grabbing my chin and tilting my head backwards so fast I'm seeing shooting stars.

I'm going to ask you once—did you or didn't you take any of the cookies I made for dinner? Standing toe-to-toe and eyeball-to-eyeball, she repeats: Did you take any of the cookies?

From deep down inside, I know the answer had better be

no. Even George Washington would not have confessed to cutting down the cherry tree if his father had been this angry. After what feels an eternity, but is probably a split-second, I say: What cookies? What are you talking about? Twisting free of her grasp, I step backwards.

Don't lie to me, she says, her sky-blue eyes narrowing to navy-blue slits.

I'm not lying, I say, trying to keep a good four feet of tabletop between us.

If there's anything I hate more than a thief, it's a liar, she says, slamming her palm on the table.

Me, too, I say, hoping we can climb that hill hand-in-hand.

Look me in the eye! If you didn't take them, who did, Eddie?

In this hold-your-breath moment, I'm weighing alternatives—being smacked or shining the chocolate-chip cheater spotlight in Eddie's direction. I hate getting smacked. Why don't you ask *him*?

With my right ear lobe clamped between her thumb and index finger, we march downstairs to where happy-go-lucky Eddie is biking up and down the driveway, oblivious to what's coming next.

She insists we go inside the garage, a two-car garage that we share with Mrs Schwartz. Her half has just a lawnmower, but ours is full of bikes, red wagons, Flexible Flyers, and my father's tools. No one, other than my dad, could squeeze a car into this garage.

I'm going to ask you just once, did you take any of the chocolate chip cookies?

In this nerve-jangling moment, I look at Eddie, but his eyes are on his floppy sneakers, the laces hanging loose. I bend to tie one for him.

If there's anything I hate more than a liar, it's a thief.

Wait a second, the last time she said she hated a thief more than a liar. Which is it? What happens next is a shock. Eddie, who first denies taking any cookies, suddenly changes his mind and says he took one. Why would he *say* that? has he lost his senses? is he freaking out? Look at him—the droopy shorts down around his knees, the belt sliding over his hips—such a colossal shrimp. Nonetheless, I'd feel terrible if he gets smacked for something that I did. However, that doesn't happen. Instead, we both lose our after-school play privileges for a few days. Whew! A narrow escape.

Later, when we're alone, I hiss: Did you or didn't you take a cookie?

Looking over his shoulder, checking to see if my mom is listening, he whispers: I don't think so.

What do you mean you don't *think* so? did you or didn't you?

I don't think so.

What's with him, and what's with Miss Marge? If there's nothing worse than a thief or a liar, why doesn't she tell him that she's really his stepmother?

WHEN THE THIRD day of house arrest rolls around, I'm lying on my bed after school reading *The Secret of Red Gate Farm*, when the doorbell rings. Hoping someone else will answer—Nancy just received a letter left at midnight by a stranger on her doorstep—I don't move a finger, other than to turn a page. Thanks to Grosset & Dunlap, I'm reading about exciting places like River Heights, where there are all these stolen documents and troublemakers. Nothing at all like Sherwood Park. What I like is that in every book, no matter what the challenge, Nancy faces it with courage and bravery. I wish I were half as brave as she is.

When reading in bed by flashlight, there are times when I'm afraid to turn the page for fear of what's going to happen to her, my girl-goddess, and times when I can't turn fast enough. Only when she returns home—what street does she live on?—and Hannah fixes her a snack, do I put the book aside for the night.

When the doorbell rings for a second time—where's everybody?—I lean out the window. It's Marla. She wants to know if I can come out to play.

I can't, not today. She says that I have to stay in my room un—

Before I can finish what I'm saying, I'm yanked by my braids straight out of the window, scared out of my wits.

Who is *she*? my mom asks, whacking me on the side of my head.

What do you mean *who is she*? I repeat, not understanding the question, wondering if it's a riddle.

I *heard* what you said! You said *she* says I have to stay in my room, didn't you? *She* is the cat's mother, that's who *she* is.

None of this makes any sense to me. This must be how Alice felt when talking to the Mad Hatter. Nervous through and through, I can't think straight.

I don't understand, I say, wishing she would stop yelling. Being cuffed is bad enough, but knowing Marla's downstairs and can hear every word is making things so much worse. I wish I could die. Go home, Marla, my heart shouts. Go home! I hope I never have to see Marla again. And I certainly don't want to go to Girl Scout camp with her next summer.

What's the *matter*? Why are you so angry?

Why? Because I don't like you calling me *she*. I'm your mother, I'm not a *she*.

What's so bad about *she*? I didn't mean anything bad by it.

You *didn't*. You think it's okay to call me *she*?

I don't know.

You don't *know*.

At which she smacks me across the face with an open hand that has the sting of a braided whip. Pressing my palm to my cheek in disbelief, I stare at her. What gives her the right to hit me? It's then all of my shame and fury boil over and I grab onto the collar of her dress and shake her like a rag doll, until she's the one who's worried about losing her balance and falling down the steps. She tries to hold me at arm's length, but she can't because I'm as big as she is and my arms are as long as hers. Then, I smack her so hard across her face that my index finger starts throbbing and turns a violet-blue. See that? God's punishing you, I tell myself.

How *dare* you hit me, I'm your mother.

You're *not* my mother, I hiss with all the venom of a rattlesnake. My mother's dead.

Who told you that?

My cousins.

In the heat of the moment, I'm saying the very thing that I've been hoping isn't true—that Aileen, Little Miss Know-It-All, doesn't know what she's talking about.

I'm telling your father what you said when he comes home.

There it is again—the Doomsday Dad, the ultimate threat. However, Miss Marge doesn't know something I know: My father never hits Eddie or me. He jokes that if he were to hit us, he'd send us straight to the moon. We laugh.

Go ahead and tell him, I don't care. But if you hit me again, I'm going to hit you back. You want to hit me? Go ahead, I dare you, I say, my chin jutting out to make an easy target. No, you can't slap me in the face. No one can slap me in the face.

I've gone off the deep end. Even my inner-scorekeeper, the one whose job it is to keep track of every slap and humiliation no matter how slight, chimes in: Stop digging yourself into a hole.

Miss Marge tells me to go to my room. I feel bad and I'm sorry I hit her, but not sorry enough to say so. Oh, no. Is Marla still downstairs?

The problem as I see it is that my Mom has never been a mother—we're new to her, and she's new to us. She's never had any kids, and we've never had a stepmother. Her mother died when she was young, and she and her sisters lived in an orphanage run by the nuns. But as each one turned Sweet Sixteen, she was allowed to go home to their apartment at 2380 Webster Avenue in the Bronx. Maybe the nuns hit her, still that's no reason for her to hit me.

After Eddie goes to bed, my father calls me into the living room. I've been waiting for this moment, but not for what comes next.

I heard you told your mother that she isn't your real mother.

Yes. She's *not* my real mother, my cousins said so.

Your *cousins*? Well, I'm telling you she *is* your real mother, and I don't want you saying that again. And you're not to hit her. Do you hear?

Okay, but you tell her not to hit me. You said that if anyone hits me, I'm to hit back.

This is different. You're not to hit your mother. If kids hit you, hit them back.

Ready to burst into tears, wanting so much for him to be on my side just once, I bite my lip and nod in agreement, relieved to find it's all so simple.

I don't want you talking about any of this with Eddie, not one word. He's not to know. You promise?

Sniff-sniffling my way to bed, I pull the pillow over my head, wishing my dad and I were a team like Nancy and her dad, Carson Drew. No matter what happens, Nancy never cries. I don't know how she does it. A ranch hand once said that Nancy had true grit. I'm not sure what he meant, but if only I had true grit, I wouldn't cry either. How do you get it?

Standing in the doorway, Miss Fee flicks the light switch off and on: Class, I'm waiting for everyone to take a seat. We have a lot to do this morning, because I want to go over your results on the New York State Aptitude Tests. I'm going to call you up one at a time, so while I'm busy, you're to work on the compositions we started yesterday. When you're finished, you can copy the spelling words on the board into your notebooks and write a sentence for each word. If you don't understand what I said, raise your hand. A few boys clowning around raise their hands. Everyone laughs.

When called up to her desk, I learn that I had the highest score in the whole Sixth Grade on the tests for spatial awareness and mechanical design: If Wheel A turns clockwise and Wheel B turns counterclockwise, which way does Wheel C turn? Here's another: How many times must the largest gear turn for the smallest one to turn over two times? three times? five times? That Miss Fee is so delighted makes me feel good all over.

It's none too early to start thinking about career choices and college, she says. College? *Gosh!* No one other than Irma's mother, Mrs Siegel, has ever mentioned my going to college. Returning to my seat, I adjust my halo.

Later that afternoon, I'm swinging on the front gate, when Marla bikes over wanting to know if I want to come over to watch *Howdy Doody*.

Not today, Marla. I'm waiting for my father. He's going to be home any minute.

Hearing voices out front, Mrs Schwartz leans over the back railing asking if I would run to Alphonse's for her. Hoping my mom's not listening, I tell her I can't right now, but later, okay? Seymour never goes to the store, never cuts the grass, never shovels the snow or fixes the furnace when it goes on the fritz—which it does four or five times every winter. When that happens, Mrs Schwartz comes to the foot of the stairs: Yoo-hoo, Mr Bracht? Could you see what's wrong with the furnace?

Which is just as well because Seymour, a bridge-playing intellectual, wouldn't know a flat-head screwdriver from a pair of pliers.

Hey, Dad, you won't believe what happened at school, I shout, as the car pulls into the driveway.

He waves—his palm is as large and square as a slice of Wonder Bread—and pulls ahead into the garage. In *The Clue in the Jewel Box*, Nancy said you could tell a lot about a man by his hands, but I don't know what she meant by that.

Hi, Dad. Guess what happened in school today? I ask,

hugging him around the waist. My brain's pin wheeling with excitement over aptitudes—I never knew I had any.

Hi, Bob, what's for dinner? he says, never breaking his stride. Where's your mother?

Upstairs with the baby.

Save it for later, I tell myself, you have plenty of time—years. After dinner, waiting for him to finish with the *Herald Statesman*, I'm sitting with one leg thrown over the arm of a living room chair when my mom walks in, takes one look and says:

Put your feet on the floor, that's no way for a young lady to sit.

What's wrong with how I'm sitting? I ask, not moving a muscle, other than raising an eyebrow.

Put your feet down. We can see all the way to China.

That's all it takes before Eddie chimes in: I see London, I see France, I see Bob's underpants. Yah-yah-yah-yah-yah.

Little brother, you are such a pain. And the name is Barbara, not Bob.

Do as you're told, put your feet down, my father says dropping the paper on the coffee table. Face up is *Gasoline Alley*, one of his favorite comic strips. It's about a guy named Walt who found a baby on his doorstep on Valentine's Day, named him Skeezix. Walt's the kind of guy who spends his days working on cars—changing the oil, rotating tires, flushing out radiators—while talking with his pals who hang out at his garage. As far as I'm concerned, that comic strip can't hold a candle to *Brenda Starr, Girl Reporter*.

Daddy, guess what? Our New York State Aptitude Tests

came back today, and Miss Fee said that with my scores, I ought to think about becoming an architect or a dentist. Which is better?

She's pulling your leg.

What do you mean? Why would you say that? Miss Fee wouldn't joke about our test scores.

Let me ask you, do you know any women dentists?

Well, that doesn't mean a girl *couldn't* become a dentist, if she wanted to. When you think about all the drills, clamps, and needles in Dr. Goldstein's office, maybe girls don't like pulling teeth and hurting people. So what about my being an architect? Then I could design us a house with a fireplace and a front door. A Colonial with pillars like Nancy Drew's house in River Heights. Wouldn't that would be nice?

Let's not start with that again, he says. I've heard enough about Colonials in River Heights and Tudors in Bronxville to last a lifetime. You're beginning to sound like a broken record.

If I had to choose one or the other, what's better—being a dentist or an architect?

There are no women dentists and no women architects. Hey, time for bed.

Leaning over to kiss him good night, I try to rub a smudge off his cheek, but he pulls away, rubs it off with a grimy handkerchief. My dad's smart and knows a lot about a lot of things. He knows how to build a house. How to fix a roof without falling off. How to repair oil burners, change a flat, and put snow chains on his truck. But he doesn't know beans about girls. For instance, he's never once said he thinks I'm smart or pretty or that he's proud of me. You can tell right away that Carson Drew's proud of Nancy, really proud. Climbing into bed, pulling the covers up over my head, I start thinking about last Sunday at church. Seated in front of me was a girl about my age, leaning up against her father who had his arm across her shoulder. My dad never sits close or cuddly like that, not even at home, no less at church. And across the aisle was another girl with shiny dark brown hair whose father kept smoothing it, brushing it with his hand. You could tell he thought she was pretty, thought her hair was pretty. I wish I was that kind of girl. Sometimes I think my dad's allergic to me.

That night I had an amazing Technicolor dream—the Barbara-and-the-Beanstalk dream. Climbing hand-over-hand up a giant beanstalk, I was trying to get to the Pearly Gates, wanting to ask St. Peter if he had seen my mother. Higher and higher I climbed—how far is it to heaven?—only to lose my grip. *Fallingfallingfalling* I landed flat on my back under the apple tree, the one at the side of the house. I had no broken bones, but I was black-and-blue all over—even my heart was black-and-blue. One minute I was so close to heaven—close enough to hear harps playing and angels singing—and the next I was flat on my back with nothing to show for all my hard work except a bunch of shoots—more like chives than parsley.

If we go to see Nana this weekend, I'm going to ask her what she thinks about that dream. Dreams must mean something, but what? And I'll ask her what she thinks is better—being an architect or a dentist. When we first moved to Yonkers,

Daddy would take us to visit Nana almost every weekend, but after a while not so much.

Nana's always Nana—always happy to see us. I think she and Uncle Fred missed us a lot after we moved out. After all, we'd been living there so long that they were used to us running through the house and playing cowboys and Indians in the backyard. Right after we moved out, Aunt Betty's husband—an Army instructor at Fort Sill, Oklahoma—came home and they moved into an apartment at 3276 Decatur Avenue. With only Uncle Fred around, the house got too quiet for Nana, so she took a job cooking for the nuns at the convent at St. Brendan's.

Staying after school to wash the boards and clap erasers, I'm waiting to talk to my teacher—if she ever stops marking papers. I'm on a fishing expedition, fishing to find out what Miss Fee likes to eat for lunch. I'd like to invite her home for lunch, but my mom's dead set against it. Whenever Nancy Drew wants to invite her friends for lunch, Hannah says: Go ahead, dear, and invite your friends. Any day you like, would be fine with me. Maybe we could have some cold sliced chicken with a few green grapes. Keep it simple.

It's that Miss Fee is my favorite teacher of all time. If she were to come home with me, she could explain aptitudes and intelligence scores to my parents. They don't seem the least bit interested. Certainly, Miss Fee must think it's important for girls to go to college. Irma's mother said it was *essential* that Irma and I get good grades and go to college.

When I mentioned inviting Miss Fee, my mom said it wasn't a good idea because of the baby's schedule.

He can feed himself, I insisted, he's almost two.

Bang-bang, she shot me down. I suspect the real reason is that she doesn't want to miss out on her daytime *soaps*, those fifteen-minute slice-of-life dramas that make the lunch hours fly by. Her favorite is *Stella Dallas*, a story about mother love and sacrifice with more pain-per-episode than any other program. A close second is *The Romance of Helen Trent*, where the announcer at the start of each program asks: Is it possible for a woman over thirty-five to find love? My mom says it is, but I doubt it. We also listen to *A Brighter Day* brought to us by Dreft, *America's favorite brand for dishes*, but we stay with Lux Flakes as they're guaranteed to take the redness out of dishpan hands.

Despite my gracious hostess inclinations, the lunchtime project never gets a thumbs-up. All the knives, forks, and spoons remain lined up in the drawer. All the cans of Bumble Bee tuna and jars of Hellman's mayonnaise stay on the shelf. And our lunch hours go by pretty much as before—my mom listening to the *soaps*, my baby brother putting more food on his high chair than in his mouth, and me running to Alphonse's for bologna and liverwurst. I have an aptitude for that.

The attic is like some half-forgotten part of the house. If it wasn't for spring and fall cleaning, I don't think anyone would go up there—other than me, that is. In the stairwell hang these pictures that someone taped to the walls—black-and-white glossies of movie stars sent out by the Hollywood studios and tinted pictures torn from the teen magazines. When Mrs Schwartz and I lug the slipcovers and rugs up the stairs, she never says a word about the pictures. It could be they've been hanging there so long—the tape yellowing, pulling away from the wall—that she doesn't see them, doesn't give them a second thought. I'd like to know who put them there.

One of the neighbors told my mom that before we moved in, Mrs Schwartz took in foster children, so maybe they lived in the garret—garret is a spelling word this week. It's a mystery: I call it *The Secret of the Narrow Stairwell.*

When no one's around, I unlock the door and curl up on the bottom step just looking. Looking at a Universal Studios photograph, an eight-by-ten, of the actress Deanna Durbin wearing a slinky black dress that's hugging all the curves. Looking at *The Queen of Tap-Dancing*, signed in a loopy little girl handwriting:

> *Best wishes,*
> *Always,*
> *Eleanor Powell*

Wearing a black dress with a diamond pin at one shoulder, Eleanor's smiling a megawatt smile, her hair blowing a mile-an-hour in the wind. Throwing her a kiss, I say: Best wishes to you, too, Eleanor.

At the top of the stairs, a couple of dust motes are doing backflips on a sunbeam. On the landing lie sunny rectangles, flat as handkerchiefs. I step around them, not on them. *Step on a crack, break your mother's back.* Opening the door to the room at the back of the house, I tiptoe in. It's a barebones room, with nothing but raw beams, not a piece of sheet rock in sight. A lightbulb dangles from a frayed wire in the middle of the room, while off to one side are the winter rugs, wrapped in tarpaper and stuffed with mothballs. An empty picture frame leans up against a wall. The room—fifteen degrees warmer than downstairs—smells of camphor, cedar, and lazy summer days. Sitting cross-legged on the floor in the middle of the room, I close my eyes and make the Sign of the Cross.

Hello, Jesus, it's me. I wait for a response, my ears aching with quiet. After a while, I switch tactics.

Mommy, can you hear me? do you remember my name? I'm sorry to tell you this, but I'm beginning to forget what you look like. Have you green eyes and freckles? are you awake when I'm awake? are you in purgatory or paradise? Sister Mary Louise said everybody goes to purgatory before going to heaven. Even if I can't remember what you look like, I haven't forgotten you—and that's the truth.

I look for a sign that she's listening. It could be anything— a spider crossing in front of me or a cobweb swaying off in the corner. There's a heavy curtain between heaven and earth, one too heavy for her to lift and too dark for me to see through. But if things keep going this way, pretty soon all I'll have left of her is a blurry memory. What does she do with all her time? Drifting on clouds might be fun for an hour or so, but after that it would get boring. Every night, kneeling at the side of my bed—elbows on the mattress, hands folded like a tent—I pray my mother will come back, if only for a minute. I want to tell her something, tell her I miss her. Of course, if she were to come back tonight, I could ask her about the scary dream I had last night. How did it go?

I'm walking in a village with narrow streets and

narrow houses. I don't know anyone, no one knows me. Everything in the dream—the cobblestones, the houses, the street lamps, even the air—is a reddish brown. Like the color of dried blood. A team of horses races toward me, their hooves clattering and sending sparks every which way. Snapping a whip over their heads, a man in a brown cape shouts at them to go faster, faster. He's after me, I know he is, but I don't know why. What's scary is that under his cape there's not a real person, only a shadow. He reaches down and scoops me up, and we race to a cemetery on the outskirts of town. The place is a muddy mess, all the tombstones knocked over. Where are all the names? Am I dying?

Scared to death, I woke up, my heart thumping like Peter Rabbit's, the collar on my pajama top damp and cool. The bedroom smelled of fear. No matter how many times I have this dream, it scares the living daylights out of me. I'd get rid of it, if I knew how. I guess I could stay awake. Nana says I'm the only one in the family with headaches, but am I the only one who has bad dreams?

BRUSHING a sticky cobweb off the window, I can see the property on the other side of the fence. It's like a jungle with broken tree limbs and blackened stumps. Out of a clear blue sky, the word *ravine* pops into my head. Yes, that's what it is—a ravine like the one St. Barbara hid in when trying to escape her terrible father. Now that was a real nightmare.

When Barbara was a young girl, her mother died leaving her in the care of her father, a wealthy merchant who sailed the Mediterranean and was often gone for months at a time. When returning from a trip, Dioscorus learned from his vassals—who may have thought they were praising the kind-hearted Barbara—that his daughter had been seen going from village to village caring for the poor. He was furious, because he knew that the teachings of Jesus of Nazareth were spreading like wildfire in the towns, and he wanted to keep her safe from the rabble and safe from any suitors not to his liking. Accustomed to having his orders obeyed, he decided to teach her a lesson and locked her in a tower. The poet G. K. Chesterton wrote:

> Her sire was a master of many slaves,
> A hard man of his hands;
> They built a tower about her in the desolate
> golden lands.

Sad to say, there was nothing Barbara could say or do to change his mind, and there was no one who dared speak on her behalf. Clever and strong-minded, she made the most of her days in a tower.

Each day a servant would bring her a loaf of bread, a jug of warm milk, and a clean dress. She led a simple life with few possessions—a bed, a writing table, a few books, and a couple of clay vessels set out on a stone counter—but what she wanted more than anything was to have a friend, someone she could talk to.

When Dioscorus went abroad again, someone—perhaps feeling sorry for the girl in the tower—slipped a book on the teachings of Jesus into the basket. Up, up, up it went, along with the milk and the bread. Knowing how to read, Barbara fell in love with the teachings of the man from Nazareth, asking the workers on her father's estate to add a third window to the tower to remind her of the Trinity—the Father, the Son, and the Holy Spirit. Upon his return, Dioscorus asked about the window.

> There were two windows in your tower Barbara,
> Barbara…Hath a man three eyes?
> Barbara, a bird three wings?

He was angry: Renounce these ideas or die! She escaped and hid in a ravine, but his men brought her back and it was then that Dioscorus beheaded his beautiful daughter.

> Blood of his blood upon the sword stood red but
> never dry.
> He wiped it slowly, till the blade was blue as the
> blue sky.

As Barbara's soul was going up to heaven, lightning lit up the sky and a bolt killed her father. After that, people the world over prayed for her protection against a sudden death and artists and poets recorded her deeds:

> Barbara the beautiful had praise of lute and pen.
> Her hair was like a summer night, dark and desired of men....

So often I've asked myself why in heaven's name would my mother, with so many names to choose from, name me after a saint with such a hard-hearted father. According to *Common English Given Names* in my Merriam-Webster, the name *Barbara* comes from the German language and means foreign or strange. If the foreign part sounded okay to me, I didn't like the idea of being strange. Then I read that it meant *the stranger in our midst.* That sounded better, not as scary.

Knowing someone might be coming home, I tiptoe out as carefully as I tiptoed in, stopping to rub my fingerprints off the doorknob with the tip of my T-shirt. To the left is Betty Grable. My dad said a Hollywood studio insured her legs—twelve-inch calves, seven-and-a half-inch ankles—in London for a million dollars! Next to her is Margaret O'Brien, who looks confused at finding herself in such glamorous company. Between the freckles, braids, and those two king-sized front teeth, Margaret and I could pass for twins.

My father doesn't want to send me to Roosevelt High next year. No, he wants me to go to St. Barnabas, a school as single-sexed as a nunnery. As tight-lipped as a snake about any of this, it's hard to know what he's thinking, but I suspect he's heard the same rumors we kids have about the wise guys at Roosevelt.

St. Barnabas, how will I get there? There aren't any trains or buses, and it must be—what?—two or three miles.

You'll walk, like everyone else.

Like everyone else? I don't know anyone who goes to St. Barnabas, except Aileen, and she takes a New York City bus.

The truth is my cousin never wanted to go to Barnabas, she always wanted to go to Cathedral High in Manhattan, but the tuition at Cathedral was five dollars more a month so she had to go to Barnabas. She says the Sisters of Charity at Barnabas are nowhere near as nice as the Dominicans at Cathedral. She makes me laugh when she purses her lips and opens her eyes wide, saying: I *hate* Barnabas! I guess she means it, because Aileen knows how she feels about everything, whereas I'm stuck with this wishy-washy brain.

Two of my classmates at PS #14 have signed up to take the TACHS, the Test for Admission to Catholic High Schools, an exam given in the fall of each year to all eighth grade students throughout the Archdiocese of New York. Students attending the Catholic elementary schools take the exam in their own schools, while those of us coming from public and private schools take it in the gymnasium at St. Barnabas.

Prior to taking the test, my mom asks my English teacher, Miss Briggs, if she would teach me how to diagram sentences. Diagramming sentences is not something we do at PS #14, but at the Catholic schools they're big on diagramming.

When Saturday morning rolls around, I'm surprised to find out that Miss Briggs is a neighbor who lives directly across from school.

Come in, come in, she says when I knock on her back door. Entering the kitchen leaves me feeling as if I'm violating her privacy.

Close the door, Barbara, she says, standing ramrod straight, wearing a high-necked dress and low-heeled shoes, as if she was still at school. Whether in front of the chalkboard or in front of the refrigerator, Miss Briggs commands attention.

What I never suspected was that diagraming sentences could be interesting. After diagramming for an hour or so, I'm beginning to get the hang of it—beginning to see how the parts of speech—the nouns, verbs, adjectives, and adverbs—relate to one another. Miss Briggs calls it *the architecture of sentences.*

Say, for example, you have the simple sentence: Glaciers melt. To diagram it, you draw a horizontal line on a sheet of paper and divide it in half with a vertical line. Then you place the subject, *glaciers*, to the left of the dividing line, and the verb, *melt*, to the right: Glaciers | melt. As you might expect, the more complicated the sentence—sentences with compound subjects, modifiers, and predicates—the more branches. I'd have to say that once you've learned to diagram a sentence, it never looks quite the same again.

After taking the diocesan exam, I forget all about it—forget I'm waiting for results, waiting for an acceptance letter for next September. Forget, that is, until February when Carol comes to school one day saying she got a letter, did I? Trying to mask my confusion—the shock, the panic, the shame—I suggest it might be there when I get home. But it's not. Nor is it there the day after or the day after that. When I hear that another classmate, one whose sister is a sophomore at St. Barnabas, received an acceptance, my poor heart loses all of its confidence. Fanciful scenarios spring to mind: was the letter sent by Pony Express? did the Admissions Office run out of stamps? did the letter go to the wrong address? did the postman ring twice? I'm fanning the embers, trying to keep hope alive.

At the end of each school day, I race home to ask if a letter has come. Unbeknownst to me, my father, who hasn't said a word about letters going astray, is hot under the collar. He doesn't believe for a moment I didn't do as well as the others on the test. No, what he thinks is that Carol got in because her father's a doctor, my other classmate got in because her father's a teacher, and that I didn't get in because he's a working stiff.

If so, he's a working stiff with an ace-in-the-hole—my grandmother. The minute Nana hears about this, she picks up the phone and calls her dear friend who's the secretary of Cardinal Spellman, the head of the Archdiocese of New York. The cardinal happens to be a great benefactor of the Sisters of Charity, so it's not all that surprising when a call comes from the principal's office at St. Barnabas telling my mom I should come for an interview tomorrow at noon. They have the TACHS results, no need for any school records.

How will I get there?

Rather than have me walk, my dad picks me up in his bright red panel truck belonging to the Great Atlantic & Pacific Tea Company—written in gold letters on the door. Bounding south—what's with the shocks, Dad?—I'm surrounded by wires and gauges, tins and tubes, and a couple of canisters of Freon. No matter what the weather, he drives with the window down, leaving him with a deeply tanned left arm and a ghostly right.

This is one of those rare times when I find myself alone with my father, but it's not a good time to ask about my mother because I'm so nervous about the upcoming interview that it's hard for me to concentrate, hard for me to breathe. Besides, after all this time, could be he's forgotten everything he knew about her.

St. Barnabas High is on McLean Avenue, the borderline

between the Bronx and Yonkers. You can tell by the mom and pop stores that it's a mixed neighborhood—Irish, German, and Italian. We pass Boehringer's Bakery where trays of crumb buns sit in the window, the crumbs the size of marbles. Across the street is a pizzeria OPEN 11:00 a.m.—11:00 p.m. On the corner, an Irish bar has shamrocks on the window. Marotta's Luncheonette offers both fountain and table service. And judging from the windows at the hardware store, they sell everything from Mason jars and batteries to snow shovels and Flexible Flyers.

Pulling to the curb at 409 East 241st Street, a three-story beige brick building housing the elementary and high school, my dad says: You go on in. I'll wait here.

You're not coming? Don't you want to meet the principal?

No, you go. I don't want to get a ticket, he says, pulling out a pack of *Old Gold, the Treasure of Them All.*

Okay, wish me luck.

The neighborhood's as quiet as sin—the moms at home doing housework, the dads off at their jobs, and the kids in school. When I slam the door, a dog across the street starts yapping, hurling himself against a fence. Down Fido, down.

Entering the office, the secretary has me take a seat. Not knowing what to expect, I'm hoping that the principal, Sister Marie Delores, will be like Sister Mary Benedict in *The Bells of St Mary's.* When the door opens, all hopes are dashed— she's nowhere near as pretty as Ingrid Bergman, not with those glasses and that expression. If Nana were here, she'd say: Look at the puss on that one.

The interview lasts all of about five minutes, an eternity, during which Sister Marie Delores never cracks a smile, never says: Welcome to St. Barnabas. Instead, she rests with elbows on the desk, fingers folded tent-like in front of her, the shaggy eyebrows making quite a fuss.

I understand you want to come to St. Barnabas.

Yes, Sister.

Why is that?

Not knowing what to say, I fudge, telling her my cousin, who is a freshman here, loves it. Crossing my fingers, I'm hoping that whopper won't be chalked up as a lie on the great scoreboard in the sky and that Sister will not detect any insincerity on my part.

Your cousin . . . who's that?

More frosty questions, more toasty answers. Talk about feeling like a bug under a microscope. Do I want to spend my next four years here? Whoa, little pony, not so fast. You're simply under consideration. When she mentions something about my purchasing the school uniform, only then does the elephant on my chest climb down.

The uniform representatives were here last week to take the girls' measurements. You'll need to go for a fitting no later than this Friday. Can you do that? I'll give you the address, she adds, the unsmiling eyes never leaving mine. I'm so nervous, I bite down on my bottom lip to keep it from quivering.

Thank you, Sister. Thank you very much.

As for any tour of the facilities, Sister Marie Delores doesn't mention it, nor do I. Wouldn't that be a colossal waste of her time? Rising imperiously, as majestic as Old Faithful, she indicates with a nod of the wimple that the interview's over. Lowering my eyes, I bow backward out of the room, hoping I haven't misunderstood her. With my nerves shot through, I wobble out of the building and slump against the front door. A horn honks: Hurry-up, I've got to get back to work.

When school lets out in June, Carol and I take the No. 7 trolley to Getty Square to pick up junior working papers at the New York State Department of Labor. In New York State, you're eligible for working papers at age fourteen, as long as you're not working in a factory or more than forty hours a week. Carol turned fourteen in January, I followed in February. Thanks to her father, who's on staff at St. John's Riverside Hospital, we have summer jobs lined up at the hospital. We're thrilled to be getting out of Sherwood Park, thrilled to be traveling to another part of Yonkers, and thrilled to be entering the Great American Workforce.

What will we be doing? Dr. Unangst doesn't know, and, to tell the truth, Carol and I don't much care. Something of an absent-minded professor by nature and a physician by training, her father says that once we have our working papers, we should stop by the hospital and fill out the forms. They'll let us know. Without knowing the specifics, we figure that we will be earning more money in a week than we could possibly earn in a month of babysitting and running errands. And we will be paid with official paychecks made out in our names and drawn from the accounts of St. John's Riverside Hospital. All of which strikes us as highly professional.

Processed within minutes, we're assigned to a muggy kitchen in a sweltering subterranean part of the hospital where the sun never shines. Standing behind a long stainless steel table, we assemble meal trays for the patients, responding with alacrity to the dietician's directions: One diabetic—no salt, no sugar. One regular, skim milk, no dessert. Our hands fly in all directions, grabbing utensils and condiments, beverages and entrées, soups and salads.

Carol, did I put a dessert on the last tray?

In short order, we catch onto the routines. Arriving at six-thirty each morning—combed, bathed, and splashed head-to-toe with Jean Naté—we are something of a minor sensation in the kitchen, where most of our co-workers are wearing yesterday's stains. One appears to be on work release from psychiatric. Carol and I—the cotton skirts, white blouses with Peter Pan collars, and loafers with copper pennies—look like two characters out of a Nancy Drew mystery; specifically, Bess Marvin and George Fayne. Like Bess and George, we are nothing if not good-hearted troopers, cheerfully overlooking any unusual behaviors on the part of the staff, including a notable reluctance to bathe. In the sweltering kitchen, armpits are rank, hair is lank.

We're especially understanding of Grace, a co-worker

who waits for us at the trolley stop each morning, so we three can walk the last quarter mile together. We don't know why she has taken this interest in us, as she appears to be a fully-grown woman—if one with the hairiest arms and legs we've ever seen. Carol and I, who have been shaving our hairless legs since seventh grade, avoid asking impertinent questions. Yet, we can't help but notice the way she walks—the hunched back, the arms swinging in tandem side-to-side like a gorilla. Unmarried and without children, it's as if she has adopted us. Mainly, she keeps us abreast of the hospital gossip—of who said what to whom behind closed doors and who's doing what with whom under the sheets.

Carol, what do you think about Grace? I ask, not sure what to think myself.

I don't *know*, she says awkwardly, her head doing this bird-y bob thing it does whenever she's uncomfortable with a question. At Barnabas, we live and die by the rule that if you can't say something nice about someone, don't say anything at all. But just once, I'd like Carol to say what she really thinks, even if it sounds mean-spirited.

Honestly, Carol, don't you think she looks more like a *man* than a woman?

Maybe, I'm not sure.

You're not *sure* if she looks more like a man or a woman?

After two weeks of working in the kitchen, the day arrives when Carol's father remembers we're working at the hospital and decides to pay us a visit. Before he can do that, he needs to find his way to our workplace, a part of the hospital he's never set foot in. Arriving after the breakfast service and before rounds, he steps into a world of leftovers and garbage, passes a steam table speckled with dried bits of scrambled eggs and almost slips on a floor slick with grease.

Seeing him coming toward us, we wave excitedly, run to greet him.

Well, well. So this is where you two work.

Full of self-importance, we walk him around the prep area, explaining our roles with great enthusiasm and in mind-blistering detail, introducing him to our co-workers—at least to those not on smoke breaks in the corridor. Despite our coffee-black esprit de corps, he notes the gritty ambiance, if not saying a word.

Arriving promptly the following morning—*shoo, shoo*—Carol's told to report to Admissions, and I'm sent to Medical Records. Miracle of miracles, two weeks on the job, and we've been promoted to nine-to-five office work. What with our new positions, we lose track of good-hearted Grace who, for all we know, may still be waiting at the trolley stop.

Mom, Clare's on the phone. She wants to know if I can go out with her brother Saturday night. Can I?

Getting no response, I put the receiver on the counter and go inside to find her up on a stepladder taking down the drapes, an essential part of that weeklong ritual known as spring-cleaning. Every year it's wash the sheers . . . check! Pin the sheers to the stretchers in the backyard . . . check! Remove the winter drapes . . . check! Store in attic . . . check! Remove the storm windows . . . check! Store in basement . . . check! Wash the windows . . . check! Hang the summer sheers . . . check! check! check!

Hey, Mom? Clare's on the phone. She wants to know if I can go out with her brother Saturday night. Can I?

Go out with her brother? On a date? No, you cannot go on a date. Here, take this, she says, handing me a drapery panel weighted with S-hooks as lethal as porcupine quills.

But Clare and Rita have dates, I plead. Their parents are letting them go. If I go with Clare's brother, we can triple-date.

Triple-date? You're too young to date, period, she says, her words sticking to the drapery pins tucked between her lips.

Why *not*? Pul-lease!

Your father's not going to let you go on a date. Ask him.

At fifteen, with my first date knocking on the door, I'm trying to think of one good reason I should be allowed to go. That my friends' parents are letting them go is a non-starter, one found in the Department of Settled Questions. What about safety in numbers? what could be safer than six?

Tell her you'll call her back, that you have to ask your . . . *which* brother?

Her brother, Will.

Isn't he the one in *college*?

Yes, he's a freshman and has permission to drive the family car, I add, grinning like the Cheshire Cat behind her back, lips stretched tight with excitement. Inhaling through my teeth, I'm trying to tamp down any irrational exuberance, trying to act blasé.

Why would a freshman in college want to go out with a sophomore in high school?

I don't know, but he asked Clare to ask me.

Clare's a forward on the basketball team, and Rita and I are cheerleaders. Which is how I met Clare's brother—all five feet, eleven inches of him, the hair parted on one side as if with a knife—when he picked her up after a game at St. Nicholas of Tontine and offered me a ride home. I could see right away that dating a guy with the keys to the family car has advantages. Until now, I haven't dated anyone. At the school dances, we meet guys from all the Catholic schools—Cardinal Hayes, Mount St. Michael, and Fordham Prep—but that's not like having a date.

They want to go to Mayer's Parkway Restaurant, I say, in a tone suggesting girls my age go to Mayer's, the epicenter of style and panache in the North Bronx, all the time.

Mayer's Parkway Restaurant? she gasps. You must be joking.

No, I'm not. You know Mayer's on East 233rd Street.

I know Mayer's, but who's paying for all this?

The boys, I guess. But Clare didn't say anything about us going for dinner, only for dancing and drinks.

Dancing and drinks? At your age? Wait until your father hears this.

Well, not *real* drinks, Cokes.

How do you think you're getting there?

That's no problem, Clare's brother drives. He's a good driver, has been driving for years, I say, hoping she won't ask how I know anything about his driving skills.

Is Clare still on the phone? For heaven's sake, tell her you'll call her back.

I come away feeling it wasn't a definitive 'no.' The major hurdle lies ahead, how to convince my father to let me go. As for asking my mom to run interference on my behalf, the odds of her doing so are less than zero. She never goes to bat for me, not when my father's pitching. I'll bet when my dad hears about us going to Mayer's—the El Morocco of the Bronx, if minus the zebra stripes, celebrities, and paparazzi—he'll be sorry he threw away his dancing shoes. That conversation never happens. I'm out when he comes home, so my mom breaks the news to him.

I can go? what happened? is this one of those moments when my stars are in perfect alignment? when Venus is making me irresistible? All I know is that *yes* comes with conditions. Do I care? Not on your life, I'd agree to anything.

For starters, my friends have to come to the house so my dad can meet them. Fair enough. Out of the corner of my eye, I'm sizing up a living room in the throes of spring cleaning—the air slippery with Old English Lemon Polish, the windows minus any curtains, and the floor missing its rug. Anyone who came by would think we had moved in yesterday.

You'll have everything in place by Saturday night, won't you, Mom?

If you lend a hand.

No matter what, you'll put down the rug, won't you? I don't want my friends thinking we don't own a rug.

Living in an apartment without a door is bad enough, but living in an apartment without a rug is too déclassé for words. Clare's family lives in a Tudor-style apartment building with an elevator on Bronx River Road, and Rita's family recently moved into a brick and fieldstone house on Kimball Avenue. Me? I live in this cockamamie—

My father interrupts my reverie, saying: And there's to be no drinking. Got that?

Drinking? You mean *alcohol*? That's ridiculous, Daddy. No one I know drinks alcohol.

And I want you home by eleven.

Oh, no! Clare and Rita have permission to stay out until midnight. The band doesn't start playing until eight-thirty. If I have to be home by eleven, it's going to ruin the evening for everyone.

It's up to you. Home by eleven or don't go.

In this take-it-or-leave-it moment, I take it, if slipping from Cloud 9 to Cloud 8. Meanwhile, I'm fretting over a half-baked apartment about as attractive as an unmade bed.

Pulling out every stitch in my closet, I proceed to mix and match blouses and skirts, dresses and sweaters in the search for the perfect outfit. Nothing's quite good enough for Mayer's. The best I come up with is to dye my eighth grade graduation dress—a summery white organza with embroidered panels— a wintry color. I call Nana to see what kind of dye is best, and she says to buy a package of RIT. Choosing a Forest Green, I follow the instructions, mixing the RIT powder with water and salt before bringing it to a simmer: *Be sure to keep the water under the boiling point and to use a long-handled wooden spoon to keep the item moving as directed. Do not let the garment remain overlong in one place.*

Stir, wash, rinse, repeat—Gloriosky!—a summertime organza turns into a minty green dress that's free of any unsightly discolorations. Adding a string of pearls and an angora shawl, I'm ready for the Big Night. Drab to Fab in under an hour. What's happening with the living room?

WILL COMES upstairs to meet my parents, while my friends wait in the car. My father stands in the living room like the original mountain man, his arms—muscular arms thanks to years of swinging meat cleavers and dragging nine-point bucks through the backwoods—folded across his chest. There's to be no shaking hands, no social niceties, and certainly no *how are you, son?* Trepidation darts across my date's face. I take his hand offering moral support, and, after a rapid-fire series of hello, good-byes, I pull him toward the stairs.

Be sure you call home when you get to the restaurant, my dad calls after us. Ah, the fourth condition. Bounding down the steps, my date in hot pursuit, I keep my fingers crossed that my father won't have any last minute change of mind.

Don't look back, I hiss, and whatever you do, don't let him catch your eye.

A curtain flutters in a downstairs window. Hi, Mrs Schwartz.

A REDDISH glow from a neon sign, *Mayer's Parkway Restaurant,* gives East 233rd Street a shady-lady feel. All six of us—night-clubbing, bright-light clubbing—pile out of the car to breeze past the doorman, our laughing heads held high as if to the manner born. Catching sight of an eight-piece band, the musicians in tuxedos—shades of Daddy Warbucks—my spirits soar, until I notice the men in dark suits, the women in basic black. The minty-green organza is about as apropos as showing up at a wake in a bathing suit.

When the band strikes up, we six take to the floor and any

concerns about an out-of-season dress fade fast. With Will's arms around me and mine draped around his neck, I'm floating in a cloud of All Spice After Shave. We slow dance, we lindy, we cha-cha-cha. What do we talk about? I don't recall a word. When you're dancing, your feet do all the talking. And when the band strikes up—*You're just too marvelous . . . too marvelous for words*—I feel I really am. Enjoying what for me is a rare state-of-mind, I recall I was to have called home.

Picking up the phone on the first ring, my dad asks if anyone's drinking.

Drinking? No one's drinking. Clare, Rita, and I have Cokes, and the guys have something called a Tom Collins. It's like Seven-Up with a cherry.

It seems as if I barely have time to hang up and get back to the dance floor—*Embrace me, my sweet embraceable you*—when Rita, signaling from across the floor, mouths three fateful words over her date's shoulder: Your father's here.

All my lightness of being vanishes like bathwater down a drain. Looking toward the bar, there stands my father in his lumber jacket, holding a plaid golf cap in hand—like a cherry pit in a bowl of diamonds. What if I ignored him? how much time would that give me before Will sees him motioning for me to join him?

I'm sorry, Will, but my father's here, I say, my voice barely breaking a whisper. Let me talk to him, I'll meet you back at the table, okay? Tears well in my eyes. I can't imagine what he's doing here, but I know this is not going to end well.

Get your things.

But, Daddy . . .

Get your things . . .

What are you *doing?* You're ruining everything.

I told you no drinking.

I'm *not* drinking.

But your friends are, so get your things.

Meanwhile, the bartender, a white apron folded at the waist and tied in the front, is taking it all in, wiping the same spot over and over. Knowing nothing I can say will change my father's mind and not wanting to create a scene, I pick up my wrap and mumble something to my friends about seeing them at school on Monday. I'm mortified.

The ride home is a white-knuckled affair. Humiliated by him in front of my friends, I vow never to talk to him again. He's ruined my first date, he's ruined the best night of my life. Meanwhile, utterly unconcerned, he makes no effort to engage me in conversation, simply burns through one cigarette after another.

Will phones the following morning, comes by the house around noon to apologize to my parents. Sick at heart, I'm too embarrassed to look him in the eye and never leave my room. As for the rug, who cares?

Your father's one helluva guy, says George Hollister, my dad's golfing buddy. The two of them are heading for the Jersey Shore, looking to rent a house for the month of August. Whether it's to save money or a poor selection, the rental they come up with is miles from Point Pleasant and miles from the ocean, but only a block off the Manasquan River in West Point Pleasant. Thrilled to be getting out of Sherwood Park for a month, I will go anywhere.

At the corner of Curtis Avenue and River Road, the house, which is divided into two apartments, bears no resemblance whatever to any seaworthy Victorian with wraparound porches and gingerbread trim I had in mind. As it was Mr Hollister's idea to rent at the shore, he gets first dibs. Naturally—he's no dummy—he takes the ground floor apartment, leaving us an upstairs with sharply sloping rooflines, intrusive dormers, and one outstanding feature—a sundeck off the living room perfect for tanning milky-white legs.

During the week, with Mr Hollister and my dad in the city, my mom and Mrs Hollister—everyone calls her Pidgie—pack lunches, and we walk to the River Avenue beach. Here the Manasquan River is broad and free flowing, with a mix of commercial fishing boats—their tall poles scratching the underbelly of the sky—and motorboats tied up at the residential docks.

Swimming out beyond the float line the first day, I'm quickly surrounded by a gaggle of guys: How long you down for? where you from? Yonkers, where's that? To a man they're from Bayonne or Jersey City, with summer homes here in *West Point*. Lucky guys who get to spend all summer at the shore goofing off—biking, swimming, taking out the boats, and horsing around—a lot of horsing around. What's more, they have big Italian dinners—veal parmigiana, chicken cacciatore, osso buco—every night of the week, whereas at my house spaghetti and meatballs is a twice-a-year happening. Best of all, they all have butterscotch tans (no milky white legs in this group) especially Mackey, who could be a model on the Coppertone billboard near Jenkinson's Pavilion.

Living at the beach is easy living. After dinner, we bike around the neighborhood to see what everyone's doing and hang out and talk. About what? About anything. About the songs working their way up the Billboard Top Forty. About the muscle cars rolling off the assembly lines, particularly a two-seater Corvette that the guys say has 160 horsepower and bucket seats. It's like being in the cockpit of a fighter plane. The billboards say: *The Corvette belongs to the highway.* Maybe so, but if the Corvette belongs to the highway and muscle cars are in our future, fat-tire Schwinn bikes are the here-and-now.

Biking over to Maxson Avenue—don't knock, walk right in is the rule at the shore—Elaine's lying on her bed with her feet up against the wall, flipping through a copy of *Seventeen,* a magazine meant to keep us current on dating and teenage fashions. Elaine and I met two weeks ago, but I feel I've known her all my life.

What did you do? I gasp at the sight of a headful of platinum blonde hair.

What do you think, like it?

Like it? I love it. You were a blonde before, but now you're a blonde bombshell. Like in the movies.

I did it this afternoon, she says, running her hands over the sides of her head, slicking it back into a duck's tail.

You did it yourself? what did your parents say? have they seen it?

Not yet, but my mom colors her hair, so what's the big deal? She won't care, she says, tossing the magazine in my direction. Hey, wanna' go into town to the boardwalk?

The boardwalk? I get it. You want to see the guys' reaction, right? But how would we get there?

Even without the platinum blonde hair, the wise guys on the boardwalk have noticed Elaine's loose-limbed walk. Most of us simply walk, but she struts her stuff like a model on a runway. We're such opposites, not because she's from Bayonne and I'm from Yonkers. Or because she's platinum blonde and I'm a brunette. Nope, it's more than that. Deep down where it counts, Elaine's as tough as nails, not afraid of anything or anyone, while I've yet to discover my inner-daredevil.

Well, we could hitch, she says matter-of-factly.

Hitch, are you serious? Have you forgotten the last time when we could have been ra—.

They were only fooling around. Opening a bottle of nail polish, she applies another coat of 'Really Red' to really red toenails.

Fooling around? Oh, please. Pulling out my lipstick—*Tangee, the lipstick that changes color to become uniquely your own*—I retouch my lips in a waxy orange.

Let's not talk about it, she says. Let's go see what the guys want to do.

A number of the kids want to go into town and why not? That's where the action is. Even for the townies who live here year round, the boardwalk is the thumping heart of a summer night. Days at the Jersey Shore are all about sun, sand, and surf, but when that sun slinks into the Pine Barrens, the boardwalk takes on a life of its own with the *ching! ching! ching!* of the pinball machines, the flippers sending a silver ball caroming from side-to-side. The call of a barker to *step right up! step right up!* The greasy smell of frankfurters splitting their sides on a grill. And then, too, there's the summertime sweetness of cotton candy and salt-water taffy. All the while, the klieg lights are turning night into day and the arcade speakers are booming songs getting regular play on the radio: *Please, Mr Sun; Walking My Baby Back Home; Peggy Sue;* and *Rock Around the Clock.* Nothing beats the magic of a summer night, the air so moist and warm on your skin, at the Jersey Shore.

On the boardwalk is where we parade our fifteen-year-old legs in our second-skin dungarees cut short. Very short. All the while, we're eyeing the older guys—shirtsleeves rolled up to the shoulder, bulging biceps—leaning against the railing, flicking red-hot cigarette butts into high arcs out onto the cool sand below. Catcalling to us: Hey, Blondie, does your mother know you're out like that? Hey, girls, wanna' go for a ride?

Laughing, we stroll on by the libidinal energy. At the very least, there ought to be a sign: Danger Ahead: Wolves Crossing.

No, I can't go into town, not tonight. My father's coming down for the weekend. He'll kill me if he finds out we hitched, and I'll be grounded the rest of the summer. He caught one of my cousins hitching home to Parkchester from school a few months ago, and we haven't heard the last of it. Besides, it's almost seven-thirty. I have to be home by nine-thirty.

Elaine, who turned sixteen a few months ago, has permission to stay out until eleven, whereas, my deal is home before dark which comes on earlier every day.

You go ahead with the guys, I say, I'll see you tomorrow.

Leaving the house, I run into Mackey, who lives across the street. He doesn't want to go into town, so we bike to the beach where we kick off our sneakers and race one another to the water's edge. A beach usually filled with families by day is deserted at night. From up and down the Manasquan River comes the slopping of the fishing boats, and when a crescent moon steps out from behind a veil of clouds, the river running black turns into a mile-long iridescent silver ribbon.

Stretching out on an overturned rowboat, face-to-face, we listen to the katydids calling in the night, the crickets in the reeds. When an old hooty-owl warbles a lonesome song, Mackey says something about the owl having marbles in his mouth, and, silly as it sounds, I laugh, at which he throws a leg across me and brushes a hand lightly over my sunburned shoulders. At which all the sounds of the night fade away, and I can hear his skin whispering: C'mere. When he kisses me on the tip of my nose, I close my eyes, and when his lips touch mine, I kiss him back. Like in the movies. Until now, kissing boys has been limited to Spin-the-Bottle or Post Office at birthday parties. This is better. And Mackey's a good kisser, so there's no bumping noses or kissing teeth. Not like with other guys.

Catching my breath, I ask about his favorite songs. He likes Joni James's *Why Don't You Believe Me*, while I'm mad for Johnnie Ray's *Walking My Baby Back Home*. We find common ground with the Hilltoppers' *P.S. I Love You*.

Wanna' come back tomorrow night?

Sure, I say, rubbing my hand over a rock-hard bicep. Must be all that rowing against the tide. And once again I hear his skin calling: C'mere. How long this goes on is anybody's guess, but the next thing I know he wants to bike me home. My heart melts faster than a Hershey's kiss on a hot summer's day.

Turning onto Curtis Avenue, we hear voices coming from across the sand-pocked lawn. Hurriedly, he kisses me good night, the bike tires getting tangled.

See you tomorrow?

See you tomorrow.

Who was that, one of those guys from Jersey City? my father asks, catching sight of me sneaking across the lawn, trying to make it upstairs undetected.

Hi, Dad, you just get here? How was the traffic?

That night before drifting off to sleep, I tie my teenaged hopes in a neat package and put them on the doorstep of a brown-eyed boy from Jersey City.

THE NEXT day, with my father down for the weekend, we head for the ocean. Parking on Atlantic Avenue, a few blocks from the boardwalk, we can hear the waves pummeling the beach.

Sounds rough today, doesn't it, Daddy?

There are no red flags flying, no warnings posted on the boardwalk. It's just another sun-bleached day at the Jersey Shore. A lifeguard paints his nose a chalky white with zinc oxide, while another coils a rope, readying the lifeboat.

No sooner have we pinned down the blankets with our sneakers and gear, than a rogue wave rushes halfway up the beach, threatening to undo all our efforts. My father says: Look over there, do you see that?

He's pointing south to where waves are coming in on an angle, powerful waves that could strand you a half-mile up the beach in no time. It's hard to tell if the tide's coming in, going out, or at a standstill. Racing to the water's edge, I pull up short, the sea-spittle swirling around my ankles, looking for an opening between the waves to jump in without being clobbered. Jumping the waves is like jumping rope—timing is everything.

Are you coming, Dad? I call back over my shoulder.

In a minute. You go ahead.

Up and down the beach, the waves are pounding the sand, creating a thunderous roar. If the calendar says August, the water says March. I'd feel better if he was coming in with me. In shallow water, thinking it's a now or never moment, I wade in a few feet, only to be pulled off balance and knocked down by a powerful wave. Before I know what's happening, I'm being dragged out to sea. I try to right myself, try to swim for shore, without success. Scared-stiff and bobbing like a plastic beach ball, I scream one word: Daddy!

Swim, a voice inside my head commands. But despite my efforts, I'm moving out to sea as smoothly as a Coca-Cola bottle on a conveyor belt. Aside from the voice in my head, I can't hear a thing. Bobbing between waves, it's as if I'm watching a silent movie. The lifeguard blows a whistle that I can't hear. My father, standing ankle-deep in foam, hands cupped around his mouth, is shouting something, but what?

The moms and dads, who had been lounging on the beach a minute ago, are on their feet, shielding their eyes from the sun and scanning the horizon. Circling overhead, a seagull that has lost its *caw-caw-caw* heads for the pier.

Between swells, I catch sight of a woman in a white bathing cap. Relieved to find I am not alone, I shout and wave, treading water frantically. She signals for me to follow, as she swims north, parallel to the beach, rather than striking out for shore. In no position to question or argue, and not wanting to be alone, I swim after her for what seems an eternity, but is probably no more than a few minutes. Then an incredible thing happens; the Atlantic Ocean, as if tiring of us, relaxes its grip. Once free of the riptide, I swim for shore—the waves doing all the heavy lifting, pushing me ahead of them as if eager to be of help. Physically and emotionally drained, I stumble onto the beach. My dad comes running with a towel asking, What happened?

What happened? What do you *think* happened? Didn't you *see* me? I say, pulling the towel over my head, not wanting to look at him or anyone. Didn't you hear me calling you? Why didn't you come out and help me?

You were going out too fast, he says. I was trying to tell you what to do.

What to do?

Swim harder.

Swim *harder*? How could I? It doesn't matter how hard you swim if you're caught in a riptide. My voice tinged with resentment, I look down to see a midriff as red and raw as hamburger meat and a polka-dotted bathing suit laced with a dozen pulls.

You're okay, he says. Catch your breath and dry off.

Having had a narrow escape, is it too much to expect a reassuring word or a squeeze of the hand from him? I'll bet if Mackey had been there, he would have jumped in and swam out to help me. At which the woman with the white bathing cap comes to mind. Shading my eyes and scanning the beach, I'm hoping to find her, to ask how she knew to swim parallel to the beach and if she, too, was scared. Soon enough I realize that all the bathing caps are white.

Dad, do you see that woman caught out there with me?

What woman? I didn't see any woman, I only saw you.

You didn't *see* her? She had on a white bathing cap . . .

My younger brother Kenny comes running over, saying: Are you all right, Bob? I was scared.

Me, too, Kenny, I say, mussing his sandy-blond hair and giving him a hug. Me, too.

It's springtime of senior year, only months to go before graduation. When the last bell of the day rings and my classmates are stomping down the stairwells, I hang back, pretending to be straightening my desk, if trying to muster my courage to speak to Sister Fideles about a serious matter: how do you know if you have a genuine calling to the religious life? After four years at Barnabas, it's clear to anyone who's paying attention that a calling to the religious life outranks that to the married life or the single state. No one has said so in as many words, but it's in the air that priests and nuns are nearer and dearer to God than thee or me. Short of waking up with stigmata on your hands or feet, how do you know?

Day after day, I trudge around with a soggy heart weighing down a foggy brain. The idea of having a calling to the religious life had been the theme of our freshman year retreat given by a Paulist missionary, Father Egan. Dare to be different, he said, and answer the call. I took it seriously for a few days, but then the idea faded, only to have it resurface a few weeks ago. Having no one to talk to—there are no guidance counselors—I'm taking a chance on my homeroom teacher. It's a longshot—both an awkward moment and an excruciating ordeal.

Preoccupied with tidying her desk, Sister Fideles, doesn't realize I'm here and jumps a mile when I come up behind her.

Excuse me, Sister. Could I speak with you for a minute?

Cocking an eyebrow—if there was a black widow spider crawling my forehead, she couldn't look more startled—she continues stuffing papers into a bulging black briefcase. Noticing her *speak if you must* expression, my voice goes wonky.

Sister, I've been thinking about entering the convent after graduation, but I don't know if this is God's plan for me.

Pray and you will find the answer, she says, authoritatively snapping the brass buckles on a briefcase resembling a doctor's satchel.

I've done that Sister, but I haven't heard a thing, haven't received any sign.

At that, she pulls back abruptly, and I see the words *foolish girl* written into the folds around her mouth.

Am I being a foolish girl? seeking attention? Maybe so, because this idea of a calling to the religious life only resurfaced after my father made it clear he does not intend to send me to college, that I am not going. Period. Why is that? As far as he's concerned, girls don't need college because they'll be married in a few years. Whether that's true or not, a number of classmates are starting a three-year nursing studies program at St. Vincent's Hospital in artsy-craftsy Greenwich Village. If the artsy-craftsy part sounds good, caring for the sick and dying doesn't.

I'll tell you one thing, missy, Nana had said. When you grow up don't be a nurse, that's not for you.

Other friends are heading for college—mainly to Mount St. Vincent over in Riverdale or to Our Lady of Good Counsel in New Rochelle. Moreover, a few of the sainted ones are buffing their haloes and entering novitiates after graduation. Why is it that all of my friends' parents are helping them get into colleges, into nursing schools, and into nunneries, but my father will not lift a finger to help? I think he cares about me, but not the way other parents care about their children—not the way Carson Drew cared about Nancy Drew. Perhaps it's just as well my mother isn't around to see this sorry state of affairs. I'd like her to be proud of me, but how can she be proud when all I'm doing is spinning my wheels and going nowhere fast? The eyes of those in heaven are better than our eyes here on earth, Nana had said. If that's true, does my eagle-eyed mother see my father is selling me short?

As I see it, my classmates are like a gathering of Monarchs emerging from their cocoons and ready to take flight. And me? Here I am stuck in a chrysalis without so much as a flight plan. Why is that? was it something I said or didn't say? something I did or didn't do?

To be honest, I haven't shown much resourcefulness along these lines, haven't made any calls inquiring about openings at various novitiates for the upcoming year. And why not? Simply because I haven't the foggiest idea how one goes about doing this sort of thing. Honestly, what do I know about convent life? Only what I saw in *The Bells of St. Mary's*. A classmate did tell me that novices at Maryknoll study the works of the great Catholic theologians—Erasmus, Thomas Aquinas, and Francis of Assisi—and master a foreign language before being sent out to the missions. All of that suits me fine, but what if I had a Mother Superior who thought me better suited to scrubbing floors at the motherhouse than to biking a dirt-packed path in the Congo or piloting a sampan up the Yangtze River? Clearly, my vagabond heart has its bags packed and nowhere to go.

Hemming and hawing, I tell Sister I've been praying for a sign, something to assure me that this is the Lord's plan for me, not mine for Him.

A *sign*, what sort of sign?

I hesitate, not knowing what to say, if fearing it would sound presumptuous to tell the truth that I'd been hoping for something definitive, perhaps something as melodramatic as the mystical visions of St. Theresa of Ávila. To my way of thinking, it's incredible hundreds of young people willingly enter religious orders each year without receiving any indication that the Lord is agreeable to such an arrangement.

Nothing special, Sister, just something that would let me feel I'm doing the right thing.

Casting a wary eye in my direction, she bites her tongue, doesn't say another word, as the four feet of space between us turns into a bitterly contested terrain. This pressure builds in my head to say something, say anything to break what has become a painful silence. She wants out; I want in.

When you were *young*, Sister, and thinking about entering the convent, how did *you* know you were making the right decision?

Sister, a model of decorum, draws a sharp breath and straightens up to her full five-feet-two. Have I overstepped my bounds? Would it have been better to ask a general question rather than delving into particulars? I don't know what to think. My brain feels as if it's swimming underwater. She glances at the clock above the door—too late in the day for gibberish.

Don't worry, dear, if God wants you, he calls you. God has a plan for each of us, and, in time, you will discover yours.

In time? doesn't she realize I'm running out of time? that the clock is ticking down?

If we all sat around waiting for signs, she says, what would happen? There's work to be done in this world. We are the hands of God on Earth. You have two hands. That should be sign enough. What's important is to be of service to others, not to be going around looking for signs.

I'm thinking, yes, I have two hands and a beating heart, but is that all it takes? Her answer is no answer—at least none I'd been hoping for. I'm trapped in a pool of sadness, unable to pull myself out, unable to find the steps or a railing. Is there no one to help me, no one to tell me what I should do?

Come, follow me, said the Lord. I love the Lord with all my heart and would be happy to follow, if I felt I was doing the right thing. There must be lots of ways to follow, other than entering a convent. Stubbornly, I persist in offering a contradictory opinion.

In the Bible, Sister, it says that we *should* ask the Lord for signs.

Where does it say any such thing?

In the Old Testament, Sister.

The Old Testament? Now, what do *you* know about the Old Testament?

Her snappy tone frazzles what's left of my composure, but not wanting her to think me a complete dunderhead, I press on.

In the Book of Isaiah, Sister, when Ahaz says that he will not put the Lord to a test and Isaiah tells him to stop trying his patience, to go ahead and ask the Lord for a favor.

Isaiah and Ahaz? The brusque manner and the up-tilted nose, suggest she has a problem—not with Isaiah and Ahaz, but with me. Picking a speck of lint off her cape, she gives me a sidelong glance, saying: When the Shepherd calls, the sheep recognize his voice. Then, without further ado, she trundles off to the cold comforts of the convent. Me and my busted halo.

LATER THAT night, around the kitchen table, my father says: What are you worried about, you'll get a job like everyone else.

Doing *what*? I can't type, I can't take shorthand. For four years I've been in the academic track, not commercial.

What are you talking about? There are plenty of jobs that don't require typing or shorthand.

Like what? Tell me one.

He's made it clear that a girl going to college makes about as much sense as taking an arts and crafts course on the Titanic. And my mom's no help. The three of us form a triangle. My dad's the Decider-in-Chief, the supreme lawgiver; my mom's the Adjutant General in charge of administration; and I'm the sharpest point of the triangle.

My dad never talks to me, not really—not the way Carson Drew talked to Nancy. No, he leaves all the girl-talk to my mom, which is a truly terrible idea because she's so bad at it. Every time she tries, she gets all choked up, stammers and blushes big time.

In sixth grade, for instance, when my friend Irma got her period for the first time, I didn't know what was happening, thought poor Irma was going to bleed to death. The news spread like wildfire, and by lunchtime, I suspect even the janitor knew about Irma's near brush with death. Arriving home that afternoon, acting blasé I said: Guess what, Mom? Irma got her period in school today. A blank expression came over her face, her eyes like saucers, big and white as Orphan Annie's. Clearing her throat, all she said was: Really? Then she went back to snipping the ends of the green beans and digging the fuzzy eyes out of the potatoes, while I made myself a snack—Ritz crackers topped with Velveeta cheese topped with a dab of Welch's Grape Jelly.

I thought that was the end of it, until a week later when

she gave me a robin's egg blue booklet showing a half-dozen diagrams of the female body and having twenty pages of fine print about something called menstruation. Men-struation? It didn't sound like anything a girl would get. I studied the drawings, couldn't make heads or tails of them. The next day, I asked a classmate who told me it was the same as getting your period and that once you got it, you keep getting it for the rest of your life. I hoped I wouldn't get it.

After a few days, my mom asked if I had read the booklet (yes) and if I had any questions (no). Is she kidding? But plucking chickens in a wind tunnel is easier than having a heart-to-heart with her.

Most of all, down deep it kills me knowing my parents, unlike all of my friends' parents, have no hopes and dreams for me. Their hopes and dreams come to an end in June. Did my mother have any hopes and dreams for me when I was young? Would she have let me take ballet lessons with Aileen and Sis? Irish step-dancing? piano lessons? I assume my parents want me to get married someday, but that's about it. The thought of sitting with my hubby watching TV, married with kids, is depressing. Besides, I'm not even dating anyone.

To make matters worse, my band of sisters at Barnabas is unraveling as fast as a loose thread on a cable-knit sweater. Carol's entering a five-year nursing program at Mount St. Vincent, and when she graduates she'll have an RN and a bachelor's degree in nursing science. Five years out, what will I have? With the year winding down and the monarchs taking flight, my only happiness is that I've met a good-looking guy at one of the Friday night dances who's invited me to his senior prom at Fordham Prep. When I told Nana, she insisted upon making my gown. The final fitting is this weekend.

Last year in English, when Sister Agnes had us read William Butler Yeats's poem *The Second Coming*, I felt the lines— *Things fall apart; the centre cannot hold*—were written with me in mind. And that falcon circling high in the sky, unable to hear the falconer's voice? That's me—a kite without a tail—so far from God I can't hear a single word. So many nights I cry myself to sleep, thinking about my mother, thinking how life would have been so much better had she lived. Before I know it, I'm feeling sorry for myself all over again—not such a good thing. But where is she when I need her?

Where do I sign? The office of North Bronx Commercial Department of the New York Telephone Company on East 193rd Street—a block north of the Fordham Road railroad station, a block west of Webster Avenue—is a twenty-minute train ride and a five-minute walk from home. Arriving early, I take a seat outside the supervisor's office and watch as Mrs Fitzgerald, the receiver crooked between her cheek and shoulder, manages to talk on the phone, make notes, file papers in a drawer, and buff her nails on the sleeve of her jacket—all at the same time. A large-boned woman—five feet nine or ten—she's wearing a charcoal grey suit that's padded at the shoulders, nipped at the waist. Which makes me double-glad I went with a Glen plaid suit and black pumps.

After watching her for a full ten minutes—crossing and uncrossing my legs, not knowing what else to do—I get up and walk around. The office is a large open floor that's subdivided into six or seven U-shaped sections, each one staffed by a half-dozen representatives and a supervisor. A business-like hum fills the room, with the representatives talking with customers on the phones, taking orders for new service and for the latest equipment—the wall phones now available in sandalwood, avocado, or white. The slim-bodied black rotary phone that looked like a deadly weapon in the hands of a Lee J. Cobb is passé.

Earlier this morning, when I said I wanted to skip the interview, my father had a conniption.

You think you can cancel the interview at the last minute? You don't realize it, but this a chance of a lifetime. Working for the phone company is as good as having a civil service job. You're too young to remember, but during the Depression, the telephone company never laid off a single employee. And after you're on the job for a year, they let you buy the stock at a discount. Your aunt must have a ton of it by now.

Barely seventeen, long-term prospects for a comfortable retirement have zero appeal. The good news is that I won't graduate for two months. But then what?

Hardly a week after parading down the aisle to *Pomp and Circumstance*—the faculty smiling, the moms carrying corsages in plastic boxes, and the dads capturing the Polaroid moments for posterity—those of us with jobs enter the Great American Work Force, our pockets stuffed with commutation tickets and timetables. Those heading for college in the fall shake out the beach blankets and drive out to Jones Beach.

My distress at missing the good times is palpable. Instead of enjoying leisurely hours basking in the sun, I'm cringing under the fluorescents—counting the minutes until the morning break, counting the minutes from the break to the lunch hour, counting from the end of lunch hour to the three o'clock break and from that to five o'clock—the real break. When not clock-watching, I'm sorting mail according to the local telephone exchanges—assigning all the Wellington 3s to one pile, the Fordham 4s to another, the Olinville 5s over there, and the Kingsbridge 6s over here.

Daydreaming the hours away, I imagine myself walking a leaf-strewn path across a campus dotted with ivy-clad buildings. Despite the time I spend woolgathering—one of Nana's favorite words—I'm excellent at my job, quick and accurate. None of my co-workers suspects a thing, least of all my supervisor. Only when I return home at night do my discontents come to a boil.

Hand me the tomatoes, will you, and call your brothers, my mom says. They're playing ball over in the schoolyard. You ought to be happy that you're finished with school and have a good job with a steady paycheck. You're not going to be doing the same thing forever. I'll bet in a year or two, they make you a business office representative. Everyone says that's a really good job. What more do you want?

What more do I want? I want to go to college like Rita. She's starting Hunter in September, and this summer she's taking a course on nineteenth century British Romantic poets. She's mad about Keats and Shelley. And me? All I'm doing is writing orders and collecting overdue bills, and I'm not mad about anyone.

No one's stopping you from learning about poets if that's what you want to do. Get a book from the library.

You don't understand, it's not the same when you're studying on your own. When you're in college, you have a professor who explains things, gives you background on authors and the period. That sort of thing. Reading on your own, you miss all that. Let me ask you, have you read any poems by Keats or Shelley?

No, they didn't teach them when I was at Walton.

See? You're making my point. If I were to go to Hunter, I could study things I'm interested in, like nineteenth and twentieth century writers, and I could be a teacher like Miss Fee. You remember Miss Fee, don't you?

Of course I remember Miss Fee. Go call the boys for dinner.

It's galling to be stuck at home, stuck in a job I don't like, and stuck without a Saturday night date—and nobody cares.

Dates are hard to come by in Sherwood Park, but I met someone at church who's sweet on me—takes me to concerts, the ballet and out to dinner. A few weeks ago, we took the train to White Plains to hear Mantovanni and his orchestra at the new Performing Arts Center. When they played this piece, *La Ronde*, I closed my eyes, imagined myself dancing the night away. Like the young women—beautifully coiffed, elegantly dressed—in the painting that hangs in our living room. But there's no chemistry in this relationship: It's a mismatch in that I think of him as a friend, whereas he thinks of me as someone he'd like to marry, and he's prepared to be patient, or so he says. Patient? I don't think it works that way. You can tell within ten minutes of meeting someone if there's a spark. When he sees me home and wants to kiss me goodnight, believe you me, there's no loitering at the front door.

Coming into the kitchen—running freckled hands through hair as white as Nana's—my father says: Why don't you go on the police force?

Are you *serious*? There are no women on the police force.

Yeah, but I know a guy who has a brother on the force,

and he says the commissioner's getting ready to bring women into the department by the end of the year.

So what if he does? The women will be sorting mail, answering phones, and writing reports. That's what I'm doing now. Only then, I'd have sergeants and captains looking over my shoulder and listening in on my calls, instead of my supervisor. If they bring women onto the force, they're not going to let them walk a beat. Besides, what makes you think I'd like a job like that?

What's with him? Does he see me packing a rod? shooting it out with bootleggers? seeing drunks home after midnight? My father, who has known me longer than anyone, doesn't know me at all. Whether he's too busy or simply disinterested is hard to tell, but if you gave him a quiz about his only daughter, he'd flunk.

Hey, Dad, what's my favorite color? Wrong, not green. Guess again.

Okay, here's an easy one for you: If I were to play a musical instrument, which one would I choose? The recorder? You've got to be kidding.

Hey, no stress, Dad, try this: What's my favorite thing to have for breakfast? Oatmeal? Oatmeal puts me to sleep. I've told that you a dozen times. You're really bad at this game, do you know that?

What it boils down to is that he doesn't understand me, and I don't understand him. To me, he's like the clouds racing by. I love watching them, even though I don't know a thing about clouds—is that a cumulus or a cirrus?—and they don't know a thing about me.

Cops make good money, he says, and you get a couple of weeks of vacation every year and lots of benefits. If you start when you're twenty, you can retire after thirty years on the job and get a pension for the rest of your life. Who can beat that?

If he's concerned about my retirement, I'm concerned about today and tomorrow.

You don't believe me? I'll bet you ten they bring women on the force by the end of the year.

It's a bet, you're on.

Did I tell you I won twenty bucks the other day from a kid who works with Hugo. You remember Hugo?

Hugo? The same Hugo you worked with at Mr Kirkbauer's butcher shop on West Farms Road?

Same guy. You know, they closed that shop when the old man died. I told Hugo to talk to the manager at the A&P on Tremont Avenue. They took him on the spot. The other day I was in the area, so I stopped to say hello. He had this kid working with him, and the kid's cutting a side of beef, doing it all wrong. So, I said to him, you could drop that side of beef twice as fast if you held the knife *away* from your body. You're holding the knife too close. He looks at me, sees my overalls and says: Hey, grease monkey, you telling me my job?

That did it. He's a punk, a kid. Who you calling grease monkey? I say. I'll bet you twenty, I can drop that side of beef faster than you can.

You think so? he says.

I know so. You wanna' bet?

I give Hugo a twenty, told him to get the kid's money.

Hugo's grinning ear to ear, because he knows what's coming next, knows the kid's out a twenty. But the kid doesn't suspect a thing. We hook up two sides of beef and two minutes later, I'm done—the meat's lying on the floor, and the kid's still getting started. When he sees I'm finished, his mouth hangs open. You should have seen Hugo doubled-over, laughing so hard.

Did you keep his money?

Nah, I took it from Hugo, gave it back. Told the kid to watch his mouth, to watch who he's calling a grease monkey. The next time he might not get off so easy. So, we have a bet, right? I'm not going to let you off that easy.

Funny, I never thought you would. But I'm not joining any police force, so get that idea out of your head.

My father and I are continually at loggerheads in that I'm talking college, he's talking police force. I'm talking present, he's talking future. It's ironic that my mother named me after a saint who didn't see eye-to-eye with her own father. Why was that? did she have a premonition? was she trying to give me a warning? My father knows as little about me as Dioscorus knew about St. Barbara.

When dinner's over, he tilts back on a straight-legged chair against the wall, saying: You get paid today?

Yes, I got paid, I say, exasperated to find him walking around with a mental calendar detailing my paydays. But I didn't have time to go to the bank, so you'll have to wait till tomorrow. You're worried I'll skip town without paying the room-and-board?

Scraping leftover shells into the garbage, I spy the tip of a school catalog poking from under a few lettuce leaves.

Hey, what's this doing in the garbage?

My mom thinks it may have slipped off the counter.

Look, I'm not asking you to send me to college, I'm not asking you to pay my way. All I'm asking is if you'd loan me enough so I could get started. I'd pay you back, I swear. And Mr Scanlon would give me back my part-time job at the A&P in a minute.

You're not going to college, forget about it. I'm through supporting you, and I'm tired of talking about this night after night. You're too late.

Too late, what are you talking about? I panic wondering if he knows more about college admissions than I do, knows something he hasn't told me. That wouldn't surprise me, but how can it be too late when I won't turn eighteen until February?

If you wanted to go, you should have thought about it a year ago.

What are you *talking* about? Tell the truth, you never intended to have me go to college, did you? Rita's father's sending her to Hunter College and her sister to Our Lady of Good Counsel. And Corinne's father, who came from Italy without a word of English, is sending her to Mount St. Vincent and her brother to Fordham University. He said he wants them to have a better life than he did. Don't you want that for me? As soon as the words are out of my mouth, I regret them. To hear him confirm what I merely suspect would be devastating.

A better life? You've got it pretty good from what I see. I got by all right without college, you can too.

What does that *mean* you got by all right? Going to college isn't about getting by, it's about having a chance to study literature, history, and art. Not spending my days sorting mail and routing orders at the telephone company. Why don't you care about any of these things?

I'm not going to be on the hook for any loans, not for you or anyone. Cash on the barrelhead, that's how I operate.

The two of us are like horses on a carousel, going round and round and getting nowhere.

Dad's pissed with you, Eddie says later, coming into my bedroom.

Who cares? Leave me alone. Why aren't you doing the dishes? Check the calendar and you'll see that this week it's your turn to wash and Kenny dries.

As far as my father's concerned, I have three choices: staying at the phone company and dying a slow death, joining the Police Department and being shot to death, or finding Mr Right and living until death do us part. Choose one of the above.

YET ANOTHER evening, yet another dust-up. My dad taps his shirt pocket, checking for cigarettes, saying: What other people do with their money is their business. You go to college, and then what? You still have to go out and get a job.

What *other* people do with their money? Is that what this is all about, the money? One of my classmate's father works for the railroad, and he's sending her to Ladycliff, a private all-girls college upstate, near the Military Academy at West Point. How fabulous would that be? Before you know it, she'll be marrying a commissioned officer in the chapel at West Point and walking the aisle under an arch of crossed swords.

Her father's not paying the bills, the aunts are.

Her *aunts* are paying her tuition?

Until now, it has never occurred to me that anyone other than your parents would pay your college expenses. This is a game changer, a brain changer.

Both of her aunts are spinsters with good jobs, he says, so they're helping out. They can afford it.

Well, how about Aunt Mary and Aunt Loretta? They're spinsters with good jobs, so do you think they might be willing to help?

Hope soars on angels' wings. Is that a light at the end of a tunnel? Is it possible Aunt Loretta—after all, she is my godmother—or Aunt Mary would be willing to help? This euphoria is nipped in the bud.

If they had wanted to help, they would have said so.

Maybe they don't know I'm interested in going to college. Can we talk to them?

No, we're not calling anyone. I don't need their help, he says, the veins on his temples bulging, and you don't either.

Okay, but what if I went to Hunter College? At Hunter, there is no tuition, I say, with the confidence of someone holding a royal flush. Not as long as you're a resident of the city, in the top ten per cent of your graduating class and plan to teach in New York City schools after you graduate. Rita uses her grandmother's address in Woodlawn for her school mail. I could use Nana's.

Marge, what's for dessert? Snuffing out the conversation, he lights a cigarette. At that, my brothers get into the act, pounding the table with their fists, clamoring for dessert: We want dessert, we want dessert. Eddie's now a freshman at Sacred Heart High in northwest Yonkers, not far from my former employer St. John's Riverside Hospital, and Kenny's at PS #14 learning, among other things, to play clarinet.

Leaving the table, I fling myself on the bed to thumb through the school catalog, but find it hard to concentrate. My mind's like a radio with all the stations playing at once. I'm blueblueblue—as blue as I can be.

A notice appears in the *Herald Statesman* that the Berkeley Business School in White Plains is offering two scholarships, to be based on the results of a school-administered competitive exam. I call my cousin Aileen to find out what she knows about Berkeley. Ever since graduating Barnabas, she's been working at the Mutual Life Insurance Company at 740 Broadway, only a ring toss from Columbus Circle. What's fantastic is that she's now engaged to a good looking guy who graduated Iona College where, at least to hear him tell it, he captained the bowling team and played a lot of golf. At graduation last June, Gene—a young Clark Gable without the Dumbo ears—was commissioned a 2nd Lieutenant: *One of the few, the proud, a Marine.* Those two go together like peaches 'n' cream—she with that china-doll complexion and strawberry-blonde hair, he with the roguish brown eyes and year-round tan. My father, on the other hand, remains skeptical:

Jaczko, what kind of a name is that?

Hungarian, I say.

You know any Hungarians? Nah, I think he's a wop.

A what?

Before I can ask her about Berkeley, she says: Babs, you won't believe it, but the other night we saw a movie—*Margie*—with Jeanne Crain. Margie lives with her grandmother, because her father is a widower. My goodness, she reminded me so much of you when you were living at Nana's. She even had your braids. The resemblance was so real. If you have a chance to see it, don't miss it. You'll see your double, I'm not kidding.

That Aileen sums up my childhood years so easily—the grandmother's house, the widowed father, the long braids—is not surprising. She's more clear-eyed and less conflicted about those years than I am, but what's missing in this picture is the bewilderment and confusion—the walking room-to-room searching for something that was lost and could not be found. St. Anthony, St. Anthony, look all around . . .

After catching up on family news, I ask what she knows about Berkeley Business.

It's like Katy Gibbs—they teach secretarial skills, typing and shorthand, and how to dress for success.

Dress for success?

You know, hats and gloves, suits and heels. Like Barnabas.

Putting the receiver back in the cradle, I check my dime-store Coty compact for any likeness to Jeanne Crain. As for Berkeley, I register and take the test, even knowing that if I won, I would likely end up working in an office, but at least I'd have some skills. When you're caught in a death spiral, you have to do something, anything to break free. But when you're down, it's hard to find the way up.

DID ANYTHING come from Berkeley? Every evening, it's the same question, same answer.

I wouldn't get my hopes up if I were you.

Mom, let me ask you, what's wrong with hoping? Alexander Pope said hope springs eternal in the human breast. By that he meant you couldn't help it—it happens.

If you get your hopes up and don't hear anything, you'll be disappointed. Think how many girls must have taken that test. More than a hundred, I bet. What if you won? You'd go back to school for two years and lose two years pay. That doesn't make sense. You're better off staying where you are.

If I went to Berkeley, I'd have some skills and could find a more interesting job, meet interesting people. Maybe be a secretary for the president of General Motors or the chairman of IBM. Working at the phone company is like being in a sorority, with not an eligible man in sight. If I were to move to Manhattan, I could skate at Rockefeller Center, hear a concert at Carnegie Hall. There's so much to do in the city, and nothing to do in Sherwood Park

Move to *Manhattan*? The disbelief in her voice suggests she equates moving to Manhattan with moving to the North Pole. You think your father's going to let you live in Manhattan?

On the front burner, the gauge of a four-quart Mirro-Matic pressure cooker is ready for blast off. We rarely make it through a month without it spewing, say, essence of lamb stew all over the ceiling. Either that or the drain hose on the washing machine, Sears' Best, jumps off the lip of the sink, sending gallons of soapy water onto the floor and into the teacups and soup bowls in Mrs Schwartz's kitchen cabinet. At which she comes to the foot of the stairs, calling: Yoo-hoo, Mrs Bracht . . .

And if you go back to school, who's going to pay your bills? Your father's not going to let you hang around like a freeloader.

I know, I know, you've told me that a hundred times.

Coming in on the tail end of the conversation, without so much as *hello*, my father lobs a grenade: Did your mother tell you we're thinking of sending Eddie to college? If he goes, we're counting on you to help pay the bills.

It's a direct hit, my heart's in smithereens—a million bloody fragments splattered over the kitchen table, the walls and the linoleum. Why would he say such a hurtful thing, knowing how much I want to go?

Are you saying you'd send *Eddie* and not me? I don't believe this. Where exactly are you planning to send him? Name me one college.

Stubbing out a cigarette butt, he says three razor-sharp syllables: Iona.

Did I forget to call first dibs? The idea that Eddie with so-so grades goes to Iona, while I stay at the telephone company to help pay his bills is infuriating. To think I never saw this coming. You can only get hit so many times before you start to feel it.

Why haven't you mentioned any of this before? Why is it he can go, and I can't?

It's more important boys go to college.

Since when? You think college is for boys? If so, why are so many of my girlfriends going to college?

Sidestepping the question, he tells me I'll be married in a few years, that no one needs college to get married and have a bunch of kids. His short not-so-sweet vision of my life is as conventional as church on Sunday. All the brightness, lightness, and rightness rushes out of me. Fingering his shirt pocket for a pack of cigarettes, he goes into the bedroom, taking with him the quiet intensity of a volcano. And my mom? She's busy being the good wife, not challenging anything he says, but letting me know by her wrinkled brow and earnest eyes that she'd like me to cut it out, behave myself.

Waiting for him to return to the battlefield, it occurs to me that were someone to walk in and meet him for the first time—see the self-satisfied demeanor, the jut-jawed grin, and the Arctic-blue eyes—they'd take him for a good-time Charley. Which he is. But they'd never see the other side—the inflexible, unbending, dogmatic, my-way-or-the-highway guy.

As a child, I wanted him to put an arm around me and tell me about my mother—tell me that she loved me, tell me that it wasn't my fault she had gone away. That never happened. Instead of sharing memories, he's done all he could to erase mine. He never loved me, not the way Carson Drew loved his daughter. Oh, who cares? I never loved him anyway.

What's wrong, Bob? Are you getting *married*? Eddie asks in that singsong voice kids use when trying to get your goat.

No, I'm not getting married, I say, giving him the once-over, checking for any princely qualities that may have emerged in the last half-hour. On the plus side, he's grown a few inches this year and, for the first time since kindergarten, he's no longer the class shrimp. Other than that, he has a long way to go to catch up with Prince Valiant.

Hey, Bob, did you hear what Dad did today?

No, I *didn't* hear what he did today, I say, in a patronizing tone that sails over his head.

When he came home for lunch, Kenny told him that the janitor had tried to hit him with a pole. For no reason.

That doesn't make sense. Why would the janitor do that?

I don't know. They were playing stickball in the playground, the way they always do. When Dad heard that, he ran over to school, climbed the fence and found the janitor in the boiler room and threw him up against the wall.

Who told you *that*?

Nobody, I was there. Dad grabbed him around the neck, saying: If you hurt one of my kids I'll kill you. You should've seen the janitor's face. He nearly peed in his pants.

Out of my way pipsqueak, I say, stomping off to my room.

For a year, I've been dating Nick Breitweisser—dating, that is, when he's not away at school. Tonight is one of those times. Pulling into the Glen Island Casino off Shore Road on Route 1-A in New Rochelle—the cradle of swing in the '30s and '40s—a parking lot attendant signals for us to pull up under a neon sign that's glowing red-hot in the night. All the great bandleaders from Tommy Dorsey and Glenn Miller to Les Brown and Claude Thornhill have played at the Casino, so the prospect of dancing the night away to the music of a live band in a legendary place has me flying high. When the parking lot attendant opens the door, I get a whiff of salt-air coming off Long Island Sound, hear the muffed strains of *Moonlight Serenade*.

The dining room—stark-white walls, with dark wooden beams crisscrossing a high ceiling—is awash with white damask cloths, glass ashtrays and a few nautical touches, including an anchor mounted on a wall. It's a Saturday night, the men natty in seersucker suits or navy-blue blazers, and the women pert and pretty in summery dresses.

When we take to the floor and Nick wraps his arms around me, he's an intoxicating mix. That freshly laundered shirt spritzed with Niagara spray starch. The All Spice After Shave. However, as good as he smells, when it comes to dancing, he lacks a sense of rhythm, doesn't seem to feel the beat of the music. You can tell right away that he hasn't spent much time at the Friday night dances. Then, too, there are the unexpected flourishes, like a double-dip that comes out of nowhere, leaving me alarmingly off-balance. After an hour or so, I suggest we take a breather, walk to the water's edge.

Off in the distance, a steamboat passes in front of Fort Slocum, while closer to shore, a one-man shell slices through inky black water.

How are things going at school, Nick?

No sooner are the words out of my mouth, when a green-eyed memory slithers from its roost. It's sophomore year, with Sister Elizabeth the Merciless playing games with my psyche. Dashing off a midterm essay on the pitfalls of envy—choose one of the seven mortal sins—I'm extemporizing on the need to be happy for others, even when their ship has sailed into port and yours is lost at sea. To be happy for Nick, for instance, who lies stretched out on the grass with all the languor and self-assurance of a well-bred character in an F. Scott Fitzgerald story. Nick goes to Boston College, a Jebbie bastion, Jebbie being code for Jesuit. Hand him a question, and he'll run a mile with it. A tad windy, but never winded. That guy loves nothing better than hearing himself talk, my dad says. Maybe so, but I like people who talk easily, who aren't stingy with their words. And I especially like listening to Nick talk about college—about his friends, the classes, and his professors.

It's then I imagine myself walking hand-in-hand with him across campus, dropping by the Admissions Office and filing an application. First name? Bob. Last name? Doppelganger. Afterwards, we stop at the chapel where Mozart is running up and down the aisles, where crumbs of incense hang heavy in the air.

On a bulletin board in the Classics Department, there's a notice—C*aveat studiosum!*—reminding those majoring in the classics that Advanced Placement courses are conducted in Greek or Latin. Be sure to pick up a copy of *Ancient Greek Writers from the Peloponnesus* before the first class. Poof!

What's new is that Nick has joined the Glee Club, and they gave a concert on Alumni Weekend, adding the song *Laura* to their repertoire. He loves *Laura*. Due to rehearsals, he missed a lecture last week given by a visiting professor from Notre Dame on the Marxist underpinnings of Catholicism, missed the Q & A that followed—some students arguing on behalf of social justice, others claiming social justice was no justice at all. He was sorry to have missed it. Me, too.

Happily, he never asks about my job, my family, or my friends for that matter. Which is okay, as I don't like conversations getting too personal, prefer to keep the serious stuff out of sight. As for the job, what's to say? That the 8:12 from Mount Vernon was twenty minutes late in arriving at the Fordham station yesterday. That the colored wall phones are selling like hotcakes. No, the job pays the bills, and I've managed to save $225 toward college tuition. What strikes me odd is that Nick has never once asked if I'm interested in going to college. Nor have I said, for fear of making my father look like a skinflint.

When I ask how he did on finals, he says he pulled a C in Philosophy. Thinking a C a waste of his parents' money, I suggest he may be spending too much time at Glee Club, not enough over at the library. He insists being in Glee Club is an honor.

It's highly selective. First you have to audition, and if you make the cut, you're interviewed by the club's officers.

If he reads music and sings *a cappella,* why isn't he a good dancer?

Hey, you're not listening.

I am so, I say, with an inscrutable smile intended to paper over any perceived slight. Not wanting him to think me a dimwit who knows nothing about the origins of Western philosophical thought, I ask if they're reading Socrates this year, though what I know about Socrates would not fill an eyedropper.

No, we read Socrates and the pre-Socratics last year. This year we're reading Locke and Rousseau, the philosophers of the Enlightenment.

His comment about the pre-Socratics, the casual way he tosses it off, sets me back on my heels. Who are the pre-Socratics? Not willing to advertise my ignorance, I mentally push them to the top of the reading list. To be sure, how can anyone develop a philosophy of life without having first-hand knowledge of the pre-Socratics?

Scooping a strand of kelp from the bay, Nick dangles it over my head, and I squeal as the icy water trickles down the back of my dress. Flinging it into the bay, he lays me back on the grass, kissing me softly. Overhead, that old painter moon is dipping a brush into a bucket of moonlight, highlighting the waves in the harbor, the chrome bumpers in the parking lot. Searching for love behind a hundred kisses, it's never been this close before.

The night comes alive with the *chuck-chuck-chuck* of a bullfrog and the *hustle-bustle* of the grasshoppers, crickets, and katydids. Somewhere out there in the night, Jay Gatsby's flicking pale gray ash off a white dinner jacket, listening to the gin-soaked laughter coming from the home of Tom and Daisy Buchanan. If only Daisy, the love of his life, were to step outside, she'd see him waiting for her on his dock in West Egg.

Nick's offhand remark about the pre-Socratics continues to rankle. I can see it all now—a chasm is yawning, with those interested in the life-of-the-mind on one side and all the know-nothings on the other. Desperately wanting to align myself with the philosopher kings of the Enlightenment, I signal my amanuensis to get serious, to buckle down and start filing college applications. Currently, I'm high on Wellesley, not all that far from his Jebbie bastion.

Tell me, he says, how do you know you exist?

Did he really say that? Sitting bolt upright, unsure if he's joking or serious, I stall, not wanting to come up with a wrong answer, asking if it's a trick question.

No, it's a philosophical problem.

Aha! Philosophy 101. Okay, so how do I know I exist? Well, for starters, I think you exist. If I didn't think so, I wouldn't be talking to you, would I? And since we agree on that, I think I exist, too.

Suspecting such an off-the-cuff response might sound lame to someone who's had a chance to waltz the question around the classroom with a college professor, it takes me by surprise when he gives my kneecap a hearty whack, saying: You got it. *Cogito ergo sum,* I think therefore I am.

Cogito ergo sum. The syllables roll around in my mouth like a couple of sour gumballs.

Yes, Descartes.

Day-cart? The meaningless name ricochets in my synapses.

An eighteenth century French philosopher who wrote the proofs of human existence.

The proofs of human existence . . .what's he talking about? I mentally scribble the Frenchman's name on a must read list, sorry to be missing the philosophical constructs and the classroom discussions. At the telephone company, I doubt if any of my co-workers would know Day-cart. Ah, yes . . . *Cogito* . . . a year or two down the road, I will be handling customer complaints, and he will be flitting the literary salons of Europe, chitchatting about Kierkegaard, Wittgenstein and Spinoza.

Cogito . . . I will be living at home and he will be light footing the world.

Cogito . . . he's going to meet Laura—the laugh that floats on a summer's night—who's on a first-name basis with all of the pre-Socratics.

Cogito...this starchy smile is making my cheeks ache.

That Nick, with gentleman Cs, holds a first-class ticket on the Lifetime Orient Express, while I'm standing on a fly-bitten platform in Mount Vernon cheering him on doesn't seem fair. Fair? Who said life is fair?

As he nuzzles my ear, tiny goose bumps goosestep the length of my spine. From the clubhouse comes the strains of *Goodnight, Sweetheart*, the song that ends all the Friday night school dances.

Goodnight, sweetheart, till we meet tomorrow . . .
Goodnight, sweetheart, sleep will banish sorrow . . .

Come, let's dance, I say, knowing that dancing has the power to lift my spirit like nothing else. Reaching the edge of the dance floor, I turn toward him and—Ouch!—he steps on my metatarsal, shredding my last good pair of nylons.

Tears and parting may make us forlorn
But with the dawn, a new day is born . . .

He apologizes, a hint sheepish, as we continue—*slow, slow, quick, quick, slow, slow, quick, quick*—elbowing our way around a crowded dance floor.

Don't worry. I'll stop by Alexander's Monday.

So I'll say goodnight, sweetheart, tho' I'm not beside you
Goodnight, sweetheart, still my love will guide you . . .

This never happens to Fred Astaire and Ginger Rogers. Watching the two of them swan a dance floor, it's as if invisible strings are keeping them in sync with one another.

Dreams enfold you…In each one, I'll hold you . . .
Goodnight, sweetheart, goodnight.

At that, Nick adds an impromptu embellishment, twirling me out and under his arm. I smile weakly, as he coos something about times like this making him wish we were married. Put that thought aside for a rainy day, I tell myself, along with *cogito ergo sum.* Truth is we're nothing like Fred and Ginger—this is a no-strings affair.

An hour later, exiting the parking lot, a sign catches my eye: Danger: Heartbreak Ahead. Did I read that right?

ARRIVING HOME after midnight, I'm surprised to find my mom in the kitchen, a newspaper spread out before her on the table.

Where's Nick?

He's gone home. Opening the refrigerator, checking for leftovers, I ask what she's doing up so late.

The weather's going to be good tomorrow, and I want to hang out the clothes first thing in the morning. We're short towels. So how's *Nick?*

The way she says his name suggests something's not right.

What do you mean how's *Nick?*

I mean, how is he, what's he doing?

He's fine, but why do I get this feeling you don't like him?

I like him, but I don't know . . . it's that he's . . . so stuck on himself. It's all about him—what he's doing, where he's going.

As she's saying this, I watch the corners of her mouth turning down with disapproval. The comment is surprising coming from her, as she never makes snarky remarks about anyone. Never. So what's it all about? Has she found all of his letters, read them all aloud? Does she think I'm giving him a pass on *plays well with others?*

Are you saying he's conceited? With one arm draped over the refrigerator door, I complain there's nothing to eat. I think you don't like listening to him talking about college this and college that.

Let not start that again. Close the door before the light burns out. Bob, give me a hand with those dungarees.

I don't mind threading my brothers' dungarees through a wringer after midnight, but I mind being Bob. When I was born, was my father hoping for a boy? The only one who would know that is my missing mother. Funny how she came to mind just then, when I haven't thought about her for ages. I don't know if that's a sign I'm growing up or giving up. What I do know is that Veronica most often comes to mind at those times when I'm dancing on the edge of the blues. As for Nick, he's like smoking—hard to give up.

WITHIN THE week, a razor-slim, businesslike, engraved envelope arrives from the Berkeley Business School:

Dear Miss Bracht:

We are delighted to offer you a two-year partial scholarship to the Berkeley Business School in White Plains. Would you be so kind as to contact . . .

Alternating between disbelief and delight, I do a little war dance—jiggling the hips, pumping a fist in the air—before flopping onto the bed with the letter pressed to my heart. I can see it now, happy skies ahead. Okay, but how will I convince my father to let me go? He's done paying tuition, done paying the bills. But hope springs eternal, so at the first opportunity I lob one rosy scenario after another at him, only to have him bat each in turn out of the park. Unable to see my way forward, I tuck the letter between the pages of my Merriam-Webster and put off writing the committee—praying he will change his mind.

Dear Sir: Thank you for your most kind offer of a scholarship to the Berkeley Business School. Unfortunately, circumstances do not allow me to accept at this time. Yours truly . . .

Seeing the words in Waterman's blue on a sheet of Crane's ivory, they're as final as the Ten Commandments carved in stone.

Nursing a cup of coffee, while reading *Atlas Shrugged* at the luncheonette on Fordham Road, a young woman sits down next to me and begins rifling through a shopping bag filled with what look to be textbooks. Out of the corner of my eye, I watch as she pulls them out, one by one. Curious, I ask if she goes to college. When she says she goes to Fordham, it's a slap-your-forehead moment.

Fordham University? I didn't know women went to Fordham! I thought it was all male, like Fordham Prep. My mind's racing, trying to find a toehold in a rapidly shifting landscape. Do you take classes up the block at the Rose Hill Campus?

She does, but only on Saturdays. Most of her classes are given evenings at the City Hall Campus on lower Broadway.

Lower Broadway? Besieging her with questions, I learn that she's accumulated fifty-four credits by taking classes at night, four nights a week. Her words fill me with hope, leave me feeling as light-headed as a helium-filled balloon. At last, I can see a way forward.

Within days, a catalog arrives from Fordham, announcing fall classes will be starting in two weeks. If eager to sign up, I'm short money, so I ask my father if he could help me out. Temporarily, that is.

I'm not asking you to *give* me the money, but I have $225 put aside, so if you could loan me, say, another $150, I could register for two courses. Otherwise, I'll miss a whole semester. He turns me down.

If you want to go to school, do it on your own dime. Save your money, start next term.

But that's not until *February*. I'll miss the fall term. I hate hearing myself whine, but sometimes I can't help myself.

What's your hurry? By February, you might change your mind.

What's my hurry? I'm late getting started. I won't change my mind. I don't want to waste a semester when I could be earning credits toward a degree.

He shoots down my hopes as easily as ducks in a shooting arcade. Ayn Rand says: Don't let anyone kill that spark in your soul. Choose your own values and hold fast. Success will come in time.

Are you sure, Miss Rand?

FEBRUARY. The night is bitter cold, the streets thronged with people hurrying home, hurrying to meet friends, hurrying to get to classes. Coming up from the subway at Chambers Street, I step into a world that's bristling with energy and momentum, with skyscrapers blocking out a wintry sky. The limestone building at 302 Broadway has a sign off to one side reading: *Fordham University, City Hall Division.* Paralyzed between dread and desire, my heart stands still, while my brain fumbles and frets. Am I smart enough to do college work or will I be exposed as an imposter who fooled the Admissions Department? Ayn Rand says when you find yourself caught in a contradiction, check your premises, for one of them is sure to be wrong. Summoning her face to mind—the sharp features, piercing dark eyes, mannish hairstyle—I hear her no-nonsense voice saying:

Don't be a fool. Open that door. If you don't open it, you will never be able to open the doors on the other side.

Shoving all the negative thoughts to the back of my mind, I allow myself to be carried forward on the wave of students heading for the elevators.

A small chapel off the lobby beckons. Thinking time spent in prayer might quiet a heart that's fluttering faster than a hummingbird's wings, I slip into a pew. There's no one around. Eyes closed and wrapped in a deep silence, I feel my mother's presence. Can she help me? Does she think I can do this? Is she disappointed that I've turned into such a pest, arguing with my father all the time? The other night, Eddie said: Why are you and Dad always arguing? I had no answer for him.

The sacristy lamp throws a reddish glow over the altar cloth, and a half-dozen ruby-red candles flicker in a rack off to one side.

Please, dear Lord, lend me thy strength. Hold me in thy

hand. Do not let thy servant go. And whatever you do, for heaven's sake, don't let any of the instructors call on me, not tonight. Get me through the panic, okay? Amen.

In front of the elevators, a student is handing out copies of *The Maroon Quill,* the Business School newsletter. I take a copy, tucking it between my books and head for my first class—Elements of Logic, 6:00 p.m. to 8:00 p.m. By the time seven o'clock rolls around, the reality of what has been an exhausting day is making it hard for me to stay awake. Up since six o'clock this morning and having put in a full day at the office, I'm bushed. How will I make it through Medieval Europe and the Rise of Universities 8:00 p.m. to 10:00 p.m.?

When we change classes at eight o'clock, I deliberately take a seat at the back of the room, hoping to stay out of the instructor's line of vision. A young woman across the aisle introduces herself. Blessed with a breezy self-assured manner— Hi, I'm Maureen Buckley from Nicholas of Tolentine—she invites me to go after class to a meeting of the IRO. (At all the Catholic schools, students usually give the name of their parish rather than that of their neighborhood.)

The IRO? What is it, a union?

No, she laughs, it's the Inter-Racial Organization. We meet downstairs at ten, as soon as classes are over.

Can anyone go, or is it members only?

No anyone can go—white students, black students, it doesn't matter. All that matters is if you're interested in making a difference in race relations. Have you heard of Dorothy Day?

I haven't. Maureen explains that black students have been arriving at Fordham in greater numbers, thanks to efforts of women like Dorothy Day and *The Catholic Worker* movement—a New York City strain of Catholic anarchism. It was they who lobbied the Jesuits to open their colleges to blacks, seeing it as a first step toward a religious transformation of society. Dorothy Day printed the first issues of *The Catholic Worker* newsletter in her kitchen, selling them for a penny a copy. Listening to Maureen with her highly developed social consciousness, the City Hall Division of Fordham University begins to feel like the real deal.

Thanks for the invite, but I've a train to catch. If I miss one at that time of night, I'll be stranded in Grand Central for an hour if not for the night.

C'mon, you'll like it. It'll be fun. The meeting's downstairs and there's coffee. Despite the full court press, being stranded in Grand Central does not strike me as fun. Promising to join her next time, I beg off.

Okay, she says, but at the next meeting, we're going to have the election of officers. I'd like your vote.

Why not? Who else would I vote for other than Maureen?

Even though I'm running on fumes at this hour, the night's shaping up better than I had anticipated. Simply being in a college environment is making me feel smarter, if not less tired. Rubbing my cheeks and yawning an exaggerated stretch-mouthed grin, I'm fading fast in the back row. Which does not escape—is Maureen kicking me?—the instructor at the front of the room.

The young lady in the back row, are we keeping you awake? Would you like to answer the question?

Leaving my humiliation at the classroom door, I step into the night to find lower Broadway deserted—not a nighthawk in sight. Clutching my textbooks to my chest, I hurry past darkened doorways and down desolate streets, my high heels tapping out a lonesome tattoo. Hoping to steady my jangled nerves, I concentrate on a jaundiced light seeping from a subway station off in the distance. Remember, I tell myself, it's hard because it's all so new—the classes, the city, the lateness of the hour, the streets empty of people. But you'll get used to it. Think about it this way—once you reach the subway, it's only a quick hop to Grand Central and then home again, home again. Inhale. Exhale.

Dashing through Grand Central Station, I'm brought up short at the sight of a dozen beautiful chandeliers in the arcade.Like a squadron of dimly lit spaceships arriving from a distant galaxy. Despite the lateness of the hour, hundreds of commuters are crisscrossing the concourse, hurrying to catch the last trains out to the Gold Coast of Connecticut and to the upscale villages of Westchester County. From my vantage, the activity on the main concourse—all the sidestepping, feinting, and dodging—is like a Busby Berkeley production punctuated by syncopated rhythms and urban jazziness.

With only seconds to spare—All aboard! All aboard!—I take a seat by a blackened window to watch the fleeting images of those behind me: a man placing a briefcase in the overhead rack; another tucking a commutation ticket into the hatband of his fedora before pulling it down over his face; a couple ca-noodling across the aisle, sharing a box of crackerjacks. There is something magical about boarding a train—destination unknown—so much so my energy level rises. Opening a text-book, intent upon getting a head start on next week's readings, I wake up as the conductor calls: Mount Vernon! Mount Vernon! Even before the train comes to a complete stop, the regulars are stampeding down the stairwells to Mount Vernon Avenue, which is every bit as deserted as lower Broadway. A taxi driver idling at the curb rolls down a window:

Need a ride, Miss?

No, thanks. I'm only going a few blocks.

Six to be exact, but taxis cost money, and I've none to spare. A neighborhood as familiar as the tops of my knees by day feels menacing at night. Unaccustomed to being out alone at this hour, nothing looks the same. What's more, footsteps are gaining on me. Or is that my imagination? Any sensory impressions my brain may have put aside for a rainy day—the toes recording the squidgy things like river sand and mucky bogs; the soles taking note of the spiky grasses and tufty-headed clover; the heels hold-ing onto the hard-earned information about potholes and cracks in the sidewalks—are swept away by a massive rush of adrenaline.

Wheeling around to confront the stalker in the night—a man with a red-hot cigarette dangling from one hand twenty feet away—I'm within a nanosecond of shrieking with fear when I hear him say: Is that you, Barbara?

Is that you, Mr Hotchkiss? You scared the life out of me.

What are you doing out so late?

I'm just coming home from school. I'm taking courses at Fordham University, near City Hall.

How's it going?

So far so good, I laugh, but this is only the first night. Hearing myself say *first night* is like promising myself there will be more to come.

I'm taking two courses this semester, I tell him, one on the rise of universities during the Middle Ages and the other on the elements of logic.

Cutting across an empty lot, the chicory snagging my nylons, PS #14 looms in the distance like a dark gray battleship.

Elements of logic? I never knew they taught logic. The way I look at it, some people are logical, some ain't.

I laugh appreciatively, telling him there's more to logic than he might suspect. For instance, there are syllogisms that allow you to check your premises.

Syllogisms? Like what?

It's hard to explain, but I'll give you the example the instructor used. Let's say that all men are mortal. Would you agree—all men are mortal?

You mean, we all die.

Exactly. Now that's the first premise. Then we say John is a man. That's the second premise. So what do we have? All men are mortal, and John is a man. So from that we can conclude that John is mortal. Do you see? It's called deductive reasoning, working from a general premise to a particular conclusion. Next week, we're doing it in reverse, inductive reasoning.

With the night falling down upon us, I suspect his eyes are

glazing over. What's odd is that this is the first conversation—other than hello, good-bye—I've ever had with Marla's dad. When I would call for her, he'd be feet up on the Barcalounger watching TV. I don't know anything about him, don't even know if he roots for the Yankees or the Dodgers. Wanting to be polite and keep the conversation going, I state the obvious:

Are you coming home from work Mr Hotchkiss?

Yep, I'm working the three-to-eleven shift this month. Here we are, he says, pointing to front steps leading to a vestibule as dark as dirt at high noon.

G'night, Mr Hotchkiss. Say hello to Marla and Mrs Hotchkiss, will you?

With one more pitch-dark, empty lot to pass, I remain alert for darting shadows or snapping twigs. When the garden gate swings closed behind me, I pause at the front door to rest my head against the rough siding, telling myself *it will get easier, it will get easier, it will get easier. Hang in there, little tomato.* Mounting the stairs, I hear: Is that you, Bob?

G'night, Mom.

ENERGETIC AND self-confident, Maureen has a plan. Run for office? Me? That's the craziest thing I've ever heard. I don't even know what the issues are.

Issues? What issues? That's not important, she says, we can figure that out as we go along. Let's run as a team, like co-secretaries. If I miss a meeting, you take notes. If you miss, I'll take notes.

Listening to her, I'm thinking: Is she crazy? Missing any meetings or classes? I've missed enough already.

Downstairs in the cafeteria, a dozen members of the Inter-Racial Organization are milling about, meeting and greeting. When the meeting comes to order, Maureen, girl activist extraordinaire, is elected club secretary and a young black man—three-piece Brooks Brothers' suit, classic striped tie—is president. When it's time to address new business, someone proposes we visit Birdland this year, an idea meeting with unanimous approval.

As the meeting winds down, Maureen introduces me to the newly elected president of the IRO who, by day, is a social worker in Rockland County. When he hears I live in Yonkers, he's quick to offer me a lift home.

That's nice of you, but I don't want to take you out of your way, not so late at night. I know it's a long trip to Nanuet.

I'm being disingenuous. Taking him up on his offer would eliminate walking the empty downtown streets, waiting on a grimy subway platform studded with chewing gum, and racing across the concourse of Grand Central Station trying to catch the last train out to Mount Vernon. To say nothing of not having to walk home from the railroad station.

You're not taking me out of my way, he insists. I go straight up on the Deegan.

Well, if you're *sure* it's no trouble. You know what, you could drop me near the raceway. I could get home from there, and that would save you a lot of time.

Am I kidding? If he takes me at my word and drops me by

the raceway, I have no idea if buses run at that time of night. I could call my father, but where would I find a phone booth? Can I run a mile in high heels?

Easing the car out of the garage, he points to a gauge low on gas. He thinks we'll have a better chance of finding a station open on the West Side Drive. Whizzing through the night, our conversation touches on the IRO, on our classes and classmates, and on his work with troubled adolescents at an institution in Rockland County. Luck of the draw, we find a station open on the Saw Mill River Parkway. When he gets out to check under the hood—what are guys looking for under the hood?—an attendant in his mid-forties comes out. Bending over to take a look inside the car, he and I are eyeball-to-eyeball, so close I can read the label on his denim cap: Imperial Esso Service. So close that if looks could kill, I'd be dead. In my mind's eye, I picture my father waiting by the garden gate. Uh-oh. My stomach double-knots.

Wallowing in unhappy memories, I'm making myself more apprehensive than need be, as my friend tries to read a dipstick under the eerie glow cast by an overhead lamp. Oblivious to any hostile glances or the rising anxiety of his passenger—an anxiety having more to do with my father than the Esso attendant—he's taking his good-old time. That this young man, a senior at Fordham and president of the IRO, is a social worker caring for troubled adolescents will mean diddlysquat to my father. *For heaven's sake, throw in a quart of oil, and let's get out of here.* When the attendant goes inside to get the oil, my thoughts turn to another young man who didn't quite meet my father's expectations.

IT WAS the night that Rita and I went to a fraternity party on the Upper West Side. By the time we arrived, the place was thick with smoke, throbbing with music. My goal for the evening was to meet a guy who did not live in Sherwood Park. With Nick Breitweisser now a Supply Officer in the US Navy sailing the high seas, that relationship is heavily dependent upon letter writing. Barely through the front door, a guy wearing khakis, a buttoned-down shirt and a lime green Lacoste sweater over his shoulders, asks me to dance. He's a good dancer, easy to follow, and when we take a break, he brings over two beers, saying: You look familiar. Do I *know* you?

I don't think so, I would have remembered you.

Hey, I know. You look like . . . what's her name? Donna Reed! Yeah, has anyone ever told you that? When he said that, he smiled and his whole face got into the act, as if happy to have made the connection.

The Donna Reed Show is on ABC on Wednesday nights. In carefully matched outfits and never a hair out of place, Donna plays the role of perfect wife and mother. Before I can answer, there's a crash in the kitchen where a number of the brothers are guzzling beers and throwing back shots. A male voice cuts through the din: All blacks, out!

Gasp! Paralyzed with fear, the happiness of the moment rushes out of me in one long swoosh. That a college student would say such a shameful thing is, for me, unthinkable. Guardedly, I glance around to see if anyone in the room is black. Noting my consternation, Jerry says: It's some jerk. He's drunk. Let's dance.

Shortly thereafter, we hear the same raucous voice: All queers…get out! This is followed by uproarious laughter in the kitchen. The evening's taking a dive. Here I had been looking forward to this fraternity party all week, but now all I want to do is get out of here before something terrible happens. When it comes to crowds—pep rallies, parades, street fairs, sporting events—I avoid them. Checking this out with Merriam-Webster, I found *demophobia*, a fear of crowds. Symptoms? Excessive sweating . . . check; breathlessness . . . check; feeling sick at heart . . . check; a fear of losing control . . . not exactly, more a fear of others losing control.

At which the voice cuts through the din: All Jews . . . out!

Now that's a sucker-punch. Instinctively, my hand goes to my throat. What if Mrs Schwartz had been here with me, or Irma, who is probably studying at Cornell?

Someone shouts: Knock it off out there, you guys!

Jerry, listen, it's been nice meeting you, but I'm leaving. I have to tell you, this is my first and last fraternity party, so I don't know when I'll be seeing you again.

He mentions a dance coming up, says Lester Lanin and his orchestra will be playing, and asks if I'd like to go.

Lester Lanin? Lester Lanin, the society bandleader, is going to play at a fraternity dance?

He explains it's not a fraternity dance, but the annual Christmas Dance at Manhattan College. He doesn't belong to this fraternity. Like me, he's come with a friend.

I'd love to, but I have to ask my father.

Okay, I'll call you tomorrow. Give me your number, he

said, rooting around for a scrap of paper on which I scribble: Beverly 7-8129.

Returning home sky high on happiness, I skip any mention of the boorishness and drinking. When my parents turn off the TV, ready to call it a night, I bring up Lester Lanin.

Who *is* he? my father said.

Lester Lanin? You don't know Lester Lanin?

No, not Lester Lanin, I know who he is, but who's the guy you want to go out with?

You wouldn't know him. He's a student at Manhattan College studying civil engineering. He calls himself a bridge, roads, and tunnels guy. That's cute, isn't it?

What's his name?

His name? Why do you want to know his name? You wouldn't know him.

Maybe not, but what's his name?

Jerry.

Does Jerry have a last name?

Jerry Kim.

Kim? What kind of a name is that?

What do you mean what kind of a name is that?

You heard me, is he Chinese?

Chinese? No, I don't think so. I think he's part Korean, part American. He speaks English as well as you do, Dad. I mean, he doesn't sound like Charley Chan, if that's what you're thinking.

Kim.

Yes, Kim.

You think I'm going to let you go out with some *chink*? he said, his face florid, the arms akimbo. Blindsided by the comment, I'm thinking: *a chink? a chink in a wall? a chink in one's armor? what does any of that have to do with Jerry?* Belatedly, I get it.

How can you *say* such a thing? You don't know him, but you must know that to be a civil engineer you have to be smart. Besides, you and he have something in common—you're both great dancers.

I don't care if he's a good dancer—

In addition, you might be happy to know, since you're the one who's always harping on guys drinking and driving, that he hardly drinks. A beer maybe, but not like the Irish guys. And he's Catholic, goes to church on Sundays. (Jumping from square to square, I'm trying to keep ahead of his queen.)

He's *Catholic*, what's that supposed to mean?

It means that you and he share a bond of faith. If you don't know that, you don't know your Catholic theology or the Church's teachings.

Catholic theology? What are you *talking* about?

What I'm saying is that according to the Church's teachings, it's best for Catholics to date other Catholics. It's better, for example, that I date someone who's Catholic and Asian or Catholic and black, rather than someone Irish and Jewish.

Irish and Jewish? No such thing. I've known a lot of Irish, not one of them is Jewish. Where do you get these knuckle-headed ideas?

No, it's true. That's what the nuns say. It's that dating can lead to marriage, and marriage to children and, according to the Church, all children have to be baptized Catholic. Right?

The nuns, who cares what the nuns say? You can forget about the dance. That's my last word.

Why *not*? I wheedle. It's a *Christmas* dance with Lester Lanin's orchestra. He'll come to the house, you can meet him. You forget I'm nineteen years old, old enough to make up my own mind about who I want to go out with.

You think so? Over my dead body. As long as you're living under my roof, you'll do what I tell you.

If we were playing Monopoly, the card I'd be looking for is *Get Out of Jail Free*.

AT THE Esso Station, my Good Samaritan counts out a few bills for the attendant. Brrrrrr, it's cold, he says, smacking his upper arms for warmth as he climbs back into the car. I make no mention of any withering glances, nor do I let on that a more harrowing scene may lie a few miles up the road. Through the side view mirror, I watch as the lights of the station fade, leaving a dim glow on the horizon. Feeling skittish, I insist he drop me off at the raceway, but he won't hear of it, not at this time of night. Barreling down Yonkers Avenue, we pass the racetrack where the klieg lights have gone dark for the night and the barns where the trotters are munching hay in their stalls. A quarter-mile on, the neon sign at the Empire Diner casts an unhealthy glow over a now empty parking lot. I'm so anxious, I can scarcely breathe. Inhale. Exhale.

You'll need to take a left at the Royal Scarlet up ahead, I whisper, too tense to make polite conversation, concentrating my energies on jumping from the car. Lady luck is with me tonight: the whole of Crescent Place is as quiet as Grant's tomb—no light on at the house, no neighbor's dog barking after midnight, and no father prowling the sidewalk.

Thanks so much, I say, closing the car door as quietly as possible. See you next week.

A notice appears in the paper that Trans World Airlines will be holding interviews at Idlewild Airport. I read it over and over. Wouldn't this be a dream come true, but what are the odds of getting an interview? Forget the odds, just show up.

Not knowing how to get to Idlewild Airport, I take the easy way out and ask my father if he would drive me or let me borrow the car. This innocent request results in my parents having a rare disagreement, not what you would call a no-holds-barred, plates-flying disagreement, but a sharp difference of opinion.

Don't take her out, Ed, my mom says. If you do, I'm warning you she's going to get that job and then what?

What do you mean *and then what?*

I mean they could send you anywhere.

Not wanting to hurt her feelings, I bite my tongue, knowing such a scenario would be an answer to this maiden's prayers.

198 | VERONICA'S GRAVE

They could send you to California if they wanted to.

What's wrong with California? I reply, as images of cable cars notching their way up Nob Hill and Hollywood starlets being discovered at soda fountains come to mind.

A single woman living on her own in California?

She sounds like a teacher who realizes that despite her best efforts the student has missed the point. Acting blasé, I downplay any possibility of California.

California? Fat chance, everyone wants to go to California. However, if you want to fly International to Paris, Rome, or Madrid, you have to fly out of New York.

Paris? Why would you want to go to Paris?

You're not serious. Who wouldn't want to go to Paris or travel the world? I'd like to go to Ireland and kiss the Blarney Stone. Climb the Eiffel Tower and see all of Paris at my feet. Visit Rome and see the Vatican and walk the Forum of the Caesars in the moonlight.

Are you saying you think it's all right for a single woman to travel the world by herself?

Mom, let me explain something—airline hostesses do not travel the world alone. They're part of a crew. As for what people will think, I think they'll be jealous. Being an airline hostess has to be one of the best jobs in the world. I've been told women passengers come on board carrying fur coats, with stone martens draped around their necks. That you meet celebrities—actors and actresses, politicians and VIPs—and you're paid for doing it. I'd do the job free, if they'd let me.

Being a stewardess is no job for a decent girl.

My mom has a way of making the word *stewardess* sound like a euphemism for prostitute. Switching tactics, I toss out an enticement, telling her that TWA gives employees and family members free travel passes. Naturally, she, the happy homemaker, is not interested in traveling.

You're planning to leave home, is that what this is all about?

No, of course not, I fib, even though it's all I can think of. At this point, my father comes in from the living room asking: When are the interviews?

Saturday.

I'm off Saturday, I'll take you out.

What happened? I'll bet he's packed for Hawaii—white anklets, black shoes, and a floral print shirt.

WE ARRIVE early at Idlewild Airport, which takes its name from the former Idlewild Golf Course. A place long on grass and short on blacktop, there are millions of birds wintering over in the marshes. We zip past the main terminal, New York International Air, where the multi-colored flags of a dozen countries are flapping in a breeze, while out on the tarmac stand the propeller-driven planes belonging to Air France, Alitalia, and Air Jordan. Although early in the day, a dozen people—including two boys on bikes—crowd the viewing stand, to watch the planes taking off and landing. You can feel the excitement in the air and see it in the architecture—a new age of aviation is dawning. At the Pan-American Terminal, a circular building with a flat-as-a-pancake roof, the planes park with their black noses touching the building. Like birds around a feeder. Further along, a billboard at a huge demolition zone indicates that this is the future home of the TWA Flight Center, designed by Eero Saarinen.

Do you think Eero Saarinen is a man or a woman? Look at *that*, I say, pointing to a sketch of the proposed terminal—it looks like a giant prehistoric bird in flight.

The interviews take place in a redbrick industrial building in the boondocks. I ask my father to come back around four, thinking I should know by then whether or not I have the job.

In a large reception area on the ground floor, some forty or fifty young women—down from Maine and Massachusetts, up from Texas and Alabama, in from Pennsylvania and New Jersey—mill about making conversation. Spirits are flying high, each hoping to be crowned Miss Congeniality. By nine-thirty, there is a brief welcome and an overview of what we should expect; specifically that each of us will have four interviews throughout the course of the day.

Around three-thirty in the afternoon, I'm called into the office of a C. E. McBride Jr. for my fourth and final interview. An attractive, slightly rotund, middle-aged man rises as I enter. From the scuttlebutt in the outer room, I already know he's the Supervisor of Employment for TWA flight personnel and has come from Kansas City to oversee the interviews. I also know that when you enter his office, he wants you to walk to a corner and turn around, so he can check out your legs. Thick ankles? Thanks for coming, nice to meet you. Piano legs? Take them with you when you leave, please. Heavy thighs? Sorry to have put you to the trouble.

After the preliminaries—Ipana smile, Katy Gibbs handshake—I'm no sooner seated when he asks: Aren't you talking to the other young ladies?

Bells clang, sirens whistle, lights flash: If he suspects I'm not talking to the other applicants, wouldn't that be a black mark against my name? Scribble-scribble: Candidate shows poor social skills.

Yes, I am talking with them, but why do you ask? I say, my hand fluttering from lap to throat, a gesture that could vaguely be interpreted as *how could you think such a thing of me?*

Because you're the first one to come through that door in the last hour who hasn't walked to the corner and turned around—without my asking them to do so. The chin is tucked, the eyes amused.

Suspecting this to be an icebreaker, I play along, telegraphing him a megawatt smile, saying, I was hoping you'd forget. My knees are a bit shaky, so if it's all right with you, I'll stay where I am. He's having none of that.

Do me a favor, walk to the corner.

At which I trot my limousine legs—Aunt Dot says all the Bracht girls have the ankles of thoroughbreds—to the corner to do a full turn.

Could you raise your skirt a bit?

Checking to see how much leg I'm showing, not wanting to look the hussy, I wait for a reaction, but after no more than a cursory glance, he continues thumbing through a folder, presumably one with my name on it, motioning for me to take a seat.

Miss Miller says you're taking classes at Fordham—

My heart goes limp, dies a little when he says Miss Miller. *Does he mean Miss Mueller? is this a ploy, a deliberate mispronunciation to see what I'll say? wouldn't the Supervisor of Employment for In-Flight Personnel know the names of the other interviewers? if I don't say something, will he think me a dimwit incapable of remembering passengers' names? if I correct him, will he think me lacking in the social graces essential for a TWA hostesses? Not sure how to play this game, I invoke Rule Number One: Don't be a Jerk. Mum's the word.*

—at night. How do you like Fordham?

I *love* Fordham—the classes are great, all the instructors brilliant and the student organizations . . .

You mean sororities and fraternities?

Oh, no. Not at Fordham. Our extracurricular groups are the Inter-Racial Organization and the Student Council for Evening Students.

Ah, yes, and I see here you've had three years of a foreign language.

Well, actually, I've had six—three years of Latin, three years of Spanish—but I don't know if Latin counts, since no one speaks it anymore. What do *you* think?

He tilts back in a swivel chair saying: I think it counts, but I'm wondering how you're going to continue taking classes while flying for TWA. Flying's not a nine-to-five job.

Not wanting to bore him with the dishwater dull details of my current nine to five, I smile saying:

That's exactly what I'd love about flying. I once read that the world is like a giant encyclopedia, but in order to read it, you have to travel. I like that, don't you? He does.

What's unsettling is how within minutes of meeting me he's zeroed in on my biggest worry: If I leave Fordham before getting my degree, will I go back and finish? I can't imagine a time when I'd quit flying to go back to living at home, working at the phone company and taking classes at night. Accumulating credits at night is as endless and exhausting as shoveling snow in a blizzard. What's more, should I leave Fordham, I'll never hear the end of it from my father. On the other hand, should I stay the course, I'll be the first in my family to graduate college. All things considered, if Mr McBride offers me the job, I'm going to take it.

The Telephone Company's paying you more than we're prepared to offer at this time.

Mr McBride, for me flying with TWA isn't about the money. I've wanted to be an airline hostess for as long as I can remember, as far back as elementary school. In fact, in my Graduation Day autograph album, there was a page with all these questions: who is your favorite actor? favorite actress? favorite film? what will be your future occupation? On that line, I wrote stewardess. Did you have those albums? Ours were navy blue leather with pastel pages in about as many colors as Howard Johnson's has ice-cream flavors.

And how many might that be? he says, the bushy eyebrows only half-hiding the merriment in the eyes.

Twenty-eight, I say, my face brightening in all the right places, tiny dimples punctuating my cheeks. Giving me an *aw-shucks* grin, he wonders aloud whatever happened to his album.

Wouldn't it be incredible, I say, if where it said future occupation, you had written, Supervisor of In-Flight Personnel for TWA?

He gives a chuckle, saying *engineer* would have been more like it. Then—too soon, too soon—time's up. He's arranging his papers, capping his fountain pen. *Don't just sit there—say something, do something, ask a question. The longer the interview, the more time you have to make a good impression.*

Well, he says, drawing out his words: I . . . think . . . that . . . we've . . . covered . . . everything. I want to thank you for coming in. It was a pleasure meeting you, Miss Bracht—firm handshake, good eye contact—but I should tell you we won't be making any decisions for at least a week or two. My colleagues and I need time to put our heads together. Have you any questions for me?

In a spilt second, I yank my ego out of my pocket and ask how many hostesses he intends to hire.

That's a good question, but hard to answer, he says pushing back from the desk. We don't have a specific number in mind. We're simply looking for young women who would make great TWA hostesses. On average, we interview forty applicants to fill one position.

One in forty? I repeat, as deflated as a punctured balloon. We want to get it right, he continues. The way we see it, our hostesses are on the front lines with our passengers. We think of them as our secret weapon—the face of TWA.

That phrase *the face of TWA* negotiates the switchbacks of my brain, triggering thoughts of a classmate at PS #14, who had been a runner-up in a Miss Rheingold contest and went on to be *the face of Revlon* on the Arthur Godfrey Show. Perhaps noticing I'm growing paler at his every word, adding a wink, he says:

As you might expect, my job's easier than it was years ago. In the early days of aviation, a young woman had to be a registered nurse to become a hostess.

A nurse? why was that?

The planes weren't pressurized. Airsickness was a big problem. And people weren't accustomed to flying, weren't used to the sensation of being airborne. I'm told they'd interview one hundred before hiring one ambassador for TWA.

A TWA ambassador? This is getting better and better, but if his congenial manner is meant to be reassuring, I'm not reassured. My heart's flip-flopping like a mullet out of water. Having canvassed the competition, I suspect he'll go with the Georgia Peach from Cedar Creek, the one who goes around saying ya'll this and ya'll that. Or the leggy blonde from Texas—*five foot nine? five foot ten?*—who tells everyone she's from Big D. Big D? Big deal. Most people don't know what the heck she's talking about.

Wiping my sweaty palms on a tight-fitting pencil skirt

riding above my knees, my mind races to find something to add that might improve my chances, something other than my vital statistics: five feet five-and-one-half inches, one hundred and twenty-four pounds, thirty-five/twenty-four/thirty-five, with seven-and-a-half-inch ankles, and twelve-inch calves. What's he scribbling? Did he just cross my name off the list? My feet don't feel like they're my own. Making a herculean effort, I push myself up and out of the chair to bow geisha-like out of the office, hoping he doesn't detect the free-floating anxiety in a forced smile. Pausing in the doorway, I hold up two crossed fingers and, giving a discernible wink, say:

I'll keep my fingers crossed until I hear from you, Mr McBride.

You do that, young lady, he says with a broad smile.

Say good night, Gracie. Exit left.

MY FATHER has the car positioned for a quick getaway, a fuzzy grey spume pouring from the exhaust. The man is like a Swiss watch, never late. But he's also like a soufflé in that he doesn't like to be kept waiting.

Waiting long, Dad?

Nah, ten or fifteen minutes. You get the job? he says, quick-checking the side mirror before making an illegal U-turn out of the parking lot onto Ocean Boulevard. With his left hand barely grazing the wheel, he roots around with his right for a pack of cigarettes, taps the pack on the dashboard in such a way that a single cigarette pops up—not two or three, just one—which he grabs between his lips. He then takes a matchbook from behind the visor, opens the cover with a flick of a finger, and bends the matchstick into a ninety-degree angle, rubbing the chemically coated tip against the striker, and lighting up. It's a deft maneuver executed with the skill of a surgeon. I don't understand why he smokes Chesterfields, when everyone knows that more doctors smoke Camels than any other brand.

Did I get the job? That's what I'd like to know, but they don't tell you, not for a week or two. Get this, they take one in forty applicants. How about those odds?

He's noncommittal, offering little more than *you'll see*. Once in a while it would be nice to hear a reassuring word, something more than *you'll see*. But sweet talking is not his style. Maybe it's that he doesn't want me to get my hopes up, but my hopes have been sky-high ever since I saw the notice.

You know, Daddy, some of the girls were so pretty, and a number of them had this way of talkin' all sweet and Southern—as if each word went into a honey pot before it came out of their mouths.

You might say that this would be a perfect opportunity for my father to say he's sure I'm as pretty as any of these Southern gals, but there are no such affirmations coming from behind the wheel.

You know, Dad, that way of talkin' sweet and sugary sounds phony. Of course, what I think doesn't matter a bit, it's what Mr McBride thinks that counts, right? No comment.

And, get this, a number of girls were college *graduates*.

Let me ask you, if you could hire someone who's been to college or someone who hasn't, who would you choose?

Knowing he finds any mention of college, no matter how inconsequential or off-the-cuff, provocative, I drop it. A ride's a ride. Getting something out of him is like nailing jelly to a tree. Off in the eastern sky, I watch a pair of silver wings fading out of sight.

A LETTER arrives from TWA offering me a job. I can't believe they want me and not the leggy blonde from Big-D or the sweet young thing from Cedar Creek. To show they mean what they say, they've included a round trip ticket to Kansas City. The next hostess training class will start Monday, July 6, if that's convenient. If that's convenient? Let me check my calendar.

The letter goes on to say that if I have any questions, be sure to give them a call. Included is a full-color booklet with pictures of TWA hostesses in form-fitting green uniforms, more sage than shamrock:

Once you have completed training, you will be meeting and greeting stage and screen stars, key figures in the news, prominent people in government, and noteworthy men and women from many nations and all walks of life.

I can hardly breathe—it's as if I've run a mile after a bus. Where's Kansas City?

On a day that would be perfect from start to finish, another letter arrives. This from the manager of the Skyline

Inn on Route 4, Box 530, in Parkville, Missouri, who writes to give us an overview of what we can expect during our month of training in Kansas City. He wants us to feel at home, suggests we think of his address as our own. (Much obliged!) At the Skyline Inn, rooms will be assigned, four girls to a room, on a first-come basis at the rate of $15 per week, with extra days charged at $2.15 per day. When we receive our first paycheck—they're paying us during training?—we need to clear our accounts. Local transportation is included, and they have a bus and a station wagon available to take us to the airport, to church on Sundays, or to go shopping after class. Should we decide to call a cab, we must pay for it ourselves. Fair enough.

The letter points out that we need to make our beds each morning—doesn't everyone? That fresh towels and washcloths are furnished daily, sheets and pillowcases weekly when the maid comes in to clean the apartment. A maid? Hannah Gruen, at last. It goes on to say that boys are not allowed in the rooms, but not knowing a soul west of Jersey City, I couldn't care less. Management explains they're not policemen, but they have a contractual responsibility with TWA to see we live in accordance with the company's rules and regulations:

We are not a bit narrow-minded. We have worked with TWA hostesses for many years, and we think we can understand almost any problem you may have — give us a try.

This might be the first time that anyone has offered to help me with anything. My mom's shocked at the prospect of my going with TWA, but my dad's okay with the idea. If only I could refrigerate this moment, keep it fresh for a month or two. When I tell Nana the news, she thinks it's positively grand.

Guess what, Nana? You can put your dress patterns away. Oleg Cassini will be making my TWA uniform.

THE FLIGHT to Kansas City on a four engine propeller-driven Constellation—a Lockheed 0-49—is a white-knuckle affair. Understandably so, as this is my first flight. At home, everyone was so excited about my going to Kansas City, they all piled into the car to drive out to La Guardia Airport to see me off. No one we know has ever been on a plane. Waiting to board, the sight of the plane on the tarmac, with the ground crew rolling out the steps—Trans World Airlines in bold red letters running the length of the fuselage—is exhilarating.

Seated at a window not unlike a porthole with tiebacks, I read everything in the seat pocket, including the fine print on a white barf bag. When a ground employee gives the all clear, the captain backs us slowly away from the gate and the Connie, as graceful as a ballerina, pirouettes on the tarmac.

Good morning, Ladies and Gentlemen. We would like to welcome you on board TWA's Flight #1 from New York's La Guardia Airport to Kansas City, Missouri. Our flying time today will be . . . Our hostesses in the cabin are . . . Please be sure to let us know if there's anything we can do to make your flight more pleasurable.

Pinch me, I must be dreaming. To think that in four weeks, the voice coming over the intercom could be mine. I sit with fingers crossed, not trusting in my good fortune, hoping that nothing—a meteorological event, a mechanical glitch, my father tearing across the tarmac—will interfere with take-off. After four desk-bound years at the telephone company, the road under my feet is moving. And today is Saturday, July 4th, Independence Day.

Taxiing past the air traffic control tower, we make a wide turn at the far end of the runway and, with propellers whirring and engines groaning, we tear down the runway—like a pebble from a slingshot—until the nose of the plane comes up, up, up and the ground begins to pull away. Clenching the skinny armrests for dear life, I sit immobilized, afraid to blink for fear of falling out of the plane.

We fly low over a hot July day. Over the Grand Central and Van Wyck parkways where traffic is flowing east to the beaches. Over a baseball diamond where a neighborhood game is in progress. Over the narrow streets of Whitestone, all the boxy houses lined up like dominoes. Within minutes, the captain dips a wing bringing us south, passing the Triborough Bridge, the United Nations—a green-tinted slab of glass and steel on the East River—and the Chrysler Building with its crown shimmering in the morning light. Beside myself with happiness, I let go of the armrests long enough to give myself a hug.

Wall Street flies by under the wings. As do the storage tanks, so many hatboxes on a shelf, over at Standard Oil in

Bayonne, New Jersey. The plane glides in and out of the clouds, playing an aerial game of hide-and-seek. Seeing the city as it might appear to a red-tailed hawk is nothing if not enchanting. Then it all comes rushing back—a child of nine or ten, shielding her eyes from the sun, trying to make out a plane droning overhead, longing to go along. It's a dream come true.

My parents have made it clear they expect me to return home when training's over. My dad says he's going to check out some second-hand cars, to make it easier for me to go back and forth to the airport. I haven't told them, but I have other plans.

K ansas City. The hostess-training program leaves nothing to chance. On Monday, July 6, we begin learning the history of the company; most significantly, that Howard Hughes owns a full 77 percent of TWA. Throughout the week, we study the worldwide routes, memorize fifty airport codes, and familiarize ourselves with the various configurations of the planes in the fleet. Starting with a two-engine Martin 404—a noisy bugger, the pilots say, but forgiving—carrying no more than forty passengers, all of whom board and deplane through a loading ramp in the tail.

Excuse me, how does that work?

We practice emergency procedures—Shoes off, ladies, jump feet first into that chute—on inflatable chutes and run through wet ditching procedures in dry landlocked Kansas City. That day, I wore a sign reading *clergyman*, while others had signs reading *military man* or *baby*. I love Kansas City, love TWA. I've sent Skyline Inn postcards to just about everyone I know—especially to friends back at the phone company. It will probably take a month for the postcard to catch up with Nick at sea.

Everything's great about Kansas City—no nine-to-five drudgery by day, no arguments at home by night. Everything suits me—even sharing a smallish motel room with three other trainees. I'm laughing louder, smiling more—without a care in the world. Other than passing the course, that is. Today, for the first time since I've arrived, Veronica came to mind. I found myself wondering what she'd think about my having such a glamorous job. A year from now, she would have been eligible for a free pass to Ireland—a chance to see Spanish Point, the seaside village in County Clare on the west coast of Ireland where her parents came from. For the first time, I was thinking about what I could do for her, not what she could do for me.

TWA is big on branding, with no regulation left unwritten. A hostess must be between 5'2 and 5'8, weigh between 105 and 135 pounds, and have 20/20 eyesight. Weight checks are mandatory, and we have to stay within 5 pounds of our hiring weight, or be taken off the line—with separation from the company a real possibility. When it comes to the minor stuff, girdles are mandatory (no jiggling in the aisles) as is *Fire & Ice*, a bright red lipstick with cool blue undertones thought to make your teeth a whiter shade of white. That said, over at Pan American, *Persian Melon* rules the skies.

The week before graduation, we're treated to hairstyles having little to do with any personal preferences—the main consideration being that the hair should not touch the collar and should look becoming with the hat. Do we flinch, do we complain? Not at all. We're flying high—tell us more.

On another day, we troop into a blistering-white room, one mirrored from the countertops to the ceiling, where we perch on white stools to learn the art of applying makeup. Particularly that of applying a lighter shade under the eyes to mask any tiredness or shadows resulting from jet lag. Jet lag? Most importantly, we're not to smoke in uniform or date the passengers. As for marriage, it's grounds for dismissal.

Who wants to get married? All I want to be is a TWA ambassador and travel the world. As far back as I can remember, I've loved being away from home, loved being on the road. Racing clouds in the high Adirondacks. Counting blades of grass in the Finger Lakes. Sunning to a lobster-red at the Jersey Shore.

Remember ladies, says our instructor Miss Massey, we're not selling sex, only the sizzle.

When graduation day rolls around, we're as ecstatic as a roomful of teenyboppers. Where are you *going*? Where are *you* going? By tomorrow, some of us will be winging it to the impossibly glamorous city of San Francisco, living on Nob Hill and riding cable cars to the Buena Vista Café for the best Irish coffee in town. Others will be heading to sunshiny LA, the City of Angels, where there's a chicken in every pot, two cars in every garage, and a swimming pool in every backyard. And those of us with our sights set on New York, will be apartment hunting in Woodside or Jackson Heights, neighborhoods home to hundreds of handsome flight engineers and pilots. Nothing beats a man in uniform.

Or a woman when outfitted by Oleg Cassini in a waist-cinching uniform meant to give each of us an hourglass figure. Before we can slip into the uniform, we need to buy it. The two-piece jade-green gabardine uniform for spring and summer is a steal at $51.75. As is the mocha-brown version for fall and winter at $52.75. Other items include a topcoat with a liner, monogrammed white blouse slips, a raincoat, a clear plastic cap, a scarf, a leather purse, and a baggage tag. All of which comes to $230.00, which we can pay in one lump sum by check or have deducted from our paychecks. I opt for the latter.

Don't we look fabulous? There must be an unwritten rule that hostesses look fresh and inviting at all times and that male crewmembers look dashing and heroic. Why not? Travel is our business.

At the graduation day ceremony, our instructors pin silver wings to our hats. Celebratory bouquets arrive for some, congratulatory messages for others. A friend receives a Western Union telegram: *Best wishes on receiving your wings and on the fulfillment of your fondest hopes. God bless you. Love, Dad and Mother and the boys.* Not a singing telegram, mind you, but a telegram even so. Late in the day, I call home to say I've been assigned to La Guardia and swallowing hard—Buck up, girl!—I break the news that I'm not coming home—not right away, not exactly—that I'm going to be sharing an apartment close-by the airport with three other hostesses.

Over the wires, I detect my mom's dismay, hear my father saying something or other in the background.

Your father wants you to come home before making any decision about renting an apartment. He's found you a good hardly used second-hand car.

My father once said: As long as you're living under my roof, you'll do as I say. I haven't forgotten that. Well, now I'm not. I explain to my mom that I'll be flying reserve for months and can't very well do that from Yonkers. That as soon as we find an apartment, I'll be home to collect my things. The disbelief coming across the wires is palpable.

Not wanting to hurt my parents' feelings, I don't mention how elated I am at the prospect of striking out on my own. TWA has been the best thing that's ever happened to me. Here I am, one-in-forty—the sweetheart of Sigma Chi.

Trying a diversionary tactic, I ask: Did Eddie and Kenny get the postcards I sent? Did a letter come from Nick?

C rew scheduling sets me up on a milk run making six or seven stops between New York and St. Louis. At the bottom of the steps, with a clipboard in hand, I'm greeting passengers when suddenly my high heels start sinking into the sun-softened blacktop. Off-balance, I instinctively try to grab onto something, anything, to steady myself and come up with the arm of an attractive well-dressed Frenchman. I knew he was French from the first *al-lo*, although I did not know that such a simple word could hold so much promise. Apologizing, I continue to cling, trying to liberate my shoes from a great sucking maw of macadam. Quick to size up the situation, he (my hero!) bends to pluck them one-by-one from the tar. Thanking him, I promise to behave myself for the remainder of the flight, at which he, the perfect stranger, says: I hope not. I'm having a good time.

Welcome aboard, Mr Bernardaud. You're in 14C.

Parading the aisle—puffing pillows, handing out gumballs in crinkly wrappers, and offering a wide assortment of newspapers and magazines—I feel his eyes on me. Seated on the aisle as he is, his colleague nodding by the window, it's not long before he sees an opening and asks a question in this Parisian-accented English that had about it the rustle of French taffeta.

Upholding my end of the conversation is easy, starting with, Why Dayton? If I understand correctly, his family's in the textile business, and he's here to visit mills in Ohio. With a smattering of French and a smidgeon of English, we flirt the flight away in basic Berlitz: *Répétez, s'il vous plait.*

He's a standout, quite unlike anyone I've known. When he mentions he'll be in New York later in the week and would like to take me to dinner, I hesitate only long enough to hear the cautionary voice of Miss Nancy Massey:

Ladies, you are not to date the passengers. Most of them are married men with families at home and wedding bands in their pockets.

Mais oui! I say, without stopping to check my calendar or asking him to empty his pockets. Slipping him my telephone number, I find that he wants something more—corny as that sounds—my TWA wings.

Absolutely not. Offering him a pair of tinny wings from the passenger service kit, he's having none of it, proposes we do an exchange. Like what? Like my wings for a tiny French flag pinned to his lapel. He says this, I say that. All the while I'm falling under the spell of his French-accented English, a linguistic deviation so delightful that it makes all things seem possible. Ultimately, I relent, suggesting that when he comes to New York later in the week, we should meet early in the day, so I can show him the city—a city he has never visited and one I barely know.

Bien sûr!

I think he likes the idea.

THE DAY dawns bright, the sky a China blue with broken clouds. Meeting at a pier on the Hudson River, the three of us (Philippe's colleague joins us) board a Circle Line Cruise around Manhattan Island. I confess that taking them on a cruise is taking the easy way out. Who wants to wait on a long line for an elevator to whisk you to the top of the Empire State Building? visit the United Nations for the umpteenth time? walk the pavements of New York in pointy-toed stilettoes?

By a process of elimination, a Circle Line cruise offered an easy way to show off the city, or so I thought until we were underway. I had not foreseen that so much waterfront property was given over to chain link fences snagging plastic bags; to junk yards with abandoned cars stacked like Aunt Jemina pancakes; and to greasy places with names like Ralph's Garage, Sam's Auto Body, and We Move It. With so much trashiness in sight, we hardly know what to say to one another. It's only when the Harlem flows into the Hudson that we breathe a collective sigh of relief. I won't do this again.

Hanging over the railing, the wind fast in my face, I turn around at one point to find the men are talking about me. What is it? Tell me.

Philippe explains his colleague thinks I'm *trés tranquille,* not like most French women. If *trés tranquille* is acceptable, the other is not. I pout. But with the Statue of Liberty steaming toward us—a gift from the French people, as Philippe reminds me—we three laugh easily in the afternoon sun.

Come to Paris, and I'll show you another Statue of Liberty.

Everything about him—the quiet bearing, intelligence, self-confidence—is appealing. A well-furnished mind has to be one of the sexiest things on earth. Then, too, he has this way of pronouncing my name that has me running on the double. With two tickets for the theater and a reservation at Sardi's afterwards, his colleague is on his own this evening.

Late in the afternoon, walking west on West 43rd Street, he spots the marquee of the Henry Miller Theater.

Barbara, zee theater is named for zee writer On-ree Mil-lair. Do you know him?

On-ree Mil-lair ? Henry *Miller.* I've heard of him, yes, but I haven't read any of his books. I stop short of mentioning that On-ree Mil-lair's works have rocketed to the top of the Catholic Index of Forbidden Books.

Not zee Tropic of Cancer?

Sorry, no.

Zee Tropic of Capricorn?

No, not yet.

Like the Princess of Parma in Proust's *Remembrance of Things Past,* I could pretend, but why bother?

You *must* read him, he insists, he's an important writer, a champion of freedom of expression.

Freedom of expression? Isn't that what landed Henry on the Index? Listening to Philippe exercising his own freedom of expression, reshaping the English language with a novel cadence and a slightly nasal intonation, *la vie Parisienne* takes shape before my eyes: Paris, a city where people sit for hours at café tables smoking *Gitanes* and *Gauloises,* the nicotine waxing the walls a Van Gogh yellow. A city where patrons passionately analyze the limits of artistic freedom and celebrate the life of the mind. And where, at Café Lipp, the crowd awaits the arrival of the power couple of the moment, Jean Paul Sartre and Simone du Beauvoir.

Philippe asks if I've seen *Wild Strawberries,* a film by a Swedish director, Ingmar Bergman. He declares it a masterpiece. When the conversation turns to music, the language of feelings, we discover a shared fondness for the Baroque, particularly for Scarlatti.

Scarlatti? Zhe father or zhe son?

Once we sort that out, he mentions a certain spirituality in Scarlatti's music . . . *n'est pas?*

All too soon, a lovely day is drawing to a close. He promises to write, and I promise to call if and when I reach Paris. In my mind's eye, I envision us walking the bridges over the Seine and stopping to buy a well-thumbed copy of the poems of Baudelaire at one of the bookstalls. What's the harm in dreaming? Were he were to dream a little dream of me and I a little dream of him, who can say?

∞

My roommate Bobbi—she with the Modigliani face and Betty Boop eyes—informs us that TWA employees are eligible for full passes on Aeronaves de Mexico. No half-fares or quarter-fares required. Working in an industry long on glamour and short on cash, free passes are the *sine qua non*. On line for nearly a year, the four of us will be eligible for passes within weeks. What to do? Go to Paris alone or to Mexico with my roomies?

Aeronaves de Mexico does not disappoint, nor does Mexico. From the moment we touch down, we're in a Technicolor dream salted with margaritas and fragrant with cilantro.

Checking into the Hotel Noa-Noa on Acapulco Bay, we head for the beach to sink our toes into warm sand the color of Kraft caramels. As content as a passel of kittens, we stretch out under tiki huts to watch the sun go down smoking into Acapulco Bay, leaving behind a sky as bruised and bloody as a handful of crushed pomegranate seeds.

My word, is that an armadillo?

The staff at the Noa-Noa treats us like visiting dignitaries, and the rooms are as promised in the brochure: *las panoramas sin igual desde todas las habitaciones.* Handwritten signs in the bathrooms warn us not to drink the water. It's not a problem as the giggling maids leave *aqua purificada* twice a day.

Hey, Dorothy, you're not in Kansas.

Entering the hotel dining room—a large open-air room alive with the hissing of cicadas looking for love in the night— we pore over the menu: *El chef sugiere Lobster Thermidor, Spaghetti Bolognese, y ancas de rana a la francesa.* Where's the arroz con pollo and chimichangas? There are no complaints to be heard from the Fabulous Four, not when a three-course meal is $2.40. When it's time to check out, we discover that the Noa-Noa gives airline employees a 50 percent discount. The only question is how soon can we come back? After dinner, I address postcards showing a sun sinking into *la bahía de Acapulco,* sending them to just about everyone I know.

Dear Nana: Acapulco is a dream! Wish you were here. Love, Barbara.

Arriving home from Mexico, there's big news. Some of us have been missed more than others. Not one, but two of my roommates—Nayna and Lynn—have received marriage proposals. Once again, my band of sisters is coming undone, one wedding band at a time. With our roomies leaving to get married and knowing things will never be the same, Bobbi and I have put in transfer requests. She's packing for Kansas City, while I'm heading for Boston.

A WEEK before I'm due to leave for Boston, my father has a heart attack. Not that this is his first, it isn't. He had open-heart surgery a few years ago. Visiting him at the hospital, I don't let on that my transfer papers have come through, or that I'm due to check in at Logan Airport next week. But after a few days, with the clock ticking down, I call my mom to explain.

You're moving out-of-state, with your father in the hospital?

I remind her that he's coming home in a couple of days and that the doctor's pleased with his recovery. Besides, I'm only going as far as Boston, a four-hour drive. It's not like I'm going to LA or San Francisco. If she needs me, I could be home in five hours. She mentions a letter from Nick, who is now stationed in Georgia.

Can you bring it with you to the hospital? I'm going to stop to see Daddy on my way up to Boston.

Arriving at the hospital, both of my brothers are there. I haven't seen them in months. When I ask Eddie how he's doing at Iona, he says he's dropped out of school, has enlisted in the Navy, and is due to ship out next month. Kenny's now at Lincoln High School. Asking if he's playing the clarinet in the school orchestra, he says he's given it up.

How come?

I wanted to go out for cross-country track, and it takes a lot of time.

I'll bet, so how's that going?

Not so good.

That's too bad. We laugh. It's good to see them, even if

we are in a hospital—one of my least favorite places. Hospitals make me nervous. Nana was right when she said: I'll tell you one thing, missy, don't be a nurse when you grow up. That's not for you.

My parents have yet to tell Eddie the details of his birth. As far as I'm concerned, there's no point in not telling him, no point in keeping up this charade, but that's not my decision. Living on my own, away from false pretenses, I don't worry anymore about making a slip of the lip. Then, again, given all the practice I've had over the years, I've become something of an expert in dodging, feinting, and skirting discussions of personal issues.

What would Veronica think about all this? would her feelings be hurt that her son doesn't know of her existence? that her husband never speaks her name? that her daughter only thinks about her from time to time? I give a holler to heaven: Hey, Mom, this isn't my doing.

Promising to call home when I reach Boston, I take Nick's letter but don't open it until I stop at a diner outside of New Haven. The opening paragraph is upbeat and newsy, but then the tone turns deadly serious. Letters have been the Elmer's Glue holding together this long-distance relationship for years. Happily enough, I was there when he graduated college and again when he graduated OCS, the U.S. Navy's Officer Candidate School at Newport, Rhode Island. For that weekend, Nana made me a pretty royal blue organza gown with two-inch bands of royal blue satin running above the hemline.

After the ball, Nick shipped out as a Supply Officer for a year or two, before being assigned to a small town in the Deep South. That's when our correspondence went off a cliff, which is what the letter's all about. He's met someone else, a Southern belle. Is it Laura, the laugh that floats on a summer's night? Sipping cold coffee—how long have I been sitting here?—I wonder if she knows the pre-Socratics, and if she makes him happy. This is no shot across the bow, it's a direct hit. Rejection sucks. Whatever happened to my ruby-red slippers? my lucky star? my rabbit's foot? I fall apart. I cry a little, cry a lot. Then I tear up the letter and leave the bits and pieces of my heart in the ashtray.

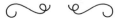

Fastest and Largest jetliner to Europe!
Daily Jet Schedules.
Just a few hours in the air and you're there on
TWA's Intercontinental Boeing 707.
So let yourself go and enjoy this Jet Age Adventure . . .
the fun, color, and excitement of London,
Frankfurt, Paris, Rome.
Don't wait . . . set the date . . . Europe will welcome you.
For reservations call: Plaza 2-2790

Talk about a game changer! After a year on Marlborough Street in Back Bay, Boston, I've transferred back to New York to fly International. Now offering daily flights to Europe, TWA has changed the rules, making it possible for hostesses with two years of seniority to fly the International routes—as long as we pass the language exam at Berlitz, which I have. As has my new roommate, Kay Galligan, who has transferred from San Francisco. Pooling our resources, we've taken a furnished one-bedroom apartment at 515 East 88th Street, at $165 a month, only a half-block from Gracie Mansion in a leafy part of Yorkville. Crew Scheduling has Kay set up to take out flight 900 to Rome later this week, while I'm going out on flight 800 to Orly.

Nana with Eddie, age 7

Before leaving on my flight, I go to see Nana who, by this time, has moved out of the house at 3272 Decatur Avenue into a one-bedroom apartment in a mid-rise building on the same block. She wants to see me in my uniform.

You've never lived alone, Nana, are you lonesome living by yourself?

Lonesome? Not on your life. When I married your grandfather I was barely seventeen, so I've never had a place of my own. I like being able to hear myself think. And your Aunt Betty's down the block if I need anything.

Hard working and good-natured, essentially Nana's been running a boarding house for her family and a hospitality center for everyone else for more than fifty years. Understandably, at her age, she wants peace and quiet and has made it clear to her children that she no longer wants Uncle Fred underfoot. This all came about after she gave up cooking for the Franciscan nuns in West New York, New Jersey. Nana's done more than her share of cooking in her time. Even before that job, she had been cooking for the nuns at St. Brendan's. Aileen remembers being in seventh grade, doing all the weekly grocery shopping for Nana and the nuns on Saturday mornings.

Sitting across from her, the cotton housedress riding above her knees, I can't help but notice the swollen ankles and the laced up shoes cutting into the flesh around them. What she calls her *elephant knees*, no longer bend the way the good Lord intended them to.

What does the doctor say about your legs?

He says, Agnes, it's old age—I knew *that* before he said it—and there's not much you can do about it. But when old age catches up with you, she says, it never comes alone. Father Brady tells me I don't have to go to church on Sunday, if I don't feel up to it. So, you see, I got me a dispensation.

Give her an egg, she'll make you an omelet. Even at her age, she has a talent for turning everything that comes her way into an adventure.

Do you miss going to church?

I miss the music, not the sermons. I've heard them all. It's easier on my poor knees to say my prayers right here.

But do you miss not having everyone coming and going all the time?

Well, it's not like when you kids were young. The latest is that your Aunt Agnes wants to move over to Perry Avenue, to a building with an elevator. But Jack's having none of it, insists it's better they take the stairs. Did you hear they had a fire?

No, what happened? That my uncle, a New York City Fire Department Chief in charge of the Medical Department, would have a fire in his own apartment is surprising.

It was up on the fourth floor. The firemen came in wearing high boots and dragging hoses and axes. Evacuated the whole building, they did. So, there's your aunt chatting with the neighbors out on 209th when she overhears one fireman telling another: Be sure to do everything by the books today. The Chief lives here. The Chief lives *here*? the other one says. I live in a better building than this.

That was enough to put a bee in your aunt's bonnet. Then your Aunt Dot got wind of Agnes wanting to move and, suddenly, she, too, wants to pull up stakes and move up the county.

In our family *up the county* is shorthand for a magical evergreen place with grass and trees, not a sidewalk in sight.

Decatur Avenue won't be the same if they all pick up and leave.

I say if anyone's looking for me, let them ring the bell.

She's adjusting to this situation better than I am. To think that by moving a half-block, she's set off a chain reaction, with everyone eager to call in the Seven Santini Brothers Movers.

Aileen told me there had been a family powwow to discuss how they were going to meet Nana's bills—what with her moving expenses and the higher monthly rent. Things got a little heated but, in due time, everyone agreed to chip in a set amount each month. When I asked Aileen how she thought Nana had managed to pay her bills all these years, she thinks Uncle Fred may have taken care of most of them.

Nana, have you seen Aileen's girls?

Yes, she came by with them a few weeks ago. The poor things have been sick ever since they moved north. See that pink dress on the chair? It has a tear. I told her to leave it with me, I'll fix it for her. When your cousin was here, her face was drooping on one side. It's Bell's palsy, and there's nothing to be done for it. Leave it alone, I told her, it will go away by itself in a month or two. It's all nerves, you know. She has a lot of pressure on her, with two young children and Gene halfway around the world in Vietnam.

Crossing to the windows, I peek through the lace curtains to find that the view—the backyards of houses facing Parkside Place—is much as before.

Where's Uncle Fred living?

He's down the block.

You mean at the *house?*

No, no. He's living with your Aunt Betty. She had a spare room and wanted him to come live with them. He and your Uncle Walter have been after me to sign the papers for the government money. I told him, no I don't want to do it. He says he'll do all the paperwork, all I have to do is sign, and the government will send me a widow's check each month.

Really? Why would the government send you money like that?

I don't know much about it, but it's some sort of law about widows and orphans. Let them keep their money for them that needs it, I told him. When I'm short, I spend less.

What interests her is the TWA uniform.

Oleg Cassini, so what do you think? I say, pirouetting.

It fits you like a glove. I like the stitching on the jacket and the buttons covered with gabardine. Very good looking.

After an hour of catching up on the family news—sipping Lipton's, nibbling Entenmann's crumb-by-crumb—the phone rings.

Who? Stop fooling around. Who? Yes, she's here, hold on, she says, handing me the receiver, the eyes rolling upward.

Is it Crew Scheduling? I ask, hoping they're not pulling me off the Paris flight.

No, it's someone's pretending he's French. Pulling my leg, he is.

Pretending he's *French?* I grab for the phone: Hello?

Al-lo, Bahrbahra? It's Philippe.

My heart leaps at *al-lo.* He's calling from Paris to say he'll pick me up at the hotel around six, wants to know where I'll be staying.

I explain I won't know until we check in at Orly, that the crews stay at a number of hotels—the California, the Celtic, the Windsor Reynolds—all a short distance off the Champs Elysées. I can have the concierge call when we arrive. Philippe, can you hear me? hello? hello?

With the connection breaking up, I come away feeling he'll find me, and I can't wait. Our letters have been winging the Big Pond for sixteen or seventeen months, so you might say we've been getting to know each other one paragraph at a time.

Nancy Drew once said you can tell a lot about a man by his hands, but I think you can tell more by the handwriting. Does your correspondent mark the lowercase i with a dot or a circle? Does the script flow uphill, a sign of optimism, or downhill, indicative of a gloomier mindset? Is it free flowing or stop-and-start? Philippe's European handwriting is electrifying, having nothing in common with the Palmer method. To think that after all this time, we have a date in Paris, the City of Lights. *Laissez les bons temps rouler.* Let the good times roll.

Nana can scarcely believe anyone would be calling her apartment in the Bronx from Paris. How did he get her number? It must cost a *fortune* to call from Paris. Here, this is for you, she says, to keep you safe.

Inside the box on a square of cotton batting lay a sterling silver St. Christopher medal.

It's lovely. Holding it in front of me, I admire the medal and myself in the mirror. Can you help me with the catch?

St. Christopher's the patron saint of travelers, did you know that?

I didn't, but that's perfect.

About to close the box, I notice a fringe of greenery poking from under the cotton batting.

What's this? ten dollars? I don't want your money. Pressing it into her hand, I tell her I don't need it, that TWA takes care of all of our expenses. They even pay us thirty-two cents an hour for every hour we're away from our home base, to cover incidental expenses. That this adds up over a month, enough to pay the dry cleaning bill.

So, you keep your money, and I'll keep St. Christopher. Don't worry about me, Nana, I'll be fine.

Don't you make me mad. You take this and buy yourself something when you get to Paris. I've always wanted to go to Europe, wanted to see where my family came from, but I haven't made it, not yet. You go and tell me all about it. Not another word. Off you go.

I pocket the money, telling her I'm going to buy her some French perfume, something nicer than *4711*. In parting, she smothers me with a bear hug. When Nana hugs you, you know you've been hugged.

＊ ＊

Working the cabin, I call the cockpit to see if the crew wants anything.

Coffee, black for the three of us, says the captain, and don't forget the saltpeter.

As if saltpeter's a variation of Cremora, I repeat the request to my flying partner in the galley, at which there are sniggers coming from a couple of male passengers within earshot.

Why are you laughing, is it about saltpeter?

One helpfully explains that saltpeter would keep the crew from getting too excited—sexually excited—at inopportune moments. Aha, so that's it.

The cockpit of the Boeing 707 is a high-tech fantasy, thirty or more dials up front, an equal number overhead. Balancing three coffees on a tray, I totter in as the captain's talking about a wine, a cabernet from Bordeaux he had on the last trip.

Interrupting himself, he turns halfway in his seat—the face as serious as any on Mount Rushmore—asking if I had brought the saltpeter.

I'm sorry, Captain, but Commissary forgot to load it today.

Well, be sure they put it on going back. Otherwise, there's going to be trouble.

Standing between the captain and co-pilot, I scan the horizon for that point where the ocean rises up to become one with the sky—completely forgetting the *no more than three minutes in the cockpit* rule.

What I have not forgotten is the section in the training manual called: *Arrangements for the Preservation of Male Pride.* Specifically, the idea that when traveling with male crewmembers, we must remember to pay our fair share of any bills, but we need to be circumspect when doing so. The manual goes on to say that when it's time to settle the bill, we should slip our estimated fair share to a male crewmember, asking if he'd be so kind as to handle the check. In all cases, a woman should avoid any public display of her financial arrangements, a courtesy that becomes more important when crewmembers are deadheading or socializing out of uniform.

Captain, are the regulations different on International? Is it okay to drink on layover?

Feigning surprise, the eyes alarmed, he asks: Don't you know the rule?

Which one? I ask, mentally thumbing a two-hundred-plus-page hostess-training manual.

When in Paris, do as the Parisians do, he says, the flashing eyes giving away what the rest of his face is trying to keep under wraps.

The way I heard it was *when in Rome.*

That, too! With a knowing grin, he insists the French drink wine with all their meals. A nip at breakfast. A glass or two, with a chaser of Perrier at lunch. A full bottle with dinner. A nighttime tipple.

The cockpit—ripe with metal, male libido, speed, and power—is a trip. As I'm turning to leave, he gives me a playful whack on my rump.

Say, how about joining us for dinner in Paris? What's your name?

Thanks, but I have a date with a friend who lives in Paris, a Frenchman.

You'd better be careful. Those French guys eat a lot of weird stuff.

Like what?

Like snails, cows' brains, intestines. Makes 'em smell bad. Don't you get too close to that guy, you hear?

EARLY MORNING, Orly. Getting an all clear from the cockpit, I open the main cabin door to find a birdlike ground hostess brimming with morning cheer: *Bonjour, mademoiselle, très fatigué?*

Smiling weakly, I offer a tentative *bonjour*, unsure what *fat-ee-gay* is all about. It appears the hostess is here to walk us to Crew Scheduling and, then, from Crew Scheduling to the crew buses waiting to take us into the city. Over her shoulder, I catch sight of a dozen planes all belonging to Air France lined up on the tarmac. This has to be Paris. In a jiff, all the passengers are out of their seats, heading for the exit—eager to start what for everyone is the adventure of a lifetime.

It's a grey socked-in morning, a trace of sadness in the air. En route to the city, most of the shops are still closed, with the exception of a boulangerie. If Paris is slow to wake, I'm quick to fall asleep. After walking the Atlantic for eight hours, I'm exhausted and want nothing more than to climb into a bed. That a new day is dawning and I haven't slept a wink, leaves me feeling out-of-sorts. Pulling up my coat collar, I wrap my arms around myself and rest my head against the crew bus window, only to startle at every bump in the road. I pinch my cheeks to no avail. Nothing—not even glimpses of France flashing by—can keep me from the arms of Morpheus. I have never been so thoroughly exhausted.

THE TWA uniform has a way of turning every street, aisle, and lobby into a catwalk. And the Hotel California on *rue de Berri,* a few steps off the Champs Elysées, is no exception. Jetlagged and weighted down with a Samsonite overnight bag, a boxy regulation handbag, and a jaunty red TWA flight bag crammed with a service manual and a pair of in-flight shoes, I congratulate myself on having crossed the lobby without a stumble.

Bonjour, mademoiselle, très fatigué?

A bright-eyed bellhop reaches for my suitcase. *Bonjour, monsieur*, I say, offering a wan smile, hoping he won't mistake me for one of those ugly Americans. A few years back, a book by that title made it clear that Europeans think Americans, particularly members of our diplomatic corps, lacking in cultural sensitivity. I'm hoping to chip away at the low expectations, one trip at a time. Catching sight of myself in a mirror, it's a good news, bad news moment. Although the uniform has come through without a wrinkle or a stain, not so my eye makeup. Rubbing a spittle-dampened finger under one eye and then the other, I brush away flecks of wayward mascara.

Bonjour, mademoiselle, très fatigué? asks the desk clerk. Put off by his chirpy tone, I paper over my irritation, but take a step backward as he reaches for my passport. The idea of handing over the passport and walking around in a foreign country without proof of citizenship seems irresponsible. Noting my reluctance, he says: It's a law, mademoiselle. A French law. We return the passport when you leave for the airport.

At this moment, the concierge—the crossed keys on his lapel a dead giveaway—says: Mademoiselle, I believe this is for you. Recognizing the handwriting, I scrunch Philippe's note into my handbag, as one of my flying partners asks if I'd like to join them for breakfast. Breakfast? The thought of eating makes me queasy. Having tip-toed the aisle all night—checking seat belts, drawing blankets over sleeping passengers, cleaning spots off the lavatory mirror, running back and forth with food and beverages, and smiling, smiling, smiling—I beg off, saying I'm *très fatigué*. The crewmembers laugh, say I'll get used to it. I'm not sure about that.

When the bellman unlocks the door to a room with the square footage of my whole apartment, I'm wondering if there's been a mistake. Off to one side stands a black lacquered writing table, its curved legs festooned with gold—perfect for stimulating the literary juices. I'll bet Colette wrote at such a desk as that. Pointing to a bell mounted next to the bed, I give the bellman a quizzical look, my hands turning up and over in a universal gesture of helplessness. In rapid French, he indicates I should push the buzzer should I want *le petit dejuener*.

Le petit dejuener?

He pantomimes drinking a cup of coffee, chewing a piece of bread.

Breakfast?

Nodding energetically, he backs out of the room.

The bathroom is a puzzle: is that stack of neatly folded sheets of brown paper French toilet paper? and what's with the second toilet bowl, the one with the hot and cold running water and hand towels? I keep my distance.

Within a half-hour of kicking off my shoes, I'm revived by the novelty of my surroundings and famished. Pulling out a copy of *Basic French Phrases*, I rehearse aloud the phonetic pronunciations before calling room service and reading word-for-word: *Je voudrais une omelette, s'il vous plait*, with *fromage*. Within ten minutes, a knock at the door.

Entrez, s'il vous plait . . . (taken from the section 'At the Hotel').

Bonjour, mademoiselle, says a narrow-hipped waiter, head-to-toe in no-nonsense black.

Bonjour, monsieur . . . si'l vous plait, I say, pointing to a writing table I've repositioned in front of the window. How can you write about Paris, if you can't see it? When he lifts the lid, there lies an omelet thin enough to make a whippet feel obese. Having used up all the freebie postcards—Wish you were here!—and hotel stationery, I point to the empty folder, asking for a few more, *s'il vous plait*. Who wouldn't love a postcard from Paris?

If there's a drawback, it's that the room is situated above the main entrance. Taxis come and taxis go, doors slam and horns honk, voices rise and voices fall. Not understanding a word of French is a blessing, in that I need not answer to anyone. Flying International beats flying Domestic in every way. In Europe, we have private rooms with baths—no sharing with another hostess, as we do on Domestic—and we can order from room service or dine out in any of the hotels where the company puts us up.

L'addition? Send the bill to TWA, *s'il vous plait*.

Thoroughly exhausted and deliriously happy, in equal measures, I fall asleep on sheets and pillowcases spritzed with the scent of lavender. Certainly, the Empress Josephine would have loved my room at the Hotel California.

∞

Philippe comes toward me across the lobby, looking as trim and cosmopolitan as the day we met. That this moment is due to a chance encounter on a flight to Dayton, Ohio, seems improbable. Closing quickly, he kisses me on the right cheek, kisses me on the left, before stepping back for a good look, and sealing it with a hug. As delighted to see me as I am to see him, he suggests we do a *panoramique* before going to dinner. Parisians dine late, he says, rarely before eight. Exiting the hotel, I glance up at a mushroom-colored sky, asking if I should get an umbrella from the concierge.

Non, c'est l'automne, he says with a lopsided grin, helping me into a Citroën about as roomy as a can of sardines.

C'est l'autome, I repeat with a wink, trying to imitate the inflection. If so, autumn in Paris is more November than it is September. The champagne fizziness of summer is long gone. Geese are now flying south in great V-formations. And Paris, having put away her summer chiffons and silks, has wrapped herself in a cashmere shawl as soft as morning mist.

Weaving through the rush-hour traffic, Philippe circles *le place Charles De Gaulle*, pointing out the *Arc de Triomphe* built by Napoleon and the Eternal Flame dating to WWI. Coming at us from all sides are kamikaze drivers converging on the roundabout from a dozen different streets.

What did you call it, an ay-twal? How do you spell that?

In the craziness of the moment, I urge him to go round again, and he does. Wherever I look—the magnificent arch, the limestone-clad residential buildings with Juliet balconies, the cafés with casual wicker furniture and waiters in formal white jackets—Paris astonishes me. As I'm watching Paris flashing by, Philippe's watching me out of the corner of one eye, commenting on this and that.

You are most observant, I tell him. Yes, my hair's longer than when I saw you last, any longer and my supervisor might pull me off the line. TWA insists the hair must not touch the collar.

They have a rule for the hair?

Absolutely, TWA has a rule for everything.

Glancing at my *hey, babe!* dress, the one I picked up at Filene's Basement in Boston before moving back to New York, he tells me that pleats are the latest thing—*le dernier cri*—this season.

Is that so? I must have missed the September issue of *Vogue*. Philippe, you never said where we're going for dinner, do I look okay? (Disingenuous to the core.)

Turning toward me, he nods, murmuring something ending in *très chic*, as he plants a kiss on my fingertips. With the temperature rising, I'm melting.

Is that *Je Reviens* you're wearing?

Is that a lucky guess or are you in the perfume business? Had he pulled a rabbit from his pocket, I couldn't be more surprised. He grins, explaining *Je Reviens* is *trés romantique, classique.* I can see why. Here I am wearing it for less than an hour, and it's already receiving good notices.

Arriving at the hotel this morning, I had asked the concierge if he'd order perfume from Catherine's on *rue de Rivoli,* a shop favored by crewmembers—*Je Reviens* for me and Chanel No. 5 for Nana. At five dollars an ounce, the perfume is a steal, and Catherine's delivers at no charge. With an exchange rate of five francs to the dollar, it's as if all of Paris is on sale.

Je reviens, he says, do you know what it means?

I will return.

And will you? he asks, good-naturedly as we zip down a doublewide boulevard where he points out a Citroën show-room, Fouquet's café, and Ladurée which he says is famous for sweets. As we're passing Ladurée, a man in a long black coat and a beret darts in front of the car, causing Philippe to jam on the brakes. Less than twenty-four hours in Paris, and already I feel like a bit player in a foreign language action film.

Bahrbahra, have you seen Notre Dame?

That vichyssoise accent is as soothing as it is sexy.

No, I've seen nothing other than the airport. I was too jet-lagged to go shopping this afternoon. Can you imagine a woman in Paris too tired to shop?

If you haven't seen Notre Dame, that's our first stop. In

France, we measure all distance from the cathedral. We think of it as the center of the nation.

Hearing the way he says *noh-truh-dahm*, I ask him to say his name.

Pour quoi? An eyebrow arches quizzically.

I'd like to hear how it sounds with a Parisian accent.

No, I like the way you say it, he assures me, giving me a hawk-eyed glance as flattering as it is unnerving. If he keeps this up, we're going to have an accident.

With the towers of Notre Dame coming into view, he says Paris doesn't change much from one century to another, that where Notre Dame stands, 2000 years ago the Romans had a temple to their gods.

Lightheartedly, I ask if Quasimodo will be ringing the bells this evening.

Ah, *yes,* Victor U-go. Later, I can show you where he—

At which the car shudders and dies. Horns honk, drivers make incensed gestures. If I understand him correctly, he plans to start it with another engine. He's so calm and collected, you'd think he was changing a bike tire in his driveway. Little hothouse tomato that I am, the *sang-froid* is attractive. Not so the car which is one homely beast—a cramped two-seater with flat metal slabs for doors. Not a T-bird or a Corvette in sight.

When the car hiccups, we bound onto *Ile de la Cit*é, to come face-to-face with Notre Dame, a miracle of stone and glass—its central window as lacey as one of Nana's doilies. Nana would love seeing Notre Dame. (Dahm, not Dame, I remind myself.)

Are you *Catholique*, Bahrbarha?

Yes, I say, wondering if there's a correct answer. It's that his family has been *Catholique* for generations. Straightaway, I envision them marching to the battlements with Joan of Arc, raising high the lily-white flag of royalty.

Crossing to the Left Bank, we run into a demonstration. Two protestors are carrying a rumpled bed sheet, a message scrawled in red lipstick. He says they're shouting about the Algerians killed last year in Paris by the police. There have been a number of bomb attacks. In fact, someone tried to kill the foreign minister André Malraux.

Philippe, look over there, what does that one say?

La barricade ferme la rue mais ouvre la voie. The barricade closes the street, but opens the way.

Opens the way? What does that mean, are they *communists*?

No, he laughs, they're veterinary students. They're protesting the use of dogs as guinea pigs for testing vaccines.

Veterinary students? Aren't they too old to be veterinary students? See that? *Aux Barricade Comrades!* Comrades? They *must* be communists.

A sharp noise—a shot—rings out, followed by students running in the street.

Philippe, watch that car!

If I'm a wreck, he's full of reassurances. A quick left, a quick right and before you can say *le cinquième*, we're in the Latin Quarter with nothing more pressing on our minds than finding a parking space.

LE COUPE-CHOUX is the epitome of country-cottage charm. Shaking off our dampness in front of a blazing fire, we pause to watch bits of bark flare up, glow brightly for an instant, and die away. In this rustic corner of Paris, all is in readiness—candles stuttering in nooks, and miniature pots of violets making bold statements against the white damask tablecloths. Nancy Drew—she who thought white linen the *sine qua non* of fine dining and who toasted the beauty of candlelight in *The Twisted Candles*—would love this place.

Bon soir mademoiselle . . . monsieur, says the maître d', not suspecting me of being an ugly American. Naturally, with Philippe running interference, the possibility of bilingual misunderstandings is less than zero. No need to trot out the over-worked: *Je suis désolé, je ne parle pas français.* And I am sorry.

As the maître d' questions Philippe about the demonstrations, I give my date the once over. Slim, serious, and on the front side of thirty, he's wearing a dark grey suit that's nipped at the waist and a shirt with French cuffs and gold cufflinks. No slouch in the dressing department, *ma petite robe noire* is garnering appreciative glances from waiters passing by. I sense a cultural divide: Frenchmen have this way of undressing you with their eyes, which is as unsettling as it is pleasing. Coco Chanel said a girl should be classy and fabulous, and that's how I feel. In less than twenty-four hours, I've morphed from mousy to marvelous—a regular Venus flytrap.

When the sommelier produces a leather-bound wine list, there's talk of vineyards and vintages. Watching Philippe—

intelligent, knowledgeable and sober-sided—holding up his end of the conversation is instructive. When a *St. Emilion Chateau Figeac* '55 comes to the table, there's talk of letting it breathe. By all means, let's let it breathe. The way they talk, you'd think the wine was a living thing.

Leaning across a yard of white damask, his nose quivering inside the rim of the glass, Philippe says something about hints of blackberry. Getting into the spirit of things—*pour quoi pas?*—I suggest a touch of velvet. With a serious mien, he laughs good-naturedly, the head cocked to one side. After a few more sniffs, a few more sips and a few more quips, a wine as silky as an Angora cat begins to purr.

By eight-fifteen, with every table taken, Philippe reaches for my hand, turning it over as carefully as you might a piece of eighteenth-century Limoges, planting a feather-light kiss on the palm—a part that's never been kissed in its twenty-three years. Inhaling sharply at the audacity, I sense Paris and I are meant for one another. Looking into his brown eyes—alert eyes with shards of amber—brings to mind another brown-eyed boy from the Jersey Shore. There is something about brown-eyed boys that tugs the heartstrings of this green-eyed girl.

When the first course arrives—No, please, you order for me, is what I say—it takes some doing to get the clamp around the shell housing an escargot. Taking a cue from Philippe, I spear one with a teensy fork to pop it into my mouth and find it's delicious. So it is we linger long over a wine that has a beginning, a middle, and an end—his words, not mine. The evening's perfect, with the universe pulling out all the stops.

Unexpectedly, I feel at ease. As if I were a world-weary traveler who, having stayed too long abroad, has returned home. And seated across from my amiable friend—his voice as intimate as the shudder of satin sheets—I could stay forever. As for the Figeac? Kryptonite in a bottle.

As if reading my thoughts, he says, Bahrbahra—there it is again, the name with all the breathy syllables—I wish there was more time to show you *all* of Paris. We could drive to Neuilly and . . .

Neuilly-sur-Seine, I say, remembering the pleasure found in writing that address on all those *par avion* envelopes. Is Neuilly a part of Paris or a suburb?

It's a part of the city of Paris, but years ago, it was a separate village. Saying this, he's studying my face—a finger tracing a line from my grey-green eyes across a scattering of Irish freckles—asking when I'll be returning.

After dinner, we stroll *rue des Carmes* to where it crosses the Boulevard Michelin—*boul miche*—to make our way to the quay across from Notre Dame, where houseboats are chafing at ropes, as if eager to be underway. A black lacquered barge, like some mystical sea creature, slinks from under a bridge carrying on its decks a full load of moonlight. With Philippe whispering sweet nothings, we stand transfixed—or at least, I am—watching tall streetlamps throwing long streamers of light onto the pitch-black water.

Contrary to what the Captain said, Philippe smells quite good, earthy and herbal at the same time. Whatever that is he's wearing, it's not Old Spice. Then, with my olfactory buds fully sated—C'mere—my head relinquishes its authority over my heart.

Ambling a quay running below street level—the dampness of the cobblestones seeping through the soles of my shoes—we're searching for a barge where they play *le jazz hot*. What surprises me is the domesticity found along the Seine: A honeyed glow seeping through lace curtains covering the portholes on a barge. Potted herbs—thyme, rosemary, longleafed French tarragon—growing on the decks. Two laughing couples seated around a table on an aft deck drinking Stella Artois. By morning, they could be on their way to Carcassonne or Beziers. By noon, biking a country path buying their baguettes at a local *boulangerie*. And by evening, drifting a countryside made famous by Monet, Van Gogh, Pissarro, and Cezanne. What a joy, the life on the Seine.

A warbling sound—high-low, high-low—cuts through the night, a police officer hurrying in our direction, shouting something or other.

What's wrong?

Come, let's get out of here. He might take us for Algerians trying to blow up a bridge. They don't like people walking below the street on the quay.

Taking the steps two at a time, we duck inside a bar with late night customers—the air thick with smoke from the *Gauloises* and *Gitanes*. We laugh easily, congratulating ourselves on escaping the flics.

What would you like to drink?

Do they have Mateus rosé?

Mateus? from Portugal? No, but we have excellent rosés from Provence. Would you like to try one?

Talk of wines comes easily to him. If one tastes of flowers, another tastes of herbs. If one's been too long in the sun, another's had too few sunny days. What's delightful is that Philippe has not once mentioned football, baseball, or basketball. When the waiter returns with a glass of a Bandol and two bottles of Armagnac, a '55 and a '57, he chooses the '55.

In France, we have a saying that when you're young, you should drink an older Armagnac and when old, a younger one.

Unable to tell if he's serious or glib, I laugh appreciatively, which triggers another Armagnac story: that cognac is like a beautiful young girl, whereas Armagnac is like an attractive older woman—*une femme d'un certain âge*—one you might not want to bring home to mother. He's delightful. Am I out of my league?

How do you like the wine? French rosés tend to be drier than Portuguese.

It's like summer in a glass.

He smiles indulgently, stroking my hand, while over his shoulder I watch the lights of Paris doing a rhumba along the quay. The city feels exotic, seductive, divine—a place where something as innocent as walking a street is filled with possibilities. How to account for the alchemy? is it the latitude or the longitude? the topiary in whimsical shapes? the chairs in the parks with pinholes in the seats? the kiosks with fanciful Turkish tops, plastered top to bottom with notices? or is it my friend who, if I close my eyes, sounds like a young Maurice Chevalier? With that goose-down voice of his, he could tell me anything and I'd believe it. At that I beg the gods of improbable happenings to stay the night, to hold back the rising dawn. Clearly, I've come undone.

When the rain lets up, we make a dash for the car, to drive ever-so-slowly back to the hotel, reluctant to call it a night. Pulling onto *rue de Berri*, he parks short of the entrance, turns off the ignition and whispers: Invite me up.

Invite him up? Well, why not, this is Paris and, being French, he's clearly interested in slowly showing me what I only know the limits of. *Où est ma tête?* What am I thinking?

Not tonight, it's late, I say, my palm lightly patting his cheek. I've got to get my beauty sleep. Crew scheduling will be calling in a few hours.

It's not late, invite me up, he croons, one hand on the back of my neck pulling me closer, the other . . .

Behave yourself! If he keeps this up, he's going to cut a finger on a pleat.

Philippe, the time you asked for my TWA wings, I was written up for being out of uniform. I thought I was going to lose my job.

Quick off the mark, a smile softening the Gallic features, he claims that's not how he remembers it. No, it was I who wanted the tiny French flag pinned to his lapel.

Come, invite me up, he murmurs, sending a bolt from Cupid's quiver deep into my solar plexus.

By the way, that flag? It's in my jewelry box, and each time

I see it, it reminds me of you, but if I invite you up that could cost me my job. We're not allowed to date the passengers.

Alors! Then you could stay in Paris.

Sensing heaven's just a kiss away, I ask how to say in French *thank you for a wonderful evening.* And repeat, best I can: *Je vous remercie d'une merveilleuse soirée.*

Which is when—my fingers tangled in his Charvet tie—he kisses me in such a way that says: Give! So I gave. Only to find myself blathering something idiotic about Paris being more romantic than New York.

Come, invite me up, he murmurs.

He is nothing, if not persistent. I swallow hard, imagining him whispering sweet nothings in French-accented English. If he asks me in French, I'm a goner. At which the doorman swings open the car door.

Bonne nuit, mon cher ami.

Crossing the lobby, I catch sight of myself in a mirror. Even the way I walk—more playful, saucy—is different in Paris. Stopping at the front desk—*trois, deux, cinq, si'l vous plait*—the desk clerk hands over a heavy brass key with a silky tassel, and I trot happily off to bed. My soul belongs to Paris.

M y roommate's new boyfriend lies stretched out on an
our unforgiving Danish Modern sofa—arms criss-
crossed behind his head—as if sunning on a deck chair on the
QE2. They met a few nights ago at Malachi's, a new watering
hole on Third Avenue that's been drawing crowds ever since
word got out that a number of young women living at the
Barbizon Women's Residence up the street were hanging out
at the bar.

What are you doing tonight?

Why, what do you have in mind?

I'm thinking I'll call a friend, see what he's doing. That
the four of us could go out, he says, flipping his feet from one
end of the sofa to the other.

I don't know. I'm not unpacked, have nothing to wear,
everything's in boxes.

Unpack on a Saturday night? You'd stay home and unpack when you could be out with a good-looking guy like

me? Saying that, his face is contorted in mock-horror, the eyes bulging, the forehead lined.

I laugh, asking his friend's name.

Dickey Dee.

Dickey *Dee*? what kind of a name is that?

Let me give him a call. Noticing my hesitation, he jumps off the sofa and grabs the phone in the kitchen, cutting off any protest.

You'll like him, I guarantee it, and I don't give guarantees. He's probably at the office.

On Saturday, where does he work?

He's a partner in a put-and-call firm, Saul Lerner Company.

I've never heard of it.

Most people haven't, but, then again, most people don't trade puts and calls.

Puts and calls? Do you trade them? Are they legal?

They're legal, but complicated. You can ask him yourself, he says, tommy gunning every word with a rat-a-tat-tat delivery.

Is that how you know him, trading puts and calls?

Nah, I've known him for years. We met on the train going up to Syracuse. I spotted the kid right away, a hayseed from Farmingdale. Taught him how to play poker. By the way, if he tells you he beat me, I say it was beginner's luck.

With images of a guy sprouting oats from his ears, an urban version of the scarecrow in the *Wizard of Oz*, I ask what his hayseed friend looks like.

What does he *look* like? He's a good-looking guy, like me.

Suave, debonair. Do I look like a loser with ugly friends? Not one of my friends is ugly, not one.

Rat-a-tat-tat . . . Rat-a-tat-tat . . . Rat-a-tat-tat.

WE MEET at Dick's apartment at 315 East 70th Street, a post-war white brick building with a sleepy-eyed doorman. If the exterior of the building is plain vanilla, the apartment is a knockout. With Dick and Stanley, an inveterate kibitzer, horsing around and fixing drinks in the kitchen, Kay and I drift room to room admiring everything from triple-matted nineteenth-century balloon prints in the foyer to small engravings over a brass bar cart.

Do you think they're Turners? Looking at the RWT penned in a corner, I ask if she knows Turner's first name.

How would I know? Kay says, the eyes rolling upwards, the deep dimples showing to full effect.

The living room is a winner furnished with a deep-cushioned sofa, a black lacquered coffee table weighted down with art books and pipes, and a six-foot long Chinoiserie breakfront. Plummy and posh, not a stick of Danish Modern in sight. Bluegrass music is playing in the background—a husband and wife duo, Evelyn and Fiddler Beers. Flipping through a stack of vinyl 78s propped against the wall, I find Pete Seeger, Patsy Kline, the Clancy Brothers, and a new group—the Chieftains. Apparently, Dick has a fondness for music with working class roots.

The martinis—on the rocks, three olives, shaken not

stirred—arrive in handsome twelve-ounce tumblers etched with bulls and bears. Asked about the apartment, Dick says he's subletting it from a British actor, Reginald Denny, who typically plays the part of the stiff-lipped British butler in films, that Mr and Mrs Denny have temporarily relocated to the West Coast where he's working on a new TV series.

When the conversation turns to horse racing, specifically to what bets the guys are placing on an upcoming race at Belmont—by their own admission, they bet anything that moves, including a full roster of football games every weekend—Dick mentions a dream he had the other night in which there was a horse named *Little Lady*. Checking the racing forms the following morning, he found a horse by that name running in the fifth, so *Little Richie from Detroit*, his betting moniker, called his bookie and the horse paid 25:1.

Okay, wise guy, Stanley cracks, you can pick up the check tonight.

Do you often have dreams of precognition? I ask, hoping that if he does, he'd give me a heads-up now and then.

Precognition? Whoa, I'd stay away from that stuff, Dickey, Stanley says on his way to the kitchen for a refill.

Dick says no, he usually has funny dreams with people running around like the Keystone Cops. The other night, Groucho Marx made an appearance, as did a childhood friend, Ralph Buffalino, with whom he once smoked a cigar behind the schoolhouse in the sixth grade.

With the martini easing my brain, I ask if he'd put me

in one of his funny dreams, that in my dreams I'm running through long dark tunnels or falling off steep cliffs.

Put you in a dream, how *cute!* Kay says, in a way suggesting she doesn't think it is. Dick laughs, even so—he laughs easily and often. Remarkably self-assured, he's an engaging conversationalist who thoroughly enjoys his own material.

Stanley suggests we go for Chinese food. Hailing a cab on Second Avenue, minutes later we're pulling up at 10 East 60th Street—the Copacabana. Understandably, the Copa has a reputation for gilt-edged ambiance, top-notch talent, and alternating dance bands, but for Chinese food? Frank Sinatra, Ella Fitzgerald, Joe E. Lewis, and Jerry Vale have all played the Copacabana, and last year the club made headlines when Bobby Darin and Connie Francis broke the attendance records.

Entering a low-slung room, the maître d' greets our dates by name and, snapping his fingers, directs a waiter to show us to a table off to one side of the stage, a stage that doubles as a dance floor. All the while, Kay and I are exchanging gleeful, wide-eyed expressions, suggesting that we got lucky tonight. Or at least I did. Stanley's a non-stop kibitzer, though Kay's holding her own.

The crowd's in high spirits—a few men in tuxedos, a few women in floor-length gowns. Wearing our knee-length black sheaths with opera length pearls, so perfect for layover, Kay and I could pass for the Bobbsey Twins in the City.

Stanley insists on ordering champagne, insists Kay take off a shoe so he can drink from her *slipper*. Fortunately, Cinderella's wearing strappy heels, so the idea goes nowhere.

A waiter hands us festive king-size menus with full-color sketches of a woman in a Carmen Miranda-style headdress. Opening the menu, I find the French dishes from *the French kitchen* to the left, and the Chinese dishes from *the Chinese kitchen* to the right. In faint script at the bottom: MINIMUM CHARGE OF SIX DOLLARS NIGHTLY PER PERSON, SEVEN DOLLARS ON SATURDAY NIGHTS.

Dick orders for the table a Moo-Goo-Gai-Pan, a Lobster Chow Mein, and a Sweet 'n' Sour Pork. Thoughtful date that I am, here I'd been considering the *omelette au fromage* at $3.50. As the waiter settles the Moo-Goo-Gai-Pan in the middle of the table, the bandleader thunders: *Ladies and gentlemen, the Copacabana proudly presents . . . Joey Bishop!*

That Richard has become something of an accidental pauper, I learn the evening we meet his partner, Herb, and Herb's wife Bonnie for drinks at Trader Vic's. Boyhood friends from Farmingdale, Herb and Richard are junior partners at the eponymously named Saul Lerner Company—a family affair as Saul, the senior partner, is married to Herb's older sister. With offices at 27 William Street, they're a block from Delmonico's, which I'm told is famous for its after-the-close bar scene and a sensational Lobster Newburg.

Located on the lower level of the Plaza Hotel at 59th Street and Fifth, Trader Vic's is a Polynesian fantasy—from the wood-planked ceiling and a dugout canoe suspended mid-air, to a collection of spears and masks mounted on a wall. Behind the bar, a couple of bartenders in floral print shirts are concocting some of the most imaginative drinks in town.

Herb and Richard order Mai-Tais, a signature drink made with seventeen-year-old imported rum, while I order one with a floating gardenia, and Bonnie one that's bristling with straws and resembling a hedgehog. To slow down the sneaky alcohol, there's a Pu-Pu platter with finger-licking spareribs, coconut-battered shrimp, and skewers of teriyaki chicken. All that's missing are the Hawaiian hula dancers making weekly appearances on the Arthur Godfrey Show.

Did Dick tell you Herb and I were married upstairs in the grand ballroom?

No, how long ago was that?

Two years ago. Our wedding was a blast, wasn't it Dick? Bonnie says, the fragile Arctic-blue eyes wide with glee. Do you remember that the rabbi was late arriving and that when he got here, my father fired him on the spot and told the cantor to marry us?

I remember, he says, your father's a piece of work.

He's crazy, you know, my father's really crazy. I'm not kidding.

Crazy like a fox, Herb says. Her father's made a fortune in plastics. His company, J. E. Plastics, is traded on the NAS-DAQ. The factory's on Nepperham Avenue in Yonkers, do you know it?

No, I don't. What do you mean he made a fortune in plastics? What are plastics?

He explains that Bonnie's father was first to discover how to turn sheets of acetate plastic into preformed boxes—the ubiquitous boxes used for corsages, nuts, and candies.

If it's a plastic box, Herb says, J. E. Plastics probably made it. They ship nationwide, which has made him a millionaire a few times over.

What stays in Richard's memory is that her father asked him to stand guard over the liquor, so the guests couldn't steal it.

Yeah, we had an open bar, and my father thought the guests would be walking off with the bottles, she says with a high-pitched laugh. I look around to see if anyone's throwing daggers, but it's a high-energy crowd and no one's paying us any attention.

After an hour or so, wanting to wash the sticky sauce off our fingers, Bonnie and I head for the ladies' room.

Did Dick tell you he's lost all his money in the market?

No, he hasn't mentioned it, I say matter-of-factly. Having no investments of my own, my interest in the stock market is casual, at best. When did this happen?

A couple of weeks ago. Herb says he's flat broke.

Not knowing what to say other than *that's too bad*, I shrug, saying, That's how the market is—up one day, down the next.

All of his stocks have tanked, she says emphatically, as if I've missed the point. Aside from her concern for my financial well-being, she's scrutinizing her face in the mirror, rubbing a finger over the bridge of her nose.

Well, I'm not dating him for his money. Retouching my lipstick, I remind her that Dick's great company, lots of fun to be with. What I don't say—after all, I only met her two hours ago—is that he's taking my heart places it's never been before. He makes me feel like an uncrowned queen. When he holds my hand—can fingers fall in love?—it's as if I've come home. I want a man I can trust—a man who treats me right, stays at home every night—and he's that kind of guy. Someone you can count on to stick around, not fool around. Who knows? He may be that once-in-a-lifetime.

If there's any downside to the relationship, it's that he has a counterintuitive sense of direction and two left feet—can't tell a waltz in three-quarter time from a foxtrot. Is that too trivial to mention? Assuredly, he could take dance lessons, but, come to think of it, he has. After serving two years with a medical unit of the U.S. Army in Saarbrucken, Germany, he returned home to have a friend ask: Do you know how to cha-cha?

Cha-cha? No, what's the cha-cha?

If you can't cha-cha, you're not going to make it with the girls out at the clubs.

What clubs?

The summer clubs on Long Beach Island— the Sands, the Colony, the Coral Reef. This year a couple of us have rented a cabana at Malibu. Want to join? To score with the ladies, you gotta' cha-cha.

Not long after, he saw an ad for Don Pallini Dance Studios guaranteeing to teach anyone to cha-cha for $100 (three times). Arriving at the studio on East 86th and Lex, he was greeted by none other than Don Pallini who asked him to dance around the room with *Miss Butler*. When the music stopped, Richard, with a full measure of bravado, flippantly asked: So, Don, what do you think? Can you teach me to cha-cha for $200?

Don Pallini laid an arm across his shoulder saying: Dick, it will cost you $200 to learn how to walk properly.

In time, he learned that Pallini had started giving dance

instruction at the urging of his friend, Rudolph Valentino who suggested he stop teaching ballet and start teaching tango. Valentino offered to be his first pupil. Months would go by before Don Pallini discovered that his friend knew all along how to tango.

You're right, Dick's a great guy, Bonnie says, but I'm telling you he's busted. You have to think about that.

Yeah, but his smile has a way of knocking me off my feet.

Changing the subject, she asks: What do you think about my nose? I want to get it fixed. Do you know anyone?

Is it broken?

No, it's not broken, it's too big for my face. See how the tip points down? When I look at myself in a mirror, I can't see my nostrils. I want a nose that tilts up, more like yours.

Looking at her—the shock of blonde hair, the Grecian nose with a small bump on the bridge—I tell her that I don't find anything wrong with her nose, which I don't. The strong nose, in fact, balances the fragile eyes, eyes so otherworldly as to fade while you're looking at them.

I've never known anyone as candid as she is. She's about as blunt as a flat-tipped screwdriver, which may be why they are having a prickly evening—she saying whatever pops into her head, Herb quickly dismissing it. Unaccustomed to hearing couples squabble the way they do, I'd have to say that for those of us with front row seats, it's been a riveting evening. Maybe firing the rabbi wasn't such a great idea.

∽

Nana wants me to come for dinner, to bring Richard. By the way, his friends and everyone on Wall Street call him Dick and his parents call him Dickey—which may explain why I've begun calling him Richard. As for going to the Bronx to see my grandmother, that's an easy sell. He's tired of eating out every night and will go anywhere for a home-cooked meal. The closest he gets to home cooking is when his mother drives into the city toting a mushroom-barley soup, blintzes, and chopped liver as good as Jenny Grossinger's. Besides, never having known any of his own grandparents, he's dying to meet her.

The D line terminates at Norwood, a north Bronx neighborhood shades greener than any in the South Bronx, but with potholes deep enough to bring a sixteen wheeler to its hubcaps. It's as if the neighborhood has slipped the radar down at the Department of Public Works.

Within minutes of meeting, Richard and Nana are getting on like old friends. Glancing around, my eye lingers on the ruby-red vase, chock-full with her novena booklets, greeting cards, letters, bills, ribbons, rubber bands, hairpins, and coins.

You know, Nana, next time I'm going to bring flowers for that vase.

Save your money. If you brought flowers, I wouldn't know where to put all the stuff that's in it. When I die, it's yours. Then you can add all the flowers you'd like.

Richard asks how she likes her new place.

I like it a lot, Richard, like living by myself. But you have to be careful around here, she says lowering her voice, as if someone might be listening. There's some monkey business going on, if you know what I mean.

What kind of monkey business?

Well, for one thing, last month they asked if I'd like them to put a peephole in the door. For security, they said. That's a good idea, I said. Sure, go ahead. This month, when I get my bill for the rent, they've raised me fifty cents. I ask you, fifty cents a month for a peephole, does that seem right to you?

Looking at her—exceedingly short, plump and animated for a woman her age, the baby-fine white hair pinned up with wavy bobby pins—she looks the same as she did years ago. It's as if, in my eyes, Nana has always been old, but has never aged. Racking my museum of private memories for more youthful images of her, I draw a blank.

Richard praises the spaghetti and meatballs, calling it world class. Italian food is his favorite, he insists, and two or three times a week, he's at Rocky-Lee's Chu-Chu Bianco on Second Avenue. Handing her a matchbook from the restaurant, he tells her if she ever needs anything, to be sure to call the number and leave a message with Sebbie the bartender. As I'm listening to all this, I notice that his blue shirt has come down with a case of the measles. Mr Spots.

As you'd expect, my grandmother has heard that Richard's not Catholic but Jewish. Within the hour, she brings up the topic of interfaith marriages, insisting there's no reason on earth why two people who love one another can't be happy if not of the same faith. Your grandfather was Protestant, and I'm Catholic. It doesn't take all that much to be happy, if you know the secret.

And what's that?

People say marriage is a fifty-fifty proposition, but that's not true. Marriage has to be 100 percent all the time, otherwise it won't work. You know, Jack Benny is Jewish and his wife Mary Livingston is Catholic. So, too, George Burns and Gracie Allen. And Irving Berlin? He fell in love with Ellin Mackay, an heiress whose family was hoity-toity—New York high society. When her father heard about that romance, he was beside himself that his daughter would consider marrying a poor Jewish songwriter, so he packed her off on a grand tour of Europe, thinking that after a few months abroad, she'd forget about him, but she didn't.

Then, her father promised to settle a million dollars on her, if she'd give up the songwriter, but she wouldn't. When Irving Berlin heard about this, he said: A million dollars? Is that all? Tell her if she marries me, I'll give her two million.

Glowing with girlish playfulness, Nana continues the saga

of Irving and Ellin, telling of the night Ellin's family had a grand party at their estate in Roslyn on Long Island. All the swells were there, even the Duke and Duchess of Windsor. At one point in the evening, Ellin went upstairs to call Irving and, as they were talking, he wrote a love song for her. Just like that.

Which one?

The one that goes: *All alone by the telephone, there's no one else but you* . . . she sings, slightly off-key.

When about to leave, she asks me to come into the bedroom, where she hands me a small box containing a gold bracelet I have never seen before.

That's lovely, but why don't you wear it?

Where do I go to wear a bracelet like that? It's been in the drawer for years. It came from Germany, a gift from your great-grandfather to his fiancée Marilyn Miller. See the inscription? Wear it when you meet Richard's mother. I don't want her thinking you don't own any nice jewelry.

The inscription reads: *T. B. to M. M. Dec, 24, 1879.* Theodore Bracht to Marilyn Miller, Christmas Eve, 1879.

A letter arrives from Philippe: *Si seulement tu savais . . .* If only you knew . . . If I understand him correctly, he feels I'm not taking the relationship seriously, dare I say too lightly. Knowing my French is clumsy, why not write me in English? Curious and exasperated in equal measure, I ask a French-speaking woman, one I barely know, if she would translate for me. A huge mistake. After reading no more than a paragraph—her face reddening, the eyes racing ahead, doubling back—she hands it back, saying it's too personal. Tucking it into my handbag—her relief tangible, so too, my embarrassment—I wondered what on earth he had said: was it a declaration of undying love? the end of a brief affair? If so, what does one do with leftover dreams? To hang my hat in Paris had been such a lovely illusion. I need a cup of coffee.

L ady, what would you like?
Let me have a cup of coffee and a tuna salad on rye, I tell a counterman at the Viand Coffee Shop at Madison and 61st Street. Everything had been perfect with Philippe, until I canceled a date last minute to have dinner at Tour D'Argent with a friend in Paris on business for IBM. *Où est ma tête?* Yes, what was I thinking? I don't know. Perhaps having seen Paris from a bateau on the Seine, from the top of the Eiffel Tower, and from the onion domes of the Basilica of Sacré-Coeur, the chance to see her in all her gastronomic glory at a legendary restaurant proved irresistible. What I didn't know then was that you could break a date and break a heart—if only your own. Open me up, see for yourself. I'm a museum of broken hearts.

Don't blame it on my heart, blame it on my head—my insecurities, my immaturity. He took the sun, left me the moon. Yet the memories of how he held his knife and fork upside down and how he kissed good night, linger on in my right-side brain. Trying to make sense of these things isn't easy—was it a misalignment in expectations? a fault in my stars? a slip-up in communications?—but a major piece of the puzzle was an inability to fully trust others—an inability having nothing to do with him and everything to do with me.

Having been charged for a lifetime with protecting the happiness of my parents and the psychological well-being of my brother, I hadn't realized I was hiding a huge part of myself— someone who was half there, never fully present. To distance yourself from others is not all that hard to do—just keep asking them questions about themselves. However, if you keep people at arm's distance long enough, they're bound to feel the chill, catch a cold. Complications set in and relationships die.

Excuse me! I say, waving to catch the counterman's eye. Could I get some milk for this coffee?

As a young girl, I trusted my father to look out for me, and where did that get me? Years in solitary, years of worry: *A slip of the lip can sink a ship.* With Philippe, I could never be sure if what meant one thing to me meant the same to him. Can you trust a smile? a glint in the eye? a refined and subtle approach? More significantly, could I entrust my battered heart to any-one? Overcoming a lack of trust in others is as challenging as overcoming a fear of diving off the high board.

On the other hand, Richard, gregarious by nature, loves nothing more than chatting up strangers and friends. When I once questioned his enthusiasm for dipping into the lives of others, he said that one never knows when you might meet the unfound friend. Don't you have enough friends? I like how he goes through life pumped up with sunshine and confidence—an embodiment of those lines by Rudyard Kipling that he's fond of quoting:

If you can talk with crowds and keep your virtue, Or walk with Kings—nor lose the common touch . . . Yours is the Earth and everything that's in it, And—which is more—you'll be a Man, my son!

Hey, Miss, did you want tomato on that sandwich?

No, hold the iceberg, hold the tomato, but toast the bread, okay?

I suspect that living so intimately with Mrs Schwartz and Seymour all those years extended my comfort zone for what theologians call 'the other'—in my case, for secular Jewishness. Had it not been for that peculiar housing arrangement, I doubt I would have been ready for an interfaith relationship. After thirteen years of upstairs-downstairs, Mrs Schwartz and Seymour were like family. All of which made it easy to fall in love with Richard—as easy as water running over stones.

A WELL-dressed man in his mid-50s—cashmere coat, wingtip oxfords—sits down, asking what I'd recommend. I laugh, telling him he's asking the wrong person because I order the same thing all the time—tuna salad on rye, hold the tomato and iceberg. Engaging and easy to talk with, it's not long before he pops the question: I don't see a ring on that finger, you're not married?

With all that cheekiness, I figure he has to be a New Yorker. You might say I'm playing the field.

Playing the field, is it? Who's on first?

Playing along I tell him a Parisian who wouldn't be caught dead eating a tuna sandwich at the Viand is on first. A doctor—a staunch Methodist from Chicago with a passion for opera—is on second. And a New Yorker, a partner in a Wall Street options firm with a liking for poetry, is on third, and heading for home.

A poet on Wall Street? That's some combination. I've done some options trading, who's he with?

Saul Lerner Company, do you know them?

Sure. I trade with Thomas, Haab, and Botts, one of their competitors.

I don't know a thing about options—puts and calls, strips and straddles. Trying to make sense of them is beyond me.

Without missing a beat, he laughs, telling me to stick with the options trader.

In a spit-out-the-coffee moment, I ask how, not knowing any of the players, he could say such a thing.

I've spent a lot of time traveling in Europe, lived a year in Paris after college. The French and Americans have very different ideas about things, especially about sex and marriage. You strike me as someone who wouldn't care for . . .

Wouldn't care for *what*?

Let's say, extramarital affairs . . .

A red flag shoots up like a flare on Bastille Day—extramarital affairs? love in the afternoon? tongue-tied divorce proceedings before a non–English speaking French magistrate? why would he think that of me? is my Burberry trench and matching umbrella indicative of a traditional mindset?

For the French, it's the pinch of salt that makes the *coq au vin* taste better. It's all about the pursuit of pleasure—in bed *and* at the table, he says with a knowing wink. We Americans tend to be more puritanical. Blame that on the Founding Fathers.

Certainly not Ben Franklin. His poor dying wife couldn't get him home from Paris.

Not Ben, the rest of them.

Okay, let's say we rule out the Frenchman, what's wrong with the doctor?

You don't want to live in the Mid-west, the winters are terrible.

My coffee has gone cold listening to him.

He calls for the checks, insisting it's his pleasure. I leave a generous tip, thinking there must be something in the water in New York—other than fluoride.

It's a hot summer evening as Kay and I head for Carl Schurz
Park—a gem of a park with up-and-down the river views.
Leaning on the railing, all the better to catch a breeze, we
watch a Moran tug chuff upriver. For me, the sight of T-shirts
and tank tops fluttering on the aft deck triggers memories of
the houseboats on the Seine—the lace curtains, the potted
herbs, and the laughing couples drinking Stella. And, as you
might expect, of Philippe.

A sailor stretched out on a park bench studying the nighttime sky, jumps to his feet at our approach. Square-jawed with
a blond buzz cut, he's a good-looking guy in his early twenties.

Hi, there sailor, Kay says, giving a sultry imitation of Mae
West. Whatcha' doing all by your lonesome in the park this
time of night?

He's doing what we're doing—taking the pulse of New
York. Within minutes, we learn he's from San Diego and a
graduate of UCLA who majored in Spanish literature.

That's interesting, I say. So who are your favorite Spanish
writers?

Here, I'll show you. Opening a duffle bag, he pulls out a dog-eared copy of *Don Quixote* by Cervantes and another, *Lazarillo de Tormes*, by an anonymous sixteenth century writer. Having walked the city all day, and not due back to his ship until tomorrow morning, he asks if we could recommend an inexpensive nearby hotel.

If you'd like, Kay says, you can sleep on the couch at our place.

Telegraphing her a bug-eyed look, she responds in kind, one reading: Did I really say that? Without batting an eyelash, he takes us up on the offer, no questions asked.

Flinging a blanket and pillow onto the sofa, I hand him a toothbrush and a mini-bottle of Aqua-Velva we've snitched from the Passenger Service Kit.

If you're hungry, there's some beluga caviar in the refrig—compliments of TWA. Help yourself.

A perfect gentleman, he's up and showered early, folds the blankets and puts on a pot of coffee. He even leaves a thank you note, including a wallet-sized photograph of himself: *To Barbara, una reina más simpática, Su amigo, Don.* What a sweetheart.

When Richard hears about this the following morning, he's apoplectic. Don't you read the papers? I don't understand you. I don't know if I can trust you in the city on your own. It's then he mentions going to New Orleans on business next week, wants to know if I'd like to go along.

Welcome back, Kay shouts over the whine of a vacuum cleaner she's bumping over a bare wood floor. How was New Orleans?

Fabulous, we had a great time. I *adore* the French Quarter—all the buildings with wrought-iron balconies and long black shutters to keep out the heat. It's quintessentially French, except for the heat and humidity. We went to Galatoire's for dinner. Between the lighting in the room, the mirrored walls and tiled floor, I thought I was in Paris. With one big exception—the waiters at Galatoire's are far nicer than those in Paris, and they go around calling everyone *cher*.

Is the food as good as they say? Kay asks, yanking the cord of a vacuum wedged under the sofa.

Yes. We started with oysters Rockefeller on a bed of rock salt—something I've never seen before. After that, I had a pompano that the waiter claimed was swimming in the Gulf that morning, and Richard had a spicy creole gumbo. It's an old-money crowd—all the men in suits and ties, the women in dresses. Here, catch! Tossing her a tin of French Market Coffee, I insist she's going to love it, that in New Orleans they blend the coffee beans with chicory.

Listen, I have to tell you something, she interrupts, her eyes flitting the room, not meeting mine. You had two calls while you were gone. One from a doctor in Philadelphia who's coming to New York and wants to take you to the opera.

I had him on flight when he was returning from a meeting of the National Medical Students' Association—get this, he was the president. Took me to his parents' country club for lunch. And who else? Don't tell me Crew Scheduling. I called in sick and went off schedule.

No, not crew scheduling. You're going to kill me when I tell you, she groans, switching off the vacuum.

Why am I going to kill you? That Kay, who is normally outspoken and direct, is shillyshallying is cause for concern. Out of nowhere, my stomach feels queasy.

You have to believe me, I didn't mean to say anything, but I couldn't help it.

Okay, okay, but what are we talking about?

She sighs, dropping her head to one side: You're going to be upset.

You're wrong. I am upset. The suspense is maddening. What's it all about?

While you were away, your mother called . . .

And?

She wanted to speak to you, said she hadn't spoken with

you in two weeks. When I told her you weren't here, she asked where you were.

And you said? Watching her cheeks and neck growing redder—it's as if she's about to have one of her cat-attacks—my heartbeat quickens, breathing slows.

I told her you went to New Orleans with Richard.

On, no! Why would you tell her that?

By now, her neck and décolletage are lobster-red—as if they've been left too long in the sun.

Why would you *say* such a thing? We agreed that if she called, you'd tell her I went out on a flight and would be back Thursday. Not that I went to New Orleans with Richard.

I couldn't lie to her, she says, her voice trailing off.

You couldn't, why not? You lie to your own mother. I've heard you tell your mother you were going out on flight, all because you didn't want to go out to Jackson Heights for dinner. You can do *that*, but you can't cover for me?

That's not a *lie*, it's a social excuse. Listen, your mother wants you to call as soon as you get in. She was upset because some guy from St. Louis called the house looking for B. J.

I can't believe you told her I went to New Orleans.

Well, I didn't want to upset her any more. Since when are you going around calling yourself B. J.?

My mom's upset some guy's calling me B. J., when she's been calling me *Bob* all my life. What's the difference?

Before I can kick off my shoes, the phone rings, my mom calling to say my father wants to talk to me.

Okay, put him on.

No, not on the phone. He wants you to come home and to bring Richard with you.

Uh-oh. In all fairness, this command performance, the meeting of the parents, is overdue. Something I've been letting slide, as my parents have been moving out of the house on Crescent Place into an apartment a few blocks away. Knowing them, they would have stayed at the old house forever, had not Mrs Schwartz decided to sell. She and Seymour—Seymour still plays bridge, has never married—have moved up the county to be closer to her other children and grandchildren in Ardsley and Scarsdale.

My brothers are still sharing a room at home, if a larger one. Eddie, having finished a two-year tour of duty with the U.S. Navy, has joined the New York City Police Department. Two year ago, when setting out to see the world, Nana gave him a key to her apartment, telling him there was always room for him at her place. No one other than Eddie, not even my father, has a key to Nana's apartment.

Kenny tells me Eddie sleeps with a gun at his side, that one night when my mom's curio cabinet holding her prized Hummel figurines came crashing to the floor, Eddie was on his feet in an instant with the gun pointing at Kenny. *Whoa!* What's chilling at three in the morning is comical at three in the afternoon. A bright spot is that my mom finally passed her New York State driver's test, which means she no longer has to wait for my father to take her to the Cross County Shopping Center, and he no longer has to wait for her while she shops. And—miracle of miracles—my dad has decided to buy a house in the Hamptons, one he can use during the summer and later when he retires.

Calling Richard, I fill him in on what has transpired. He listens, says Kay ratted me out deliberately.

Don't be silly, why would she do *that*?

She's jealous.

Not agreeing with his off-the-cuff assessment, it's wonderful finding a second in my corner. Someone to patch me up if I get a cut over my eye. To cheer me on—get up! get up!—when down for the count. When I lost my mother, I lost my best friend. Ever since I've been searching the world over, hoping for a love like his to come along.

Listen, don't worry. My father got rid of his hunting rifle years ago, so he can't shoot you.

On our way to Yonkers, it's as if we've switched roles for the day, with Richard the one in need of emotional shoring up. In no hurry to get there, he suggests we walk from the station rather than taking a cab. I chart a route that takes us along Bronx River Road, bypassing the house on Crescent Place.

My parents are delighted with the new apartment, the modern appliances in the kitchen, and the up-to-date tiled bathroom. Gone is the old claw-foot bathtub with its blue-green water stain around the drain, a stain resistant to elbow grease and Bon Ami scouring powder.

After a round of introductions, my father, directing his comment to Richard, says: Barbara's mother and I want you to know we're not happy she went to New Orleans with you.

Period. That was it. He said his piece, was done with it. Which is not all that surprising, for as soon as Richard walked through the door, my father would have realized that he was no young whippersnapper in need of a lecture, but a thirty-two year old options dealer with clients in far-flung places. Like New Orleans.

With everyone putting a best foot forward, it takes a while for me to realize that something new has been added to the equation, something unexpected. Having Richard here is having a tempering effect on family relations—I feel less aggrieved, less raw-edged. And it's forcing my parents to see me in a new role—as the object of this young man's affection—not that of the dutiful daughter. Which, truthfully, is how I saw myself until TWA came along. But could it be that after all years of going it alone, I've found someone to square the triangle?

My mom serves coffee and cake, emitting little half-laughs at everything Richard says. Perhaps she's relieved to find everything going along amicably. Afterward, stacking the cups and saucers in the dishwasher (a family first), I overhear my father telling Richard he needs to watch me with the money, that my grandmother and I are two of a kind with champagne tastes and beer pocketbooks.

On the way back to the city, Richard—snapping his heels together, doing a Gene Kelly impression—says: He never laid a glove on me.

Is that what you thought, he was going to hit you?

As the train pulls into the station, I notice a homeless man sleeping on a bench, all of his possessions in plastic bags around him.

Good night, sweet prince, I whisper. May flights of angels sing thee to thy rest . . .

And flights of angels.

And flights of angels? Are you sure? I think *may flights of angels* sounds better.

It's Shakespeare, you can't improve upon Shakespeare. It's what Horatio says when he sees the dead Hamlet: *Good night sweet prince and flights of angels sing thee to thy rest.*

I like Shakespeare's use of *thee* and *thy*, don't thee? His mind is on other things.

Do you know what your *father* told me? He said that when you get your period, I should give you a shot of blackberry brandy.

My father said *that?* The man is impossible.

FAIR IS FAIR. Now that Richard has met my parents, I'm to meet his. We drive out to Farmingdale, a small town on Long Island that during WW2 was a manufacturing dynamo, turning out thousands of fighter planes. Major companies— Republic Aviation, Seversky Aircraft, Fairchild Aviation and Grumman—all called it home.

Driving Conklin Street, the main drag, he points out what had been the office of the New York Telephone Company, at a time when you told the chief operator who you were calling and she'd connect you. No numbers needed.

Mary, I have a flat tire. Can you get me Mr Otten at the repair shop?

He's at the bank. Hang on, I'll ring him there.

As he's telling me this, we pass a tiny Tudor-style house

belonging to the chief operator, Mary O'Connor, his mother's best friend and co-conspirator. There was nothing those two loved more than betting the horses at Roosevelt Raceway in Westbury, a harness track known throughout the island for its panache and excitement.

We swing by his parents' former stationery store, a *dry* store without a soda fountain, one his father opened at six each morning to stack the papers—*The Daily News, The New York Daily Mirror, The New York Herald Tribune, The New York Times*—that had been dropped during the night. The late afternoon papers—*The Sun, The World -Telegram, The New York Journal-American,* and *The New York Post*—had to be picked at the railroad station. Once in a blue moon, Richard would lend a hand.

Hooking a left on Grant Avenue, a street named for Ulysses S. Grant, we pull up in front of a lovely white stucco house with a glassed-in porch, its windows sparkling in the noonday sun. After the introductions and a round of small talk, we sit down to a feast. As requested by her son, his mother has made her Farmingdale-famous blintzes—thin as crepes, light as feathers. The talk around the table centers on food—on kasha, kishke, and knishes, on gefilte fish, noodle kugle, and chopped liver—all of which she makes from scratch.

This chopped liver is *delicious*, I say, going back for a tad more of the starter.

Delicious, is that all? My friends tell me it's as good as Jennie Grossinger's.

Oy, vey! Lillian, Lillian, look at that! Look, his dad says, pointing to my plate, a contender for the clean plate award.

The last girl who came out with Deeky picked at her food like a bird, his father confides as we push away from the table. She was so thin, he says from behind his hand so Lillian can't hear him, I thought she had consumption. The bones on her neck were sticking out like chicken bones. I told Deeky she's sick already, stay away from her.

When he offers to show me the garden, I call over my shoulder that Richard should ask his mom for the recipe for the blintzes. With the door closing, I hear: A *shiksa* cooking Jewish? When I have a chance to pull him off to one side, I whisper: What's a shiksa?

A woman who's not Jewish, a gentile.

What's a gentile?

Someone who's not Jewish.

Are you sure it's not something else?

Like what?

Maybe a woman who's not Jewish dating your son who you sent to Syracuse in a snazzy red convertible, hoping he'd meet a nice Jewish girl from Long Island whose father's a doctor? The way she said it didn't sound like an endearment.

He laughs, saying, it doesn't matter *what* she says. Seeing him more amused than annoyed, I laugh and follow suit.

On the other hand, his father is the most contented of men, walking around in bed slippers, a corncob pipe tucked into one corner of his mouth. It's been forty years since he stepped off the boat at Ellis Island, but with that accent, you could have fooled me.

Vy do you call him Richard?

Why do I call him Richard? I repeat, thinking I may have heard him wrong. That's his name, isn't it?

Vell, yes, but vee call him Deeky. Vy not call him Deeky?

Dickey? I like calling him Richard.

Vell vat about Deek? All his friends call him Deek. Vould you like to call him Deek?

Sitting there, wrapping my ears around his Yiddish-inflected English, I'm half-expecting the milkman to bring the cows up Grant Avenue.

Not sure of the definition of consumption, I look it up later that evening to find it's an old-time name for tuberculosis, a highly contagious wasting disease that's been around for thousands of years. Having lived his first fifteen years in a shtetl—a ramshackle Jewish settlement with wooden houses, unpaved streets, and horse-drawn wagons in Belorussia—Richard's dad knows his mind. Consumption, which has decimated great swaths of Eastern Europe for centuries, is a greater threat than a lone shiksa with a good appetite. I've made a conquest.

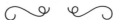

Calling Richard from Crew Scheduling, we arrange to meet at Café Argenteuil, a country-French restaurant midtown where you can always count on a warm welcome and fine cuisine. Where better for a Valentine's Day celebration? A number of food critics rank it right up there with the crème de la crème of French restaurants in New York—La Caravelle, La Cote Basque, Lutèce, and Le Pavilion. At lunchtime, Café Argenteuil attracts VIPs in the fields of publishing and advertising, most of whom have offices nearby. But come evening, it's another story with the cognoscenti beating a path to the discreet entrance on East 52nd Street.

In keeping with the spirit of the day, small red hearts dangle from red streamers above the gleaming dark mahogany bar. I head for the ladies' room wanting to change into something more festive than my uniform. When the maître d' shows me to a table by the window, I pause long enough to look over a dessert cart that's an ode to autumn—a genoise decorated with dark chocolate curls, a crystal bowl filled with puffy meringues floating in a pond of custard, and two glazed tarts, a pear and an apple. For someone who snacked her way through high school on Ritz Crackers and Velveeta cheese, Café Argenteuil is a gastronomic step up.

Arriving early allows me time to wallow in the ambiance: the lace curtains filtering the lights of cars moving slowly down Second Avenue; damask napkins as starchy as a nurse's cap; and lighting so flattering you could mistake a dowager for a damsel. When Richard arrives in his Wall Street uniform— a Hart Schaffner & Marx single-vent three-button pinstripe with spit-shined Johnston & Murphy's—I watch as he jokes with the hatcheck girl, handing over a camel-hair coat.

If Nana could see him, she would say: He's full of the dickens.

Each time I pick him out in a crowd—at a corner waiting for a light to change, getting out of a cab, in line at a movie theater—my heart does a little dance. His presence comforts me—he cares where I am, cares what I'm doing—and that caring papers over that old hole-in-the-heart. I've never felt more content in my life than when I'm with him.

Hi, Sweet Pea, how you doing? I say, as he leans over to

kiss me. A waiter coming up behind him, smoothes a ripple in the tablecloth: *Bon soir, monsieur* ...

Hello, Yves, how are you? Richard says, his face lighting with a full-hearted grin.

Very well, monsieur. Good to see you and mademoiselle again, he adds, nodding in my direction.

Richard orders Bombay martinis, shaken not stirred with three olives, asking Yves to chill a bottle of the Louis Jadot Pouilly-Fuissé, the same one we had last time.

I like a chin-up dry white French, don't you?

Absolutely, I say, what I don't like are oaky chardonnays. They give me such a headache.

Have you looked at the menu?

No, I was waiting for you, but I'll probably have what I had last time, starting with escargot. They're every bit as good and garlicky as those at the Hotel Celtic in Paris.

Flying with TWA, we crew members can dine and sign at any of the hotels where we stay—the Hotel Celtic on *rue Balzac*, the California on *rue de Berri* and the Windsor-Reynolds on *rue Beaujon*. All close to the Champs Elysées in the upscale eighth arrondissement, all within easy walking distance of the Arc de Triomphe.

For the main course, I order the *sole Veronique*. How could I not, when the name itself calls up thoughts of my long-gone mother. How many years has it been?

When the dish comes to the table, the body of the fish—having a light white sauce and a scattering of pale green grapes—glistens like that of a well-oiled swimmer. Two-thirds of the way through the *Pouilly-Fuissé*, I reach into my flight bag for a gift I bought Richard in Paris. Window-shopping on *rue du Faubourg Saint-Honoré*, a pair of silver cufflinks—*les boutons de manchettes en argent*—caught my eye.

Happy Valentine's Day, darling, I say, sliding the box across the table, a little something from Par-ee. Expecting his face to light with pleasure, I'm surprised when it doesn't. Pushing back from the table, he stares at the box for what seems an eternity, his expression that of someone who might prefer opening a gift when alone, lest his enthusiasm not match that of the giver. As he slips the ribbon off the box, I'm studying his flawless complexion and the evenly matched teeth that give him such a boyish air.

These are nice, he says, but, you know, I don't wear shirts with French cuffs.

You don't? I did *not* know that, I say, as he holds up a barrel cuff for my inspection. Color me crestfallen.

Are French cuffs too flashy for Wall Street? I know what I'll do. First thing tomorrow, I'm going to buy you a shirt with French cuffs to go with those cufflinks. Every man needs a shirt with French cuffs, if only for special occasions. Take my word for it, a shirt with French cuffs will take your wardrobe up a notch—from tried and true to suave and debonair.

No, I don't want you to do *that*. Shirts with barrel cuffs can go anywhere, day or night.

Resting my case, I remain apprehensive about returning anything in Paris where sales assistants understand better when you're buying than returning. What would I say? *Bien*

que mon ami aimait les boutons de manchette, il ne les aimait pas.
My friend liked the cufflinks, but didn't love them.

As matters stand, my tentative French grates on Parisians' ears. Not on Philippe's, of course, but on those of his fellow citizens. Ah, Philippe—yes, we had a harmony that I never meant to spoil. Even loving Paris as I do, it's not the same without him. I see him coming toward me across the lobby of the California, see him behind the wheel of every funny-looking Citroën that passes. Next month, I'm flying Madrid, staying at the Castellana Hilton where the Madrilleños don't show up before ten for dinner and every night is a fiesta.

Removing a cufflink from the box, I hold it next to the sleeve of my dress, wanting to see it up-close, wanting to show it off to best advantage. They're really great looking, I say.

They are, but why should I keep them if I can't use them?

Sweetie, I think you ought to hang onto them. Think of them as good luck charms. If you hold onto them, there might be a few black-tie events in your future.

Without comment, he slides a royal-blue velvet box across the table—Leapin' lizards!—taking me by surprise. I ask you, what's more promising than a royal-blue velvet box? Blue is the color of the sky, the color of the sea, the color of infinity. We've been dating for ten months, so could this be an engagement ring or does that sort of thing only happen in the movies?

The box opens with an authoritative snap, and inside lay an elegant eighteen-carat gold pin in the shape of a tulip, with a scattering of diamonds offering the illusion of dew-drops on petals.

It's lovely, I say, swallowing hard with regret. Sensing something lacking in *it's lovely*, Richard says that if I don't like it, we can exchange it.

No, no, I love it.

Are you sure? I bought it on 47th Street at the Cohen Brothers. They're good about returns. I've bought things there before, and it's never a problem.

He's bought things there before? what does *that* mean? I brush away a tear threatening to slip its sluices, not wanting him to notice. Nancy Drew never cried, not once, not even when bound and gagged in a deserted attic. And Coco Chanel knew that teary-eyed young women were neither classy nor fabulous.

Are you crying? I feel terrible seeing you cry. Wait a second, if you like the pin, why are you crying?

I don't know, but when I saw the box—the size and shape of it—I thought it might be an engagement ring.

An engagement ring? *You've* never mentioned anything about wanting an engagement ring.

Well, I hadn't given it all that much thought, at least not until I saw the blue velvet box. I guess I was waiting for you to come up with the idea.

An engagement ring? So, that's it. Okay, we'll go tomorrow and pick out a ring. You know this reminds me of that story by O. Henry.

Which one? I ask, happy for a chance to shake off my dampness, get out from under the weight of my tears.

The Gift of the Magi.

What's it about?

It's about a couple who have no money to buy gifts for one another at Christmas. The wife's crowning glory is her long dark hair, and the husband's prized possession is a pocket watch. What happens is that the wife sells her hair to a wig-maker to buy a gold chain for her husband's watch, while he pawns his watch to buy her a set of combs.

That's so *sweet*. As for the pin, I wouldn't dream of parting with it. I've never seen another like it.

You really like it? I assure him I do.

As for an engagement ring, why not? My heart's free. Aside from all the good times—the days of wine and roses—Richard with his agile mind, first-class temperament and heart of gold never fails to make me laugh. Having lived so long with family secrets, this is the first time I've been in a relationship where everything is out in the open. Then, too, there's that boyish smile and the way his eyes narrow with merriment.

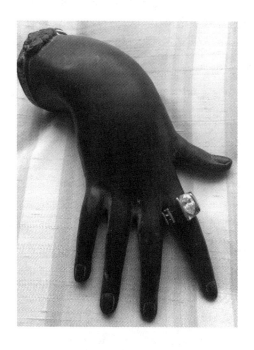

❧ ❧

Late the following afternoon, we drop by the Cohen Brother's on West 47th Street, a long narrow store lined with glass cases filled with diamonds—diamond watches, diamond brooches, diamond necklaces, and diamond rings. When it's diamonds you're looking for, this is the place. When Richard asks for a jeweler's loupe, I'm not sure if he knows what he's doing, but when he starts discussing color and carats, I feel as if I'm in good hands.

A slightly balding Lenny Cohen, the white dress shirt open at the collar, takes out a black velvet tray holding a number of possibilities—round diamonds, oval diamonds, square diamonds, and emerald cuts.

Which do you like? Richard asks. How about that one, the one with the high-pronged Tiffany setting?

I don't think so. Round stones are for friends, not romantic commitments.

Where did you hear *that*? Okay, how about that marquise, he asks, pointing to a sparkler full of fire and light.

Too edgy. A ring like that's bound to end up in a divorce proceeding.

Picking out an oval-shaped diamond, he slips it onto his pinkie for a close-up: This?

Nope, too princess-y.

All the while, Lenny's patiently taking us through a well-practiced tutorial on the Five C's of buying diamonds: cut, color, clarity, carat weight, and confidence. Confidence? In the Cohen Brothers, who stand behind all their diamonds. We learn that well-cut diamonds have more brilliance, which is what makes them more expensive, and that diamonds range from crystal-clear winter-whites to yellow-golds. The best having no color at all.

Color isn't the whole story, Lenny insists. Clarity counts, the best stones are flawless, not easy to find. I'm thinking, who wouldn't want a flawless diamond? Richard says he's not interested in diamonds with specks.

Specks? Nature's fingerprints we call them, Lenny says with a half-hearted chuckle.

Dirty fingerprints, Richard replies.

After an hour, the tutorial on diamonds having run its course, we spot a ring we both like—Lenny wipes his brow—a pear-shaped 1.75 carat diamond with a unique cut-away setting. A classic with a twist.

I slip it on. What size is this? a scant seven?

Go ahead and take it over to the window. See the brilliance of that stone. If you take it and decide it's not what you want, bring it back. As I told you, that's what the fifth 'C' is all about, confidence in the Cohen Brothers. We're a family business, and we want our customers to be satisfied. Do you *love* that ring? Diamonds are forever, you gotta' love it.

I do, I do, I say trying it first with the tip of the diamond facing toward me and then away.

When you're ready to trade up for a larger stone, we have the best upgrade policy on the street.

Do people trade up their engagement rings?

Give it to me, Lenny says, so I can clean it. When he disappears into the back, I'm worrying that once out-of-sight he might substitute another with nature's fingerprints.

You don't want to think that way, Richard says. You want to have confidence in your jeweler, as you would with a doctor. After he cleans it, do you want to wear it?

I'd love to, I say, even if the idea of the jeweler slipping a ring on my finger in a shop on West 47th Street doesn't match any engagement scenario I may have entertained.

Be sure to tell your friends about us, Lenny says, walking us to the door. From there, it's an easy stroll to the bookish realm of the Algonquin Hotel on West 44th Street. Where better to celebrate our love, good fortune, and engagement ring? Gift-wrapped in happiness, we walk arm-in-arm through a darkening winter afternoon. People scurry by with heads down, while I walk dreamily down the street, my left hand extended a foot or so in front of me, wondering how long it will be until church bells chime.

The hotel lobby's quiet. Waiting for drinks to arrive, I excuse myself to find a phone and call home to share the news.

Mom, guess what? I'm engaged! Yes . . . no. Engaged to be *married*. Will you do me a favor and call Nana? Tell her I'll call her tomorrow.

Hanging up the phone, I stand stock-still wondering if I should send a telepathic message to Veronica. She doesn't come as readily to mind as she once did, but then, she's been gone for twenty years—an eternity. Of course, what seems an eternity to me may be no more than a blink of the eye for her.

The ghosts of the Algonquin Round Table—Dorothy Parker, Robert Benchley, Robert Sherwood, Harpo Marx, and Harold Ross—gather round and raise a glass to cheer us on. Sipping well-chilled martinis poured from an icy silver beaker, the room slowly fills with the bantering of the *Vicious Circle*, as they liked to call themselves:

So, you've found yourself a diamond!

Yes, I've plucked me a diamond from the tree of life.

Rich, do you want to call your parents?

On the evening news, the weatherman's promising a good day tomorrow—blue skies and light breezes. Richard suggests we drive up to Westchester to visit my mother's grave at Gate of Heaven Cemetery in Valhalla, something I've been wanting to do but haven't done. After I moved out of the house, the pressure to double-check myself at every turn has lessened dramatically, to the point where I rarely think about those years anymore or about the ever-present fear of making a slip of the lip. A slip of the lip? So what. Not that I've become a blabbermouth, for I haven't. However, if I accidentally spilled the beans—to someone other than Richard, that is—I no longer fear that my parents' lives would fly apart, that the neighbors would be gossiping about us at all hours, or that Eddie would be psychologically damaged by learning the finer points of his birth. When you walk around harboring a family secret, the fear of revelation colors everything you do or don't do, everything you say or don't say. There's a price to be paid for harboring secrets, but as far as I was concerned, I had paid it long enough. My conscience was clear.

The turning point for me was going with TWA. Until then, if chafing under my father's house rules, I never knew how liberating it would be to live away from home, away from all the arguments and dissatisfactions—not until I arrived in Kansas City and all the restrictions fell away. I awoke the first morning feeling wonderful, feeling as if I had been in a straightjacket all of my life—my mouth padlocked, my arms tied behind my back—and, miraculously, had found a way to slip free of my bonds.

But how will we find the grave? There must be thousands of graves at Gate of Heaven, and I haven't a clue where my mother's would be. We can't very well walk up one row and down another, can we?

Cemeteries all have registries, Richard says. Let's make a day of it. We'll find your mother's grave, pay our respects, and then drive over to Banksville for lunch at this new French restaurant that was written up in *The New York Times* a few weeks ago. Here, he says taking out a neatly folded scrap of paper from his wallet on which was scribbled: *La Crémaillère a-la-Campagne.*

Okay, but I don't see how visiting her grave is going to change anything, not after all these years.

We're not looking to change anything, we're simply paying our respects. Do you remember the article you read, the one about the tribes in the hill country of Mexico? How when someone died, the whole village turned out to say good-bye. You were too young to say good-bye. Now's your chance.

WE MEET at Avis the following morning, Richard offering to drive. Given our antithetical driving styles, I refuse his offer preferring to be behind the wheel. If you were to ask him about my driving skills, he would tell you I drive with a heavy foot and delayed braking. Whereas if you asked me, I would say that once behind the wheel he morphs into a Walter Mitty, daydreaming the trip away at twenty-five mph in the passing lane. Road rage follows wherever we go—the drivers wigwagging around us, making unseemly gestures. None of which Walter Mitty notices.

Turning off the Sprain Brook Parkway, we zip north on Route 100 to find the woods still lounging in their winter weeds. Hungry for signs of new life, I call his attention to forsythia budding next to a dry-stack stonewall, to the scent of wild onions coming in through the vent, and to tendrils of ivy breaking out from under clumps of roadside snow. When not pointing out these harbingers of spring, I'm trying to dredge up a few lines by T. S. Eliot having to do with the season.

Rich, do you remember that poem by Eliot, the one about

March being the cruelest month of all? How does that go? Folding the newspaper, slipping it into a side pocket on the door, he inhales deeply—one hand on my knee, the other on my heart—saying: It was April, not March.

Are you sure?

> *April is the cruelest month, breeding lilacs out of the dead land,*
> *Mixing memory and desire, stirring the dull roots with spring rain.*
> *Summer surprised us, coming over the Starnbergersee with a shower of rain.*
> *We stopped in the colonnade and went on in sunlight into the Hofgarten and drank coffee and talked for an hour.*

What a memory you have, say it again. Which he does in a stentorian voice sure to have pleased Demosthenes.

There's so much truth to that line about *mixing memory and desire,* isn't there? And what about Eliot's personification of summer? *Summer surprised us, coming over the Starnbergersee with a shower of rain.* Where is the Starnbergersee? He thinks it's in Bavaria. I accept that, knowing full well he had been the geography champion in fifth grade.

Spotting a roadside diner up ahead, I suggest we stop for coffee—*We stopped in the colonnade and went on in sunlight into the Hofgarten and drank coffee and talked for an hour*—but he nixes the idea. Wending and winding through the rolling hill country, we pass houses set far back from the road with whimsical weathervanes—flying geese, red-tailed foxes, black stallions—and simple black mailboxes stenciled with names, but no numbers. At an intersection we pause, trying to make sense of a cluster of signs—signs for Mt. Calvary, Mt. Eden, Mt. Pleasant, Kensico, and Ferncliff, but not a one for Gate of Heaven. When in doubt, go straight.

Give me the first line of a poem, he says, any poem.

Coming up with a first line isn't as easy as it may sound, but after a few moments, Elizabeth Barrett Browning comes to my rescue: *How do I love thee? Let*—at which he interrupts: *How do I love thee? Let me count the ways. I love thee to the depth and breadth and height my soul can reach, when feeling out of sight for the ends of being and—*

Hey, there's a florist up ahead. Let's stop and get some flowers.

Miffed at being cut-off, he mutters something about a poet being without honor in his own country. With the car tires crunching the bluestones in the parking lot, I ask what he thinks I should buy.

It's your call, you know more about flowers than I do.

Okay, but what's better? A bouquet or a grave blanket?

A grave blanket?

I laugh, explaining it's a coverlet of flowers and greens.

That sounds a shade much, but your call.

No preference?

My preference is to find your mother's grave, he says, somewhat exasperated. If I'm hanging back, he's having none of it.

The parking lot, edged with purple and yellow crocuses, would have delighted Mrs Schwartz who always liked gardens that had mixed borders. A bell jangles overhead as I enter a shop ripe with the scents of hyacinth and narcissus. An attractive middle-aged woman—a string of pearls half-visible under a long white shirt and a pair of forest-green clogs splattered with mud—asks if she can be of help. I point to a twiggy basket filled with tiny daffodils on the table behind her.

This? They're tête-à-têtes. They bloom in pairs, facing one another.

Tête-à-têtes? That's exactly what I want, even though I didn't know it until a second ago. No need to wrap, they're for a grave. We're looking for Gate of Heaven, would you know where it is?

You're almost there. Keep going straight. You won't miss the sign. It's a mile or so down the road.

My stomach knots. Why so nervous? When I climb back in the car, Richard says: I've been meaning to ask you, when you are going to quit flying?

Quit flying? Didn't I tell you? There's no need to quit as TWA has changed the rules. Hostess turnover is way too high. They say, on average, a hostess flies a little more than a year before getting married. So now we can fly even if we're married, but not if we have children.

Wait, do I understand this? You want to continue flying to Europe each week after we're married? I wouldn't like that, would you? I love you, he says. I want to be with you every day, not have you jetting around the world.

I love you, too, darling, but I'd only be gone two nights a week. If I continue flying, we'd have all those free travel passes to Rome and Cairo.

We can afford to travel without worrying about passes. There's more to life than free passes.

Not for airline hostesses, I say with a wink. Seniority and passes are what it's all about. Besides, what will I do if I quit? I'm not going to hang around the house waiting for you to come home at night, and, to tell the truth, I'm not cut out for office work.

Why not go back to school and get your degree. You liked taking classes at Fordham, didn't you?

In a flash, a world of possibilities opens, an academic world where I had always felt at home. You wouldn't mind if I went to school instead of working?

Mind? Not at all. Then I can introduce you as my wife, the student.

If you did that, I could stay young for years.

What a gift this is, a completely unanticipated gift. If I weren't so nervous about visiting the cemetery, I'd be laughing out loud.

Driving between Gothic stone pillars, we hold to the ten mph limit, inching downhill through what could pass for an open-air museum of memorial architecture. All around us are handsome mausoleums with flat, gabled, or mansard roofs. With clear, tinted, or stained glass windows. And with more than a dozen styles of lettering.

How much do you think a mausoleum like that one costs?

J. P. Morgan said if you have to ask the price, you can't afford it.

That I'm sure of, but let's stop and take a look.

We're not here to look at real estate. Let's find the grave.

Pulling over to let a cortege pass, a teddy bear with a bandaged eye in a window of a burial crypt offers us a woeful look. Richard lights a pipe, a straight-stemmed beauty that gives him an introspective air. Between the pipe, the buffed oxblood loafers, and that Harris Tweed jacket, he looks like a professor who stepped away from the halls of academe.

The cemetery's profoundly quiet, so much so that the sound of laughter from a group of men walking toward us is jarring.

What's with the Yankee caps? Do you think they're going to play ball in the cemetery?

Continuing downhill through a swale of gravestones, we cross a small bridge with spires and gargoyles that brings us into a parking lot. Not a soul around—the only sound being that of the wind moving through the branches of the trees.

Inside the Information Center, balancing the telephone receiver between cheek and shoulder, a receptionist with tightly curled gray hair is on the phone. On a counter between us lay a half-dozen ledgers, the linen covers the color of corn silk and the pages filled with hand-written entries. Waiting for her to finish, I leaf through a stack of promotional materials. One pamphlet reads like a Who's Who at Gate of Heaven. Sports fans might give a rousing cheer knowing The Babe is buried here. Enquiring journalists can pay respects at the grave of Westbrook Pegler.

Musicians and composers have a choice of communing with Tommy Dorsey or Rachmaninoff. Criminal investigators might want to check out the grave of Dutch Schultz, the kingpin of crime. Last but not least, intellectuals and iconoclasts can take comfort in knowing the perspicacious Ayn Rand is nearby.

If you don't know the date she died, you're out of luck. If you know it, you can go through these books to find the information, says the receptionist, buffing a nail on the sleeve of her blouse. The date? That's easy, November 3rd, Eddie's birthday.

What's the name?

Veronica Shanahan Bracht.

In short order, she locates the information and writes down the section, row, and grave number, saying: There are markers along the roads indicating the different sections, but it's easier to watch for the Stations of the Cross.

The Stations of the Cross?

The Stations of the Cross run throughout the cemetery. The grave you're looking for is across the road from the sixth station.

The sixth, which is the sixth?

Veronica wiping the face of Jesus.

I swallow hard, thinking it appropriate. Thanking her for her help, I ask which of the graves gets the most visitors.

That's easy. Not a week goes by someone doesn't come looking for Babe Ruth. Want me to write down the location for you?

No, thanks, I think we know where it is.

After a few false starts and with the help of a gardener,

we locate the sixth station. Richard places the tête-à-têtes on the hood of the car and then, under a canopy of lindens and oaks, we tiptoe up one row and down the next, as if fearful of waking the dead. All the while, we're calling softly to one another: She's not in this row. Not here either. Did you look on that side? I'm not sure, the rows are beginning to look alike.

Some thirty minutes later, thinking we may have misunderstood the clerk, we return to the office for clarification. There's a mix-up, but not any we had anticipated. It's that my mother lies in an unmarked grave. The news is electrifying and dismaying.

Are you *sure*? The idea that my father would have left my mother in an unmarked grave for more than twenty years is unthinkable. She's sure.

Could there be a mistake?

No, there's no mistake. That grave never had a marker.

As if she had thrust an icepick into my heart, I'm seesawing between sorrow and fury. I hardly know what to say, what to do. Was it a matter of money? If so, wouldn't other family members have helped my father give his wife a decent burial? I didn't come here today expecting to find, say, an imposing angel with outstretched wings keeping watch over her grave, but neither was I expecting to find an unmarked grave. What if my father had been called off to war? who would have cared for the grave? was he fearful if he put up a stone bearing her name—Veronica Shanahan Bracht—someone passing might put two-and-two together and realize that he and my mom were living under false pretenses? What a bitter pill for her sisters to swallow—they who never forgot her children on our birthdays or at Christmas.

Pocketing the clerk's hand-written instructions, we return to park in front of the Sixth Station.

Your father's one cheap bastard.

You think it's about the money?

You can put that in the bank and draw interest on it.

Raised by parents harboring high hopes—my son, the doctor—Richard feels I've been short-changed when it comes to parental hopes and dreams.

But I don't know, maybe it was all about parental power. After all, the power to talk to me about my mother belonged to my father. So, too, the power to prick that bubble of silence, to let my aunts and uncles talk about her with me. He had the power to explain that Veronica's going away wasn't my fault. Instead he chose to ring-fence the truth. Who was I but a child wanting to please him, if all the while trying to hold onto the jigsawed fragments of my life.

What I don't mention is a conviction that children can read the unspoken but powerful messages encoded in body language, can feel their parents' emotions. Instinctively, I knew my father didn't want to have that conversation and, with my silence, I was hoping to win his love. All I wanted was to come in from the cold. If I could do that, I'd have more color in my cheeks.

The power of a secret lies in its repression. Hang it on a clothesline at noonday and it fades in the sun; keep it hidden in a closet and it's yours forever. It's one thing should you decide to keep a part of your life hidden from others, for whatever reason, but quite another if you're a child and the choice is not yours. Plain and simple, when authority figures take advantage of their position, the damage done makes it all the more difficult for the child going forward to trust others.

The weather's changing, starting to drizzle—so much for clear skies and billowy breezes. Staring intently at a patch of scruffy grass, as if expecting the grave to open, to tell its tale of woe, from off in the distance comes the lonesome whistle of a passing train. I sigh, thinking I've missed the train, have come too late—*a diller, a dollar, a ten o'clock scholar.*

Hello, Mom, it's me, Barbara. I'm sorry things have worked out this way, sorry it's taken me so long to get here. Please forgive me.

What I don't say is how she continued to flit the back corridors of my mind for years. I must have been fifteen or sixteen before I sat myself down and gave myself a good talking to, like a proverbial Dutch uncle, telling myself in no uncertain terms that she was never coming back—not for an hour, not for a minute, not even for a split-second. You're on your own, kiddo, I told myself, like it or not. Unlike *The Miracle on Thirty-Fourth Street*, mine would not happen. At which my jaw fell open, my heart dropped dead. It was as if—desperately seeking Veronica all those years—my poor heart had run the distance, could go no further. Feeling abandoned by my mother—as illogical as that might sound—and knowing there would be no help coming from beyond the grave, I abandoned her.

Then a strange thing happened—a rock-hard scab grew

over the hole-in-the-heart and, tough as it was on the outside, inside it remained soft and tender to the touch.

Kneeling at the side of the grave, feeling self-conscious about talking aloud—it's not the same as talking to her in my thoughts—I rake the grass with my fingers and it's then that tears fall like the petals of a dying rose.

Offering me a handkerchief—It's clean, Richard says—I dab my eyes. He places the tête-à-têtes on the grave, handing me a couple of photographs I'd left lying on the front seat of the car. In one, Veronica's standing with her sister, Mary, at a farm in Pennsylvania—two city-girls in summer dresses and high heels. In another, she's seated next to me on the floor by a Christmas tree. Judging from the expression on her face, I'm the spirit of Christmas, the star on the tree.

Looking at her—young, smiling—it's hard to imagine why things have worked out this way. Or maybe not. There was that childhood dream, the one in which I was walking empty streets in a village where I knew no one and no one knew me. A shadowy figure driving a team of horses plucked me off the street and raced with me to a cemetery on the out-skirts of town. It was a muddy mess—the tombstones toppled, the names hidden. Frightened out of my wits, I awoke in a panic telling myself it's only a dream, dreams can't hurt you. What did I know? I was six. I was seven. I was eight.

You're going to catch cold sitting there, Richard says. Come, let's go. I'll buy you a glass of wine.

Rich, I can't get it through my head that there's no marker, that there never has been one.

We can put up a stone. What's the big deal?

When he says *what's the big deal*, the persistent knot in my stomach begins to loosen. Until now, everything has been a big deal. But lucky me, I'm in love with my best friend. Lucky me to have found someone with whom I can share all the colors of my heart.

Can I have some of your tobacco?

What for?

To sprinkle it on the grave. You know, like bringing water from a spring or flowers from a field. Of course, we brought the tête à têtes.

Did your mother smoke?

I doubt it, I say with an unintentional laugh. Very few women smoked in those days, although one of my aunts had this way of holding a cigarette at shoulder-height, the fingers outstretched in such a way that made smoking look terribly glamorous.

A bagpiper might have been a better choice.

What's with you and bagpipers? I've never known anyone who likes bagpipers as much as you do—and you're not Scots or Irish. No, I think Veronica loved the music of the Big Bands—Glenn Miller, Benny Goodman, and Tommy Dorsey. Hey, come to think of it, Tommy Dorsey's up the road. Who knows? By now, the two of them could be tripping the light fantastic. I know what, I'll sing *Danny Boy*. Every Celtic woman has a soft spot in her heart for *Danny Boy*. After the opening bars, I fudge the middle, ending strong.

And I shall hear, tho, soft you tread above me
And all my grave will warmer sweeter be
For you will bend and tell me that you love me
And I shall sleep in peace until you come to me.

I hope she has slept in peace—hope it wasn't the nightmare for her that it has been for me. Bending to lay my hand on her grave, I tell her that I love her and have missed her all the days of my life.

EPILOGUE

Richard took the lead that day in confronting my father, telling him we had stopped at Gate of Heaven, but couldn't find my mother's grave as there had been no headstone.

Funny you should mention that, my dad said, because we were talking only the other day about what to do about the grave.

The other day? Her mother has been dead for twenty years, so if it's all right with you, we'd like to put up a stone.

There's no need for that. I'm going to take care of it.

When?

Maybe later this week. What I want to do is to put up a stone with room for all three names.

He did not explain why the grave had been left unmarked, nor did we ask. We avoided recriminations, preferring to focus on what was to come. And my father did as he had said he would and put up a handsome granite marker—clutches of flowers engraved in the upper corners, the surname writ bold at the center—that would eventually bear the names of Veronica,

Edward, and Marguerite. It was a long time in coming, but Veronica had her name back, and even a casual observer could see that she, too, had passed this way.

Although Nana never mentioned Veronica, not once in all those years, I suspect the loss of my mother continued to weigh on her mind, color her perceptions. From time to time, she would dig into her top bureau drawer to give me a piece of jewelry I had never seen her wear—starting with the gold bracelet from Germany. After that came a double strand of antique stones. Polished oblong stones in muted shades of grey, beige, and terra cotta—the likes of which were all the rage, *le dernier cri*, in Paris only a few seasons ago. An elegant thirty-inch strand of faceted amber beads, as deep and rich as any spotted at the Amber Room in St. Petersburg. A Franciscan rosary with seven decades of well-thumbed small oval beads that had belonged to Sister Bernadette of Lourdes, who—like Veronica—had died young leaving a wound in my grandmother's heart that never fully healed. Curiously enough, attached to the rosary beads is a tiny devotional medal, not much bigger than my pinky nail: Our Lady of Loretto, Pray for Us Who Fly. (The image that springs to mind is that of Sally Fields in *The Flying Nun*.) Perhaps these treasures came my way because my grandmother knew there were no keepsakes from Veronica, other than the ruby-red vase.

Nana remained true to her word, saved her pennies, cashed in her insurance policies, and bought herself a piece of property up the county—a plot at Mount Calvary in White Plains, where she lies surrounded by her daughters and their husbands. Alert to the end of her eighty years, she loved nothing more than hearing about the comings and goings of her twenty-two grandchildren and thirty-one great-grandchildren. After her death—*Things fall apart; the centre cannot hold*—we had to learn new ways of connecting with one another. Nothing was quite the same after Nana died and, to this day, the talk at family reunions is full of reminiscences of that greathearted, extraordinary woman.

When Nana moved out of the house at 3272 Decatur Avenue, Uncle Fred moved in down the block with Aunt Betty and her family, and he would remain with them for the rest of his days. Uncle Fred never married, never said hello to love. When I tried, unsuccessfully, to plumb my aunt's memories of him in later years, she recalled him as a quiet man who loved gardening and playing checkers with her children, whereas I remember him in his younger days, playing boisterous games of pinochle and hearts with my father and uncles in Nana's front parlor on Sunday afternoons.

Aunt Betty spent the last eight years of her life at the Mary Manning Walsh Nursing Home in Manhattan. I'd time my visits for days when they were having a musical program, because having a conversation with her, as she slipped further and further away, had become increasingly difficult. A visitor asked if she was my mother. No, I replied, my aunt. At which he said, your aunt's one helluva dancer. Yes, Betty was a dancing girl—a pretty woman, as sweet and thoughtful as they come.

As for my mom—she with the cornflower-blue eyes, a self-effacing smile, and never an unkind word about anyone—

how could any flesh-and-blood person hold a candle to an ethereal being, the idealized mother? After my father died at the relatively young age of sixty-nine, she lived on for another twelve years, if not as happily as when he had been with her. Theirs was a good marriage, a close marriage with scarcely a whiff of disagreement, which for me, like my namesake St. Barbara, meant that there was no one to speak on my behalf—no one to challenge my father's decisions or engage his heart.

I was a child suffering multiple losses—the loss of my mother; the loss of contact with most of her extended family, including my maternal grandparents with whom my father had had a falling out; and the loss of all the pleasures of what social scientists call the *uber place*—the house that danced on Ryer Avenue.

Survivors' tales—be they from those incarcerated in brutal prisons, concentration camps or shipwrecked at sea—point toward the brain's ability, when under stress, to retreat from the unrelenting fears and find sanctuary in memories drawn from more hospitable times. The memory of that morning at 2180 Ryer Avenue—sunbeams slipping between the blinds; my fingers tripping over a million silky tufts on my mother's chenille bedspread; the music of the Big Bands coming from the radio; and my mother, propped up on pillows in bed, sipping a cup of tea and reading the paper—was such a sanctuary.

Too young to understand the concept of death, I was left bobbing in a sea of incomprehension and bewilderment, searching for my *missing* mother and for all I had lost when

I lost her—for all the pleasures of the house that danced and for that singular smiling face. Losses compounded five years later when my father remarried, and we moved away from the beautiful Bronx. This time, I lost my surrogate mother, my grandmother, and all the hustle-bustle of the house that laughed at 3272 Decatur Avenue. Losses that went largely unrecognized by those around me. What to do? Go out and play. Don't talk about it. A slip of the lip can sink a ship. Clearly, the theories of child development being advanced by Dewey and Thorndike at Columbia University had yet to hop the D train to the Bronx.

My father took all of his memories of Veronica to the grave. He never talked about her, never even spoke her name. Undeniably, as an adult, I could have taken the initiative and asked, but I shied away from that. No sense in opening a can of worms, Nana had said. But it was more than that—there was an awareness that were such a conversation to take place, it would make my mom, who consistently went out of her way to avoid confrontations, deeply uncomfortable.

Assuredly, my dad had experienced deep grief in his lifetime—the loss of his own father while still in high school and, a dozen or so years later, the death of his twenty-five year old wife. Life teaches us lessons. Energetic and hardworking, not a lazy bone in his body, he may have thought the best way to deal with tragedy was not to talk about it, but to roll up your sleeves and get to work. And that he did. As for my brothers, Eddie and Kenny, they have no complaints about parental neglect, which leaves me to think my dad may have been a better *boy* father than a *girl* father. Not sure what to do with a young daughter, he simply called me *Bob*.

Although he would put up a headstone, he never got around to offering any of the affirmations—was I pretty? smart? funny?—I hungered to hear as a child. Of course, that was a time when fathers, generally speaking, were not as expressive of their emotions, not as affectionate or as involved with their children as nowadays. It would be left for my mom to tell me—after I graduated Hunter College *magna cum laude* and was elected to Phi Beta Kappa, Sigma Tau Delta, and Kappa Delta Pi—that my father was proud of me. Naturally, I hoped he was, but that acknowledgement came years too late for it to do much good.

With family, friends, and neighbors, my dad was a hale-fellow-well-met, a prime ribs and Dewar's guy, and often the life of the party. At his funeral, scores of people whose lives he had touched with his laughter and good-natured ribbing came to say a final good-bye.

Nancy Drew once said that you could tell a lot about a man by his hands. My father's hands—large, powerful hands accustomed to doing heavy manual work—were strong enough to slice and dice a carcass of beef in a matter of minutes. Strong enough to drag a nine-point deer out of the backwoods and haul it up onto the carving block. But they were not strong enough to open the chamber of his heart where he had salted away all the sweet, kind, and loving words that would let someone know you loved them.

I suspect that my youthful attachment to Nancy Drew—

girl-detective extraordinaire, super-sleuth—grew out of a kinship I felt with that matchless, motherless girl. There we were, the two of us, endlessly searching for something or someone, staying on the alert for any clues, signs, or signals that might help in solving the mystery. Beginning with *The Secret of the Old Clock*, *The Hidden Staircase*, and *The Bungalow Mystery*, Nancy went on to solve countless whodunits, but never that surrounding the death of her mother. Having lost our mothers by the time we were three, Nancy and I would spend the rest of our days searching for what had been, trying to make things right for ourselves and for others, trying to find the missing pieces of our lives—for only then would we be able to put down our magnifying glasses and take off our Sherlock Holmes caps.

Eddie feels that our parents' decision to keep the story of Veronica hidden from him and others was made to protect the family and that any consequences were unintentional. Even so, given the best of intentions, damage done has a way of walking hand-in-hand with you down the years. You can push it under the rug, but it only stays out of sight for a while. When Veronica rolled the dice, they came up snake eyes. Of course, you could say, as I do, that not all was lost in that she got what she wanted—that I not go through life as an only child. Without doubt, my life has been blessed by my brothers and sisters-in-law, and by my nieces, nephews, and their adorable children.

If there were years when Veronica scarcely entered my thinking, she never completely faded from consciousness.

Why this should be is hard to say, but perhaps she was hanging on in the synapses, waiting for a whiff of recognition, and for that she needed my help.

Psychologists are prone to ask: Who loved you when you were a little child? I'd say that when I was a little child, my mother loved me. Nana loved me. Aunt Betty loved me. But Uncle Fred loved Eddie best. My father certainly loved me, but not enough for a child who had lost her mother and was walking around in a daze, unable to find that missing part of her life. Then I wasn't young anymore.

I was living in a world of half-truths and evasions, trying to piece it all together, hoping to fix what had gone wrong. What I learned along the way is that while you may push a lot of stuff under the rug, you never forget about it. Not completely. And— for whatever it's worth—I learned I was strong enough to go the distance and trustworthy enough to keep a secret. What I never learned was what happened to Veronica's silver boudoir mirror, the one engraved with the fabulous peacock with cambering plumage. Just as well. Peacocks in the house spell trouble.

As do family secrets. When a child is forbidden to say what he or she knows to be the truth—when a part of the brain is placed off-limits and the mouth sworn to secrecy— the heart is never free and easy. The best you can hope for is to hide the all-pervading anxiety with a smile and a laugh, hoping no one will notice. What's more, whenever anyone with authority over a child—a parent, teacher, or religious figure— abuses that trust, it makes it all the more difficult for the child going forward to have confidence in others.

Looking back over those years, the image that springs to mind is that of Kabuki Theater, with the three of us wearing masks to hide our identities from those around us—including from Eddie and Kenny—all the while contending, or at least I was, with the worrisome half-truths and evasions. If this is a story written with love and understanding, it's likewise a cautionary tale about family secrets. Not wanting to injure my family in any way and incapable of rewriting a script handed me as a child, year after year, putting on the greasepaint to play the role of a lifetime—that of the dutiful daughter.

At a certain point, you have to let it all go. Let go of the vexing unanswered questions. Let go of the judgments. Let go of the disappointments, frustrations, and anger. For only then are you free to wipe off the greasepaint and take off the mask. That was my parents' story, this is mine. The story of Veronica's daughter, she who could never quite forget a morning in the beautiful Bronx—the sunlight slipping between the blinds, spilling over the wood floor, and the radiator adding a shrill note to the music coming from the radio—yet never quite remember the details of her mother's face.

IF MY parents told Eddie the facts of his birth, they never told their friends. It remained for the three of us—Eddie, Kenny, and me—to out them with a surprise twenty-fifth anniversary party. Surprise is an understatement, as everyone thought the kids (or the printer) had made a mistake. The gathering took place at our home—a Colonial the color of summertime butter with forest-green shutters—in the bucolic village of Oyster Bay Cove, twenty-eight miles east of Manhattan. Ours was a house that danced, a house that laughed, a house that sang in moonbeams—and on the dining room table stood the ruby-red vase, a reminder of Veronica to whom it first belonged and of Nana who filled the emptiness of the vase with the wondrous bits and pieces of her life.

AUTHOR'S NOTES

As memoir is sometimes a suspect genre, I wanted to address a few issues. The question for memoirists is what do we remember and how do we manage to remember it? For me the answer is simple: we remember best the emotionally charged instances and happenings—especially those related to such hot-button feelings as shame, embarrassment, and humiliation. Indeed, neuroscientists tell us that the more painful and agonizing the reaction to the original incident, the more likely it is to be remembered.

So, too, it is with family secrets. This book involves family members, many of whom have died, and neighbors with whom I have not been in contact for years. Assuredly, they would all have their own reminiscences of those years to draw upon, but these are mine. To protect the privacy of others, the name of a minor character has been altered and another minor character is a composite.

The rest is factual—the happenings, the interchanges, and the fallout—if compressed. Scenes depicted are impressionist snapshots, fleeting moments in time meant to be representative of the fuller picture. All conversations within took place, even if some of the more repetitive and digressive ones have been condensed. If there has been selective editing, it has not been done at the expense of truth.

Lastly, I should say that when writing one looks to avoid clichés, but a few have been included—blonde bombshell—as they were not clichés when they entered the language during the period being depicted.

In closing, I'd like to ask a favor. If you have benefitted from the reading of this memoir, would you be so kind as to post a review—even a line or two would be greatly appreciated—on Amazon (www.Amazon.com) or Goodreads (www.Goodreads.com). It would mean a lot to me.

ACKNOWLEDGEMENTS

I always thought that someday I would write a book, if not this one. At least, not until that fateful morning when, by chance, I picked up a Gotham Writers' catalog at a neighborhood kiosk in Manhattan and registered for a memoir-writing course. Entering the classroom the first evening, it was as if I had stepped into a parallel universe populated by an engaging, constructive, and interesting group of writers. My thanks go to all of them, my first readers—particularly to Annette Berkovits, Jim Cooper, Patricia Smith, Joyce Maio, and Steve James—a number of whom have published memoirs.

Then came the online writing courses under the expert hand of the perceptive and encouraging Kyle Minor—Show, don't tell!—a talented author. My sincere thanks to Kyle, who opened my eyes as to what memoir writing is all about, and to a number of my online writing buddies—Amanda Skelton, Charlotte Decanter Chung, Ingrid Ricks, and so many others whose names I no longer remember but whose enthusiasm and comments sparked this journey. So, too, a debt of gratitude is owed Stanley Weil and his mother, Peggy Weil, for their unflagging interest and enthusiasm.

Special thanks go to my former flying partners, lifelong friends—Bernadette Adamcyk, Kay McGrath, Barbara Blum, and Farrolyn Lanigan—who so generously shared flight manuals, mementoes, and memories of our years flying with TWA. So, too, my thankfulness extends to my large and loving family, especially to "the cousins" who were such an integral part of growing up in the Bronx.

A huge debt of gratitude is owed my editor, Elizabeth Kracht of Kimberley Cameron & Associates, of San Francisco and Paris, without whose incisiveness and unerring sense of how much is enough, this book would never have come to light. And thanks, too, to my publisher, Brooke Warner of She Writes Press; editorial manager Lauren Wise of SparkPoint Studio; proofreader Megan Rynot; book cover designer Julie Metz; interior designer Tabitha Lahr; and to all those who labored to turn the manuscript into this beautiful book.

As for my husband, Richard Donsky, who has been there every step of the way, believing when I did not believe, I can never adequately thank him. He has been the wind in my sails, and without his conviction that this was a tale worth telling, *Veronica's Grave* would have fallen by the wayside. Writing is not for the fainthearted.

∞

AUTHOR BIO

photo by Lindsay May for Classic Kids Photography

Barbara Donsky, a former reading specialist with a private practice in Oyster Bay, New York, served as president and capital campaign coordinator of the Boys and Girls Club of Oyster Bay-East Norwich. A *magna cum laude* graduate of Hunter College, with an MS from C. W. Post, Long Island University and an EdD from Hofstra University, her publications include a doctoral dissertation *Trends in Written*

Composition in Elementary Schools in the United States, 1890—1960. Articles in educational journals including *Writing as Praxis* and *Trends in Elementary Writing Instruction.* A short story—"What's the Matter with Harry?"—published in *the Naples Review* culminating in a reading at a Barnes & Noble in Naples, Florida. Promotional pieces written on behalf of the Boys and Girls Club of Oyster Bay-East Norwich for a capital campaign, for which she was honored by the club as "Woman of the Year" (1994) and by the Town of Oyster Bay for her public-spirited contributions advancing the general welfare of the community. She lives with her husband in Manhattan where she blogs at: http://www.Barbaradonsky.com/

SELECTED TITLES FROM
SHE WRITES PRESS

She Writes Press is an independent publishing company
founded to serve women writers everywhere.
Visit us at www.shewritespress.com.

The Coconut Latitudes: Secrets, Storms, and Survival in the Caribbean by Rita Gardner. $16.95, 978-1-63152-901-6. A haunting, lyrical memoir about a dysfunctional family's experiences in a reality far from the envisioned Eden—and the terrible cost of keeping secrets.

The Butterfly Groove: A Mother's Mystery, A Daughter's Journey by Jessica Barraco. $16.95, 978-1-63152-800-2. In an attempt to solve the mystery of her deceased mother's life, Jessica Barraco retraces the older woman's steps nearly forty years earlier—and finds herself along the way.

The S Word by Paolina Milana. $16.95, 978-1-63152-927-6. An insider's account of growing up with a schizophrenic mother, and the disastrous toll the illness—and her Sicilian Catholic family's code of secrecy—takes upon her young life.

Don't Call Me Mother: A Daughter's Journey from Abandonment to Forgiveness by Linda Joy Myers. $16.95, 978-1-938314-02 -5. Linda Joy Myers's story of how she transcended the prisons of her childhood by seeking—and offering—forgiveness for her family's sins.

A Different Kind of Same: A Memoir by Kelley Clink. $16.95, 978-1-63152-999-3. Several years before Kelley Clink's brother hanged himself, she attempted suicide by overdose. In the aftermath of his death, she traces the evolution of both their illnesses, and wonders: If he couldn't make it, what hope is there for her?

Where Have I Been All My Life? A Journey Toward Love and Wholeness by Cheryl Rice. $16.95, 978-1-63152-917-7. Rice's universally relatable story of how her mother's sudden death launched her on a journey into the deepest parts of grief—and, ultimately, toward love and wholeness.